MESSERSCHMITT Me 321/323

MESSERSCHMITT Me 321/323
The Luftwaffe's "Giants" in World War II

Hans-Peter Dabrowski
Translated from the German by David Johnston

Schiffer Military History
Atglen, PA

TWO GROUP'S END
In the desparate attempt to support the besieged *Afrikakorps* in late 1942, three transport groups of TG 5 equipped with the immense Me 323 "Gigant" were sent into the fray,. Tragically, the Gigants only provided the most vulnerable of airborne targets for the superior Allied DAF fighters. On April 22, 1943, P-40 Warhawks of the SAAF shot down a dozen Gigants of II./Gruppe in a single intereception off Cape Bon, Tunisia, resulting in the loss of *Gruppenkommandeur* Stephans and more than one hundred officers and crewmen. The survivors returned to Germany to rebuild the group, only to be sent to the onslaught of the eastern front where they were devastated once again.

Book design by Robert Biondi.

Copyright © 2002 by Hans-Peter Dabrowski.
Library of Congress Catalog Number: 2001090729.

Printed in China.
ISBN: 0-7643-1442-4

We are always looking for people to write books on new and related subjects. If you have an idea for a book, please contact us at the address below.

Published by Schiffer Publishing Ltd.
4880 Lower Valley Road
Atglen, PA 19310
Phone: (610) 593-1777
FAX: (610) 593-2002
E-mail: Schifferbk@aol.com.
Visit our web site at: www.schifferbooks.com
Please write for a free catalog.
This book may be purchased from the publisher.
Please include $3.95 postage.
Try your bookstore first.

In Europe, Schiffer books are distributed by:
Bushwood Books
6 Marksbury Ave.
Kew Gardens
Surrey TW9 4JF
England
Phone: 44 (0)208 392-8585
FAX: 44 (0)208 392-9876
E-mail: Bushwd@aol.com.
Free postage in the UK. Europe: air mail at cost.
Try your bookstore first.

Contents

Foreword

"That was half a century ago … You have taken on something there … I doubt very much that I can help you …" These are typical of the comments I received when I approached those who had been involved with the Me 321 and Me 323. Nevertheless, over the course of time I collected much interesting material, enabling me to piece together much of the story. The relatively brief but complex history of the *Giganten* made a complete description from planning to the scrapping of the final remnants seem almost impossible.

In fact, the planning of the unpowered Me 321 went back to the time when Hitler, convinced that he was "the greatest military commander of all time", had decided to conquer the British Isles. The Me 323, on the other hand, did not enter service until much later.

The war diary of KG.z.b.V. 323 and TG 5 had survived, however only fragments of the combat reports remain. The members of the various *Gruppen* knew little or nothing of each other, while many pilots were assigned to other units after only a short time. Given the changeable nature of the *Gigant*'s missions and the scant coverage they received, a complete history of the *Gigant* was impossible and what follows is a collection of essays on the history of the *Giganten*.

Hans-Peter Dabrowski

Introduction

To the present day the name Messerschmitt is associated with aircraft which combined speed and elegance. The best known Messerschmitt aircraft is undoubtedly the Bf 109, which became famous for setting a world speed record and its combat record. These attributes were also shared the Bf 108 Taifun, a single-engine sport and touring aircraft which was flown by aviatrix Elli Beinhorn, and the Bf 110. The company designation Bf was used by all aircraft designed by Willy Messerschmitt until the Bayerische Flugzeugwerke became the Messerschmitt AG.

Another famous Messerschmitt aircraft was the Me 262, the first jet fighter to be produced in numbers and committed to combat. It came too late and its operational use was hampered by the fuel shortage and Hitler's order to use it as a "Blitzbomber." Not to be forgotten is the Me 163, the "Power Egg", a rocket-powered interceptor. Designed by Alexander Lippisch and built by Messerschmitt, it also came too late.

Long before the war and even prior to 1933, Willy Messerschmitt designed and built several single- and multi-engine transport aircraft while concentrating mainly on sporting aircraft. Messerschmitt's entry into the field of military aircraft came with the Bf 109.

Messerschmitt created the *Giganten* (giants), the Me 321 and Me 323, huge aircraft with wingspans of 55 meters. When, where and why is described in the following text. For various reasons, significant gaps and contradictions still exist in the "when" and "where." Generally speaking, special-purpose transport groups were not formed until the war (usually the aircraft came from schools) and were temporarily combined into *Geschwader* (KG.z.b.V., or special purpose battle wings). After completing their assignments these units were often disbanded. Until May 1943, when the KG.z.b.V. were reorganized and renamed Transportfliegergeschwader, there were numerous formations, redesignations, disbandments and even more exceptions and deviations. In considering the story of the *Giganten* it should be remembered that the Me 323 did not enter service until November 1942. The time of victorious battles gradually came to an end for Hitler and his allies. (For example, the surrender of the German 6th Army at Stalingrad on 02 February 1943 is generally regarded as one of the war's major turning points.)

Originally designed as offensive assets (tank-carrying glider), the later Giants developed into a means of transporting vitally-needed equipment. The powered Me 323 was used to evacuate wounded and was often the last chance for many persons to be flown out of threatened areas. The *Gigant* crews experienced the growing weight of the enemy's air superiority in the skies over Africa and Italy and his ceaseless bombing and strafing attacks on the ground. Losses outstripped replacements and there were few rest breaks when the call came to support the hard-pressed German ground forces or evacuate wounded.

Insofar as one can speak of a conventional structure when referring to the transport units, then the *Gigant* units – KG.z.b.V. 323 and, from May 1943, TG 5 – deviated even from that. The Me 321 transport glider was employed in *Gruppen* which included the *Giganten* plus Bf 110 and later He 111 Z towplanes. The Me 323 entered service with *I. Gruppe* of *KG.z.b.V. 323* in the Mediterranean in November 1942 and with *II. Gruppe*, also in the Mediterranean, in April 1943. *III. Gruppe* came into existence on 1 March 1943 (created from *K.Gr.z.b.V. 900*) and was disbanded in June 1943. A number of its aircraft went to *I. Gruppe*. The *5. Staffel* of the Replacement Transport Geschwader (*E.T.G.*) was formed in Schönwalde in June 1943 with five Me 323s. Based in Leipheim, the *Staffel* was used for conversion training (while still flying transport missions in France and to the Balkans). From then TG 5 consisted of the Stabsstaffel, I. *Gruppe* with three *Staffeln* and II. *Gruppe* with four *Staffeln*. The authorized strengths may well have remained pure theory. One can assume that the *Stabsstaffel* had three *Giganten* and the other *Staffeln* six each. In addition the *Geschwader* had a Bf 108 for use as a courier aircraft, while *I.* and *II. Gruppe* each had a Ju 52 for use as utility transport (*I. Gruppe*'s aircraft was C8+DB, WNr. 640191).

The last Me 321 gliders (about twenty) were scrapped in December 1943 when the GS-Kdos 1 and 2 were disbanded. It is likely that only two or three of the aircraft were still serviceable.

The trail of the last Me 323 *Giganten* disappeared toward the end of the war between Chrudim and Skutsch (Protectorate of Bohemia and Moravia). IV./TG 4, which received almost all of TG 5's aircraft when that unit was disbanded in August 1943 and possibly those of 5./E.T.G., was based in the Protectorate until the end of 1944. Most sank into the soft earth and were attacked by enemy aircraft. It is not known if any *Giganten* managed to return to Reich territory toward the end of the war. What was left of TG 4 was disbanded at Mühldorf/Mettenheim in January 1945. It is extremely likely that there were no *Giganten* there when Allied aircraft attacked the airfield on 26 April 1945.

The Me 321 was aptly named Gigant (Giant). With a wingspan of 55 meters it was by far the largest glider the world had ever seen. (Nowarra)

Similar in size to the Me 321, the Me 323 dwarfed all previous transport aircraft. (Griehl)

The Ju 52 was the most numerous German transport aircraft, outnumbering by far all other types, which included a small number of foreign machines. (Dabrowski)

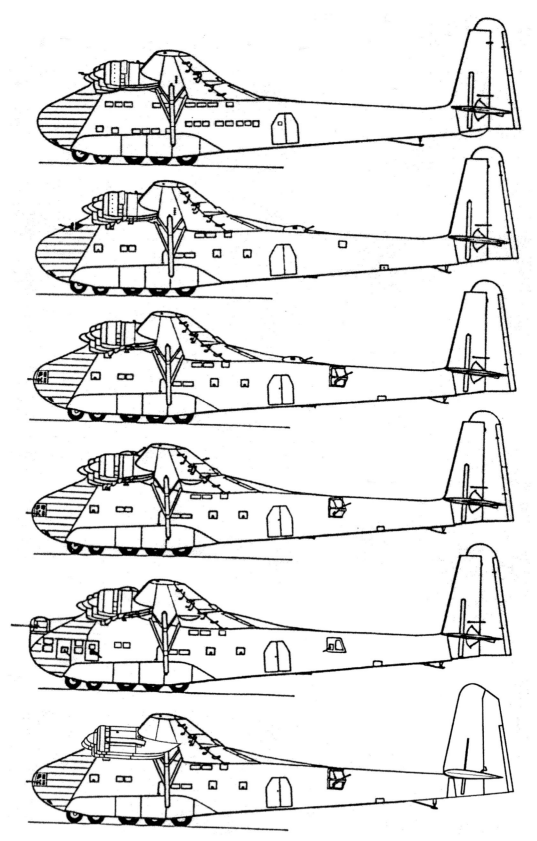

The Me 323 was produced in a number of versions. From top to bottom:
The Me 323 V2, converted from an Me 321, forerunner of the D-series, equipped with Bloch power plants with Ratier variable-pitch propellers.
Me 323 D-1 with Bloch power plants and Ratier variable-pitch propellers.
Me 323 D-2 with LeO power plants and Heine two-blade propellers, D-6 with LeO power plants and Ratier variable-pitch propellers, and the E-1 with strengthened airframe and revised armament plus, in some cases, more powerful Gnôme-Rhône 14 R engines (1,180 H.P.).
Me 323 E-2 with LeO power plants and Ratier variable-pitch propellers and strengthened armament. The E-2 designation has yet to be confirmed by any document, however it will be used here to distinguish between aircraft with very different armament packages.
Me 323 E-2/WT with LeO power plants or Gnôme-Rhône 14 R engines with Ratier variable-pitch propellers. Heavily-armed escort aircraft built in very small numbers.
Me 323 V16, prototype for the planned F-series with improved airframe, modified tail section and Junkers Jumo 211 F engines. The various prototypes were used for a wide variety of tests and in some cases exhibited clear external differences from production aircraft.

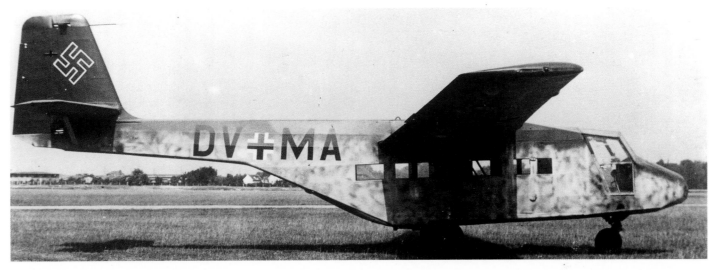

Dipl.-Ing. Kalkert designed the Ka 430 transport glider in 1943, long after production of the Me 321 had ceased. Twelve examples are believed to have been built by war's end, however they saw no action. The Ka 430 V1 (DV+MA) made its first flight at Erfurt in 1944. Its last flight was on 1 March 1945. (Nowarra)

The DFS 331 was an attempt to provide a more capable successor to the DFS 230. Only one example, KC+HB, was built, making its first flight on 30 September 1940. The RLM decided in favor of the Go 242, however, and the DFS 331 program was halted. The aircraft was designed by Hans Jacobs. Wingspan 23 m, length 15.81 m, empty weight 2 300 kg. (Nowarra)

The Go 244 was a powered version of the Go 242. Equipped with two Gnôme-Rhône 14 m engines each producing 715 H.P., the Go 244 was underpowered and incapable of single-engined flight when loaded. The aircraft was soon withdrawn from service. (Nowarra)

1

From Concept to First Flight

At the end of August 1940 the *Wehrmacht* began preparations for the invasion of Great Britain, code-named "Operation Sea Lion." Hitler apparently felt strong enough to take this step after his military successes in Europe. A fleet of 155 transport ships, 1,277 ferries and lighters and 1,161 motor vessels was assembled. The invasion force consisted of the 9th and 16th Armies with the 6th Army in reserve.

On 13 August 1940 the *Luftwaffe* launched "Operation Eagle", an intensification of the air war against England, with the objective of achieving air superiority over the island. Air Fleet 2 (GFM Kesselring, based in Holland), Air Fleet 3 (GFM Sperrle, based in northern France) and Air Fleet 5 (*Generaloberst* Stumpf, based in Norway) took part with a combined force of 2,355 bombers, fighters and dive-bombers. The initial phase of the invasion was supposed to see three regiments of the 7th Air Division parachute into England while an assault regiment was to land in gliders. As many as 100 training gliders (*Kranich* and some Horten all-wing gliders) were assembled and given a camouflage finish. When the moment was right they were supposed to transport up to 100 kg of ammunition each. This was apparently seen as a back-up measure, "just in case."

On 4 October 1940, in a letter to Ernst Udet, the Chief or Air Armaments and head of the Technical Office of the RLM, the prominent aircraft designer Willy Messerschmitt proposed a "tank-carrying glider" to be towed by four Ju 52s. The idea of a large-capacity glider for the transport of heavy and bulky loads had been put to paper for the first time. Udet obviously considered the proposal feasible and useful in the invasion, for on 8 October 1940 a team personally assembled by Messerschmitt began initial work on the project. In charge of the project was *Oberingenieur* Josef Fröhlich, who had come to Messerschmitt from Arado in 1937.

All did not go as planned, however: Hermann Göring, *Reichsmarschall* and Commander-in-Chief of the *Luftwaffe*, was unable to achieve his *Führer*'s wish for air superiority over England. The RAF had destroyed the myth of the *Luftwaffe*'s invincibility.

On 12 October 1940, two months after the start of "Operation Eagle", Hitler was forced to postpone "Operation Sea Lion." The plan was kept alive until spring of 1941, but merely as a means of exerting pressure on Great Britain. In spite of this, three days later on 15 October Messerschmitt began design work on the as yet unnamed large-capacity transport glider. The first technical description of the glider project was dated 1 November 1940 and was initially designated Me 261 w (w = *weiterentwickelt*, or further developed, possibly a cover designation) and was produced by Josef Fröhlich and Walter Rethel, who had also come from Arado to Messerschmitt, in 1938. The proposed aircraft was 28 meters long with a wingspan of 56 meters and was capable of transporting 22 tons, equal to the weight of a Panzer IV tank.

On 5 November 1940 in Berlin, Willy Messerschmitt spoke with Adolf Hitler and described his idea for a large-capacity transport glider. As Udet had done before, the designer was obviously able to sell his idea to the dictator, for just one day later the RLM issued high priority development contracts to Messerschmitt (whose project had been designated the Me 321 *Gigant*, code name "Warsaw South") and a second to Junkers (Ju 322, initially called *Goliath* then *Mammut*, code name "Warsaw East"). The Messerschmitt design was to be built of steel tube, wood and fabric, while the Junkers aircraft would be of wooden construction. Messerschmitt was able to win the contest with its design, which was based on the earlier M 20 commercial transport. Junkers was unsuccessful, in no small part because of its lack of experience in building wooden aircraft. And, unlike Messerschmitt, Junkers had no experience in designing gliders.

On 26 November 1940 Messerschmitt proposed the idea of a powered version of the *Gigant*, designated the Me 323, to the RLM for the first time. While design work on the Me 321 was under way, the head of the project bureau, Dipl.-Ing. Woldemar Voigt, and his assistant Dipl.-Ing. Wolfgang Degel had made the first calculations for a version of the *Gigant* powered by four DB 601 engines. The technical description of the Me 323 was completed on 1 February 1941. Initial shop work on the Me 321 began in January 1941 at the Leipheim airfield near Ulm. Work on the huge glider had been moved there for reasons of secrecy and capacity.

The necessary glider training had begun some weeks earlier, at the end of 1940. At the DFS in Ainring the pilots first practised towing *Kranich* gliders with He 72 *Kadett* and Fw 44 *Stieglitz* biplanes. Then, on 18 November 1940, an attempt was made with four He 72s towing a DFS 230. This experiment failed when the left outer towplane developed a problem. The next attempt was a success, as were several subsequent tests with just three He 72s. In the days that followed, further flights were made with four He 72s again and on 26 November with five. The pilots were Kurt Oppitz, Karl Schieferstein, Paul Stämmler, Erich Klöckner, Fritz Lettmayer, Heinz Schubert and Hermann Zitter, and no set order was followed. The pilots took turns flying the left, right and center towplanes and the glider. When five towplanes were used Klöckner or Lettmayer usually flew the glider. They were also the pilots in subsequent towed flights which took place at Leipheim. There the DFS 230 was exchanged for a Ju 52 (D-AOQA). The propeller of the Ju 52's central engine had been replaced by a coupling to which tow cables were attached. Three other Ju 52s served as glider tugs. During takeoff the towed Ju 52's outer engines were kept idling so that the "glider" might land safely in the event of a failed takeoff or separation from the tugs. Towed flights were also made with three He 111s crewed by members of the *Luftwaffe*. The Ju 90 KB+LA, WNr. 002, was also used as a tug, even though it had not been designed for that role. After extensive formation flying practise, tests began with three Bf 110s as towplanes. The DFS provided four aircraft (VJ+OF, VJ+OI, VJ+OJ and VJ+OL), one of which was a spare, plus pilots Zitter (center), Schieferstein (right wingman), Oppitz (left wingman) and Stämmler (reserve). The initial flights from 17 February to 7 March 1941 were conducted at Leupheim with Ju 52 D-AOQA simulating the glider. On 10 March this aircraft was again towed, with Lettmayer at the controls, and this time the Bf 110 tugs were flown by *Luftwaffe* personnel. Following these preliminary trials, *Gigant* tow trials began on 8 March. The use of three Bf 110s, which had come to be generally referred to as the "*Troika-Schlepp*" (triple tow) method, was soon found to be the most effective way of getting the Me 321 off the ground. Tests with the Ju 90 KB+LA had shown that that its effectiveness decreased sharply as the glider's loaded weight increased, and the trio of Messerschmitts was used from the very beginning when the Me 321 V2 began flight trials.

Later, in the period from 22 August to 25 October 1941, ten flights were made from Obertraubling with an Me 321 towed by three He 111s (DF+OQ, DF+OR, DF+OS) flown by Zitter, Schieferstein and Oppitz. Afterwards the He 111 was used as a glider tug to some extent, however the Bf 110 continued to shoulder most of the burden.

The "*Troika-Schlepp*" was always "pure acrobatics" as Ernst Udet once phrased it, and in spite of meticulous preparation remained a very dangerous procedure. The loss of an engine by one of the tugs during takeoff could have catastrophic results, as was later demonstrated. Even the experienced pilots of the DFS initially had great difficulties with the couplings on the rear of their machines. In particular, the aircraft on the left displayed a tendency to swing to the left. The relocation of the tow coupling to the right wing root, which aligned the direction of tow with the aircraft's center of gravity, helped alleviate the problem. Nevertheless, it is perhaps understandable that the accident rate rose sharply when less highly-trained pilots began flying the glider tug Bf 110s. This high accident rate prompted Ernst Udet to sponsor the development of one of the most unusual aircraft of the Second World War, the He 111 Z, which was a combination of two standard bombers. More about this later.

While the DFS was responsible for the majority of Me 321 testing, at an early stage the *Luftwaffe* began preparing for the new task of towing the giant glider. Toward the end of 1940 *Oberstleutnant* Karl Drewes, the Kommandeur of *II./KG.z.b.V. 1*, was given the job of establishing a "*Luftwaffe* Tow School" which was to be based at Jesau airfield near Königsberg. The purpose of the school was to train Bf 110 crews to tow the Me 321 heavy transport glider. In spring 1941 the tow school moved to Stuttgart-Echterdingen. Training began with the Messerschmitts flying as flights of three towing a secially modified DFS 230 glider (CB+MW). To accustom future Me 321 pilots to the height of the glider's cockpit above the ground (approximately 6 meters), the DFS had fitted the DFS 230 with a special tall undercarriage. These measures raised the cockpit to a height of 3.2 meters above the ground. Many years after the war one of the former *Gigant* pilots still remembered the long-legged aircraft well. It was a very odd looking aircraft but it did the job, and training on the Me 321 and the *Troika-Schlepp* combination could begin.

In addition, two training detachments were formed in Leipheim. These began operations in 1941 from airfields at Leipheim, Obertraubling, Merseburg and Langensalza. The detachments were commanded by Hptm. Mauß and Oblt. Kalthoff.

On 10 January 1941 preparations for a landing in England were cancelled for good, making it unnecessary to form a complete Me 321 *Geschwader*. The mission of the tow school and the detachments under its command was reduced to training additional pilots and readying Me 321-glider combinations for operations on the Eastern Front in autumn 1941. With the start of Me 323 production (and the conversion of a number of Me 321 gliders into Me 323s through the installation of engines), the entire glider school became redundant.

But this was not the end of the *Gigant* story. The first Me 321 was ready to take to the air at the end of February 1941 and pilots began acquiring experience on the largest glider ever to fly.

At the turn of the year 1941-42 the headquarters and elements of the two training detachments moved to Posen. Four transport glider *Staffeln* were formed there for the purpose of training glider pilots (DFS 230 and Go 242). The Posen air base also included auxiliary landing fields at Schroda and Bednary. *Oberstleutnant* Drewes left the school, which was renamed *Ergänzungsgruppe (S) 2* (Replacement Training *Gruppe* – Glider) in April 1942. In mid-June 1942 the *II.(Go.)/LLG 2* was created from one part of this *Gruppe*. This unit existed for just a few weeks before it was disbanded. In command of *Erg.Gr. (S) 2* was *Oberstleutnant* Snowadzki with Oblt. Winkler as adjutant. The *Staffeln* were commanded by Hptm. Buchmann, Hptm. Grotzke, Hptm. Gruber and Hptm. Eckstein. It was assumed that, once on the ground, the glider pilots would have to fight with the troops and they received the necessary training. This may have been the reason why *Erg.Gr. (S) 2* was turned into an infantry battalion and its pilots and technicians employed as grenadiers and machine-gunners in North Africa. Only a small remnant remained in Posen. Following the surrender of Army Group Africa only a few members of the battalion were able to

reach Sicily. Meanwhile, in Posen an active Gruppe had again been created under the command of Hptm. Nevries and it resumed the work of training glider pilots. *Oberstleutnant* Snowadzki assumed command of the detachment again after recuperating from wounds suffered in Africa. On 9 September 1944 orders again came for *Erg.Gr. (S) 2* to disband. The unit's most capable people were ordered transferred to the Parachute Army's replacement and training division.

Adolf Hitler fell into the role of the infallible military leader. At first it looked as if he was right – until he decided to conquer the British Isles. (Nowarra)

Professor Willy Messerschmitt (right) and Generaloberst Ernst Udet (left) during a factory inspection. Udet became Generalluftzeugmeister (Head of Air Armaments and Supply) on 1 December 1939. (Roosenboom)

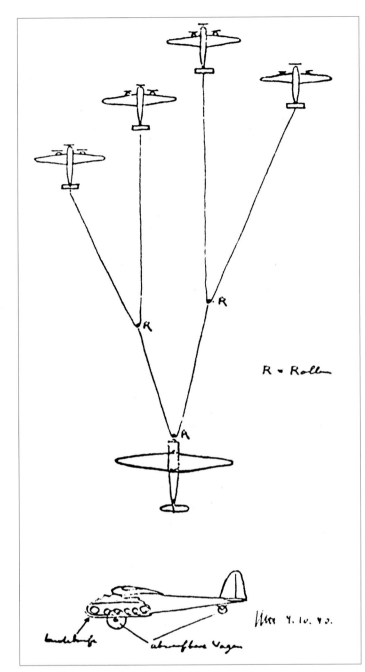

Rough sketch by Willy Messerschmitt for Ernst Udet for his proposal for a "tank-carrying glider." (MBB)

Oberingenieur Josef Fröhlich after the war. (Vogel)

Reichsmarschall Hermann Göring delivers a speech to Junkers employees in Dessau. He failed to achieve air superiority over England as he had promised his "Führer." (Nowarra)

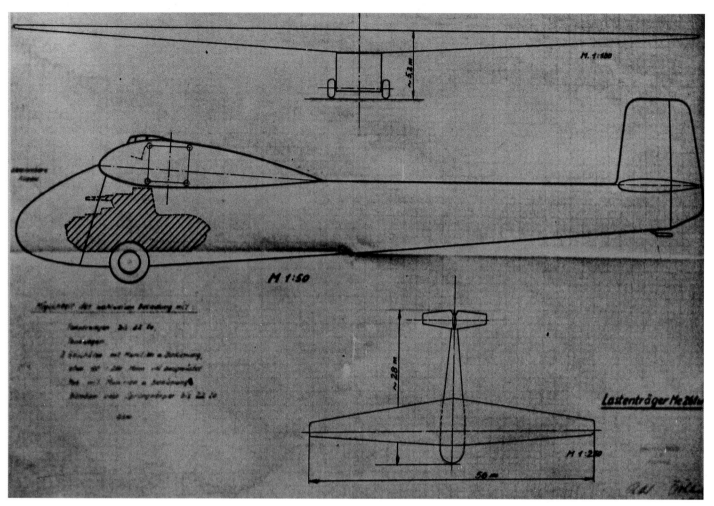

The basic design of the Messerschmitt glider dated 1 November 1940, initially designated Me 261 w (w = Weiterentwicklung, or further development). (Radinger)

Design predecessor for the Me 321 was the M 20 commercial aircraft designed by Messerschmitt in 1928 and built by the Bayerische Flugzeugwerke. (Nowarra)

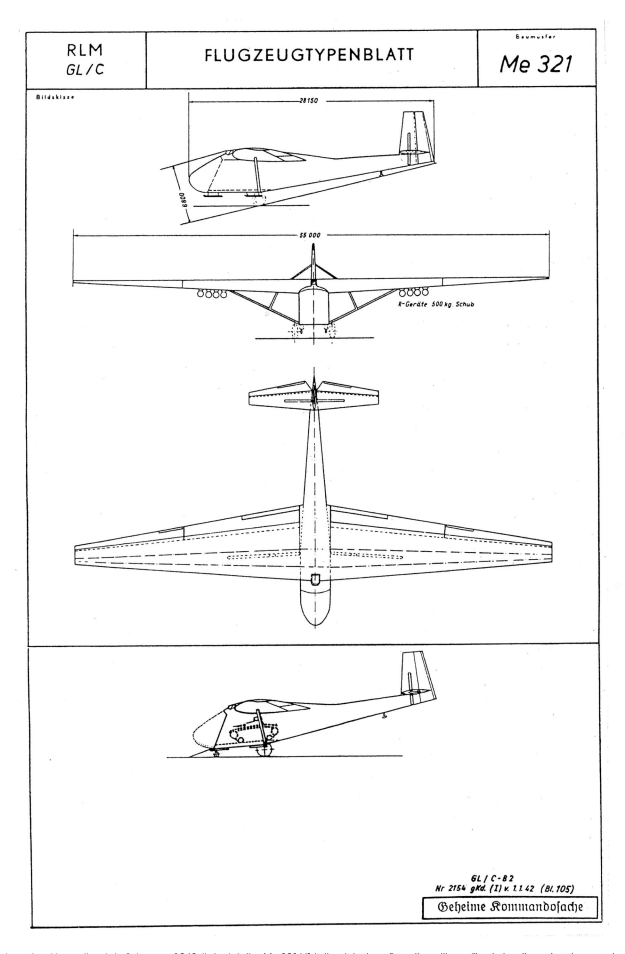

| RLM GL / C | FLUGZEUGTYPENBLATT | Baumuster Me 321 |

Bildskizze

28150

6800

55 000

R-Geräte 500 kg. Schub

GL / C - B 2
Nr 2154 gKd. (I) v. 1.1.42 (Bl. 105)

Geheime Kommandosache

While this type sheet bears the date 1 January 1942, it depicts the Me 321 V1 in its original configuration with no dihedral on the outer wing panels and the no horn balances on the rudder. (Radinger)

Right: Dipl.-Ing. Woldemar Vogt, who became head of Messerschmitt's project bureau in 1938. (Radinger)

Far right: Postwar photo of Dipl.-Ing. Wolfgang Degel. He was Voigt's co-worker and later headed development of the Me 262. (Radinger)

Below: The DFS in Ainring used an He 72 Kadett biplane in its initial towing trials. (Nowarra)

Three Bf 110s and a Ju 52 during towing trials in Leipheim. (Nowarra)

Troika-Schlepp "train" ready for takeoff. (Nowarra)

Successful takeoff by a Troika-Schlepp flight, with three Bf 110s towing an Me 321. (Nowarra)

Troika-Schlepp with three He 111s. This formation was tested in Obertraubling, however it was used little in practice. (Schlaug)

The He 111 Z towplane was created in 1941 as an alternative to the dangerous Troika-Schlepp method. The type entered service in 1942 and was capable of towing a fully-loaded Me 321. (Roosenboom)

The long-legged undercarriage of this DFS 230 raised the cockpit to a position approximately 3.2 meters above the ground. (Petrick)

The special undercarriage was obviously built using undercarriage parts from the Fieseler Fi 156 Storch. (Petrick)

2

The Ju 322 *Mammut*

On 6 November 1940 Junkers received a development contract from the RLM for a large-capacity transport glider. Code-named "Warsaw East" it was to be of all-wood construction with a maximum payload of 20 metric tons. Since the vehicle was to be designed to be used in action just once, simplicity and speed of manufacture had to be stressed in the designing the machine.

The director of the Junkers design bureau, Dipl.-Ing. H. Gropler, was therefore instructed to provide an aerodynamicist and a project engineer "for a highly secret special project." Neither Gropler nor his staff were told what the project involved. Prof. Heinrich Hertel, head of the Junkers development bureau, may have been one of the few people who was told. It is possible that he was responsible for the basic design. Merseburg airfield was selected as the site of this "special project." When the Second World War began, Junkers had transferred some of its Ju 88 production there (final assembly, equipment installation and factory flight testing). In charge of the secret development team was *Ingenieur* Paul W. Hall (previously with Fieseler). Other members of the team were Steinbach, Fölz, Merten and Fritz Freitag. From the EF 94 project evolved the Ju 322 (design sketch dated 3 December 1940), a transport glider. The design initially had a wingspan of 82.35 meters, however, as this exceeded the dimensions of every existing hangar, it was reduced to 64.8 meters. The proposed aircraft was 26.3 meters long and 11.6 meters high. Wing area was 638.54 square meters and takeoff weight 45 219 kg. Initially dubbed *Goliath* and then *Mammut*, the RLM gave the aircraft its approval while it was still in the preliminary design stage (November 1940).

Junkers based the design of the Ju 322 Mammut on its G 38 commercial aircraft of 1929, which in turn was based on a Junkers patent from 1910. It was planned that the deep, thick cantilever all-wing aircraft should carry its payload within the center-section, while the sole purpose of the box-shaped fuselage was to support the tail surfaces. The first problem arose from the RLM's demand that the aircraft be built exclusively of wood and fabric. For 25 years Junkers had been the leading German manufacturer of all-metal aircraft, and it had a great deal of experience in building large aircraft, however it had none in the manufacture of wooden machines. It was for this reason that the company's directors opposed the plan to build the aircraft of wood, however they were unable to change RLM's mind. The second area of difficulty was the procurement of materials. Sufficient wood to construct the initial batch of 90 Ju 322s had to be procured in a very short time (planned production total 200 machines). This proved possible, however in some cases the materials were on inferior quality. Like Messerschmitt, Junkers had to proceed with great haste and begin construction of the first aircraft while design work was still going on. Ju 88 production at the airfield was halted and in November 1940 every available carpenter and woodworker in the area was drafted. By the beginning of March one Ju 322 was complete and the manufacture of components for another 90 had begun.

Loading of the Ju 322 was to be accomplished using a loading ramp, as the aircraft had to be on the takeoff trolley before loading began. No external aids were required for unloading, because the leading edge folded down to form the necessary ramp. The cockpit was off-centered to port in order to maintain a uniform height in the cargo area (11 meters wide, 14 meters deep). Designing the takeoff trolley was difficult, for the large glider required an undercarriage of considerable strength. Several versions were tested, trolleys with 8, 16 and 32 wheels. The structure was made of steel tube and when complete weighed 8 tons. The Ju 322 with its four skids sat on top of the trolley and was supposed to lift off as soon as the necessary speed was reached. Initial trials with models produced doubts that this method would be practical. Various takeoff trolleys were later dropped from heights of two to five meters. Evaluation of test results revealed that, depending on ground clearance, the trolleys rebounded to almost the height from which they had been dropped.

Meanwhile the company's lack of experience in wooden aircraft construction led to differences of opinion between the design bureau and the experimental department. The statisticians had calculated that the wing spar would be able to bear a load factor of 1.8, a figure which the experimental department doubted. In an effort to prove the claim, the first spar was jacked up in one of the aircraft hangars at Merseburg and placed under stress. It broke at a load factor of 0.9. The subsequent investigation revealed that the spar been improperly glued. The second spar broke at a load factor of 1.1. At that time components for the first thirty Ju 322s had already been manufactured. The first loading experiments also ended in failure. The prototype was placed on its takeoff trolley and a Panzer IV weighing approximately 18 tons was driven up the steep ramp leading to the cargo compartment. It reached the top of the ramp, tipped forward and broke through the floor of the cargo compartment. Reinforcement of the affected areas raised the empty weight of the Ju 322 by four tons, reducing cargo capacity from 20 to 16 tons. Revised calculations, however, showed that in the best case no more than 12 tons could be loaded.

Like Messerschmitt, Junkers faced the problem of finding a suitable towplane. It was originally thought that the Ju 322 would be towed using the *Troika* principle proposed by Messerschmitt (three Bf 110s or He 111s), however this method was still unproven. Junkers was thus left with no other choice than the Ju 90, which had already successfully towed the first Me 321.

Unlike Messerschmitt, Junkers failed to keep the existence of its big glider a secret. The British had become aware of the activities going on at Merseburg from agents and aerial reconnaissance, and the BBC had broadcast details of the "Merseburg Giants." Final preparations for the first flight of the Mammut were completed in March 1941, or approximately two months after the final decision was made to abandon then idea of an invasion of the British Isles. *Generaloberst* Udet came to examine the Ju 322. He stated openly what more than a few skeptics at Junkers had been fearing for a long time: "This aircraft will not fly, the proportions of the tail are wrong. The machine will never be stable." The first flight was to demonstrate the correctness of Udet's prognosis. At least an attempt was made to correct the problem of the aircraft's center of gravity, which was too far aft when the machine was empty. Two drum-shaped tanks each capable of holding two tonnes of ballast were attached to the nose of the aircraft on either side of the cargo compartment.

The first flight was planned for 6 March 1941 but was postponed due to technical problems. The second attempt took place on 12 March. *Flugkapitän* Peter Hesselbach and Alfred Funke took their places at the dual controls of the Ju 322 V1. The glider was connected to the tug, Ju 90 Z-3 KB+LA (WNr. 002), by a 16-mm tow cable which was 120 meters long. The four-engined machine was flown by *Flugkapitän* Konrad Pernthaler and *Flugversuchs-*

ingenieur (Flight Test Engineer) Anton Endres. The two pilots applied full power for takeoff, however the aircraft did not reach flying speed until just short of the airfield boundary, while the Ju 322 was still rolling. The glider's skids had become hooked in the 8-tonne takeoff trolley, however the badly-damaged undercarriage separated just as the glider reached the airfield boundary. The glider's pilots were barely able to keep the machine in the air. The aircraft was so unstable about the normal axis that it yawed badly, almost causing the towplane, which was barely above stall speed, to crash.

The pilots of the Ju 322 immediately released the tow cable and went into an extended glide while the Ju 90 pulled away in a wide arc. Course changes in the low-flying *Mammut* were impossible and the so the two pilots put the machine down onto a freshly-plowed field between the villages of Blösien and Knapendorf near Merseburg. The area around the landing site was immediately cordoned off. Several days later, after the ballast tanks had been drained and necessary repairs had been made to the takeoff trolley, two tanks towed the aircraft back to the airfield.

Following repairs to the *Mammut* and considerable enlargement of the undercarriage, one more flight was made at the end of April 1941. Prior to this much thought was given as to how to get the big glider into the air more safely than on its first flight. The solution to the problem seemed to lie in the *"Troika-Schlepp"* method then being used by Messerschmitt. The necessary aircraft were ordered to Merseburg and training began. In addition, a new tow coupling with three lugs had been fabricated in a workshop in Weißenfels. The *Mammut*, with a new fin and rudder, was now ready for its second flight with three Bf 110s as tugs.

The Ju 322 again exhibited instability about the normal axis, making it difficult for the towplanes to maintain course. Two of the towplanes collided, causing the third Bf 110 and the Ju 322 to crash northeast of the airfield. At the beginning of May 1941 the *Technische Amt* ordered a halt to the tests and to the "Warsaw East" part of the program. Soon afterwards all of the *Mammuts* under construction were sawn up and the wood used as fuel for wood-gas generators in motor vehicles. This ended an undertaking by Junkers which had cost 45 million *Reichsmarks*. There are virtually no surviving documents concerning the testing of the Ju 322. Officially there were no photos of the aircraft in the Junkers photo archive: all documents pertaining to the aircraft were placed under lock and key and were ultimately destroyed.

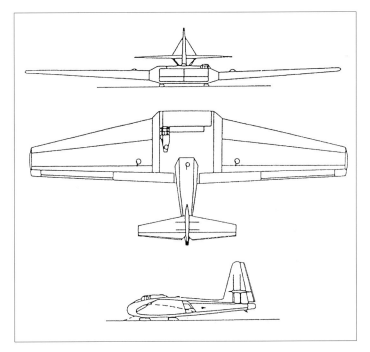

Junkers EF 94 (EF = Entwicklungsflugzeug, or development aircraft), the predecessor of the Ju 322. This giant had a ten-meter-wide loading door and a wingspan of 82.35 meters. (Dabrowski)

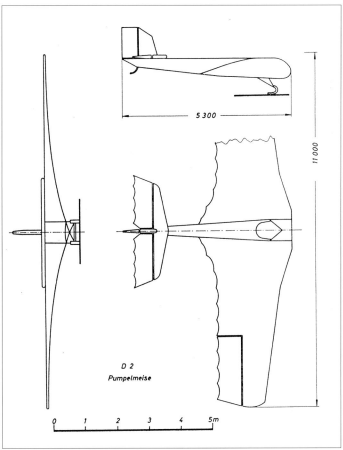

Below: The Junkers G 38 (first flight of D-2000 on 6 November 1929) is believed to have provided the inspiration for the Ju 322's design. (Nowarra)

The D 2 "Pumpelmeise" glider built in Darmstadt in 1920 bore an amazing similarity to the "Mammut" design. (Zacher)

While of poor quality, these photos prove that this glider did in fact exist. (Zacher)

Taken from almost the same angle as the one depicting the Ju 322 after its forced landing, this photo in particular shows its similarity to the "Pumpelmeise." There is no evidence to suggest that this glider's creator brought his experience to the "Mammut" project, however the possibility cannot be ruled out. (Zacher)

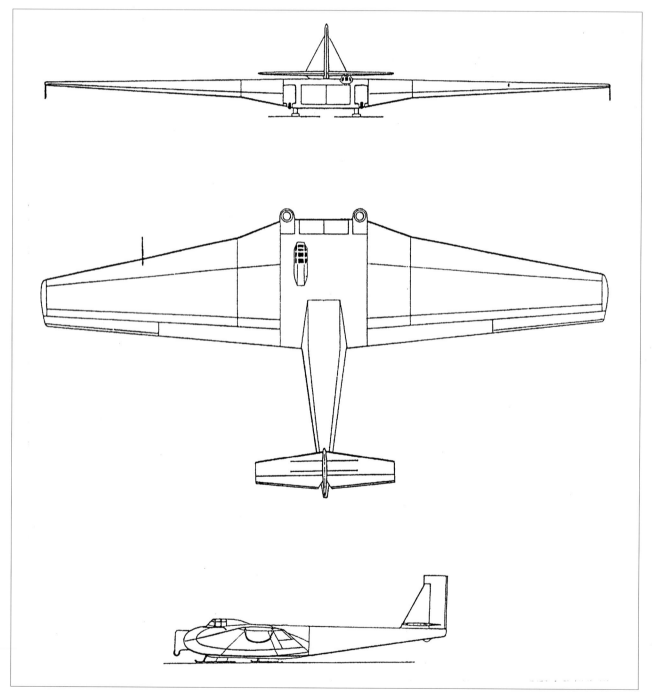

Three-view drawing of the "Mammut." (Dabrowski)

In spite of efforts to camouflage it, the Ju 322 was discovered by Allied aerial reconnaissance in April 1941. (Schlaug)

The Ju 322 on its takeoff trolley, Merseburg airfield, April 1941. (Schlaug)

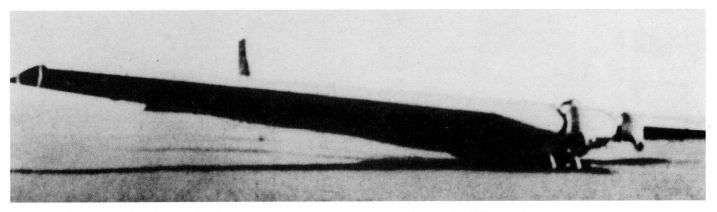

The "Mammut" after its forced landing in a freshly-plowed field. (Nowarra)

3

The First Giants

The first to take a *Gigant* into the air were Messerschmitt company pilot *Flugkapitän* Karl Baur and observer *Ingenieur* Curt Zeiler (area of responsibility: handling characteristics). At 1720 hours on 25 February 1941 the Me 321 V1 took off from Leipheim towed by Ju 90 KB+LA, WNr. 0002. The flight lasted 22 minutes. At the controls of the Ju 90 was *Flugkapitän* Peter Hesselbach of Junkers, as always accompanied by his flight engineer Paul Heerling (flight test engineer Anton Endres also went along on some subsequent flights). The flight by the huge glider ended with a smooth landing. Baur's chief complaint was the high control forces, which later led to the installation of a seat for a second pilot.

The same crew took the V1 up on its second flight at 1142 hours on 5 March 1941. This time the flight lasted 33 minutes. Each new type had to be certified by the *E-Stelle Rechlin*, and flight testing began on the prototype's third flight on 7 March 1941. Baur and Zeiler again formed the crew. Takeoff was at 1241 hours and the flight lasted 42 minutes. On its fourth flight (takeoff time 1729 hours) the V1 was piloted by *Oberstabsingenieur* Karl Francke, then head of the E2 department at the *E-Stelle Rechlin*. Curt Zeiler went along as observer. The next day flight testing resumed at 1022 hours. This time the Me 321 was piloted by the famous aviatrix Hanna Reitsch. Zeiler once again flew as observer and the flight lasted 38 minutes. The sixth flight saw the Ju 90 replaced by three Bf 110s. The towplanes were flown by DFS pilots Hermann Zitter (VJ+OL), Paul Stämmler (VJ+OJ) and Kurt Oppitz (VJ+OF). The Me 321 was piloted by *Feldwebel* Bernhard Flinsch, a well-known glider pilot seconded by the *E-Stelle Rechlin*. Curt Zeiler once again served as observer. Other glider pilots took part in the flight trials that followed, including Otto Bräutigam, holder of several records and now a *Leutnant* in the *Luftwaffe*.

Meanwhile, development of the motorized version, to which the RLM had assigned the designation Me 323, was proceeding well. At that time plans called for the machine to be powered by four Gnôme-Rhône 14-N motors, numbers of which had been captured in France.

Testing of the Me 321 V1 resumed on 14 March 1941. For the seventh flight (takeoff time 1155 hours) the aircraft was flown by a *Luftwaffe* crew for the first time. For safety reasons the Bf 110 *Troika-Schlepp* was replaced by the Ju 90, as always flown by *Flugkapitän* Hesselbach and flight engineer Heerling. At a height of about 150 meters the tow cable coupling was torn out and after just four minutes in the air the *Gigant* made a forced landing. The aircraft overturned on landing but fortunately no one was injured.

The Me 321 V2 took to the air for the first time on 24 March 1941 using the *Troika-Schlepp* method. The crew of Baur and Zeiler apparently aborted the flight due to technical problems, as it lasted just two minutes. It was not until 3 April that the aircraft made its second flight, with the same crew. The flight lasted 28 minutes. Just one day later the V3 made its first flight, which lasted 31 minutes. On 9 April 1941 the V4 took off on its first flight, towed into the air by a Bf 110 *Troika-Schlepp*. The aircraft was crewed by Flinsch and Bräutigam and the flight lasted 17 minutes. One day later the same crew took the V5 into the air on a flight which lasted 27 minutes.

Beginning on 29 April 1941 different crews conducted further test flights in the Me 321 V2, each time with a higher takeoff weight. Acceptance flights of production aircraft began at Obertraubling on 7 May, and from then on test flying gradually came to an end. The surviving prototypes were reclassified as service aircraft, but with one difference. The first Me 321s had a small cockpit designed for a single pilot, with the capability of accepting a second pilot in an emergency. This variant was designated the Me 321 A, while the second variant with a larger cockpit (two pilots side by side with emergency seating for a third man) was dubbed the Me 321 B. Only the later version was considered for conversion to the Me 323.

Since it occurred during testing of the Me 321, the first flight of the motorized *Gigant* will be mentioned here. On 21 April 1941 Baur and Zeiler flew the first motorized version, the Me 323 V1a, at Leipheim. It was a conversion of the Me 321 with four engines and a provisional four-wheel undercarriage. Takeoff-assist rockets mounted beneath the wings helped get the rather underpowered aircraft into the air. Zeiler recalled this notable event: "Baur and I managed to hold the aircraft straight. With the extremely heavy control forces the machine turned sluggishly and stalled very quickly at low speeds. And the Günzburg church tower, which we could not avoid, was coming ever closer. I realized that we must ram it if we were not able to either put our huge crate into a fairly steep right turn – with the danger that we might fall into the middle of Günzburg's marketplace – or gain a few extra meters of altitude – both of us were pulling on the control yokes like mad. I closed my eyes and Karl Baur screamed `Look out!' As we passed overhead there was no more than half a meter clearance between the spire of the Günzburger Frauenkirche and the left wing of the *Gigant*." In spite of everything, testing of the aircraft continued in the days that followed.

It is a little-known fact that a number of flights were made from Obertraubling with three He 111 H-6s as towplanes. The crews consisted of personnel from the DFS and the *E-Stelle Rechlin*. The He 111s were flown by Zitter, Schieferstein and Oppitz, and occasionally also by Fl.Ing. Werner Altrogge of the *E-Stelle Rechlin*. The Me 321 was usually flown by Walter Starbati, who reported serious problems as a result of the left-hand He 111 towplane veering left. Ten such tow flights are known to have taken place in the period from 22 August to 25 October 1941. The heavy glider *Staffeln* which were transferred to the east from July 1941 also had He 111 towplanes on strength, flown by *Luftwaffe* pilots.

The "*Luftwaffe*'s Tow School" was formed in Jesau near Königsberg at the end of 1940. Commanded by *Oberst* Drewes, its instructors were experienced glider pilots. More about this in the chapter "The Concept."

Tragically, there was a serious accident during flight testing which claimed the lives of the Me 321's crew of five. On 28 May 1941 the machine, which had been ferried from Leipheim to Obertraubling the previous day, was loaded with 15,000 liters of water. The *Troika-Schlepp* aircraft took off using takeoff-assist rockets and completed the planned flight program. While on approach to land at Obertraubling airfield the *Gigant* flew into sudden updraft (40 m/sec according to the meteorologist) which caused the tail section to fail. At 2055 hours the aircraft crashed near the village of Barbing from a height of 120 meters. The crew, which consisted of pilots Bräutigam and Finsch plus Lt. Fritz Schwarz, Gefr. Adolf Engel and engineer Josef Sinz (Messerschmitt) had no chance.

There were various other accidents on the ground and in the air during testing and acceptance flights. For example, on 2 June 1941 one of the *Troika-Schlepp* Bf 110s failed to become airborne and crash-landed just beyond the airfield fence. No one was hurt, but the aircraft was a write-off. The other two towplanes just managed to get the *Gigant* to an altitude of 150 meters, then they were forced to disengage. With no other alternative, the crew of the Me 321 made a successful forced landing in a field west of Barbing. On 17 June 1941 a Me 321 made a forced landing near Niederleierndorf after the tow coupling separated. A takeoff strip had to be cleared to get the glider airborne again. *Flugkapitän* Hesselbach landed his Ju 90 KB+LA in the field and positioned it in front of the glider. Using takeoff-assist rockets, he succeeded in getting the *Gigant* airborne again. The list of accidents and forced landings is long. The list ranges from minor damage to total write-offs, from bad scares for the crew to fatalaties. On 12 November 1941 at Obertraubling a Me 321 made the first successful landing using a braking parachute. On the same day, however, another Me 321 made a forced landing near Monheim, a second between Neuburg/Donau and Öttingen and a third near Nördlingen. On 7 December 1941 a storm damaged five Me 321s at Obertraubling air base and tore 15 more from their moorings. On 10 December 1941, while on a transfer flight from Obertraubling to Leipheim, a Me 321 rolled inverted and crashed vertically into a wood near Kelheim. All three crew members were killed. On 25 December another storm damaged several *Giganten* at Obertraubling.

As may be seen, the populace around Obertraubling and Leipheim lived in constant expectation of seeing one of these giants land in their fields. Fortunately, only rarely were buildings damaged.

Flugkapitän Karl Baur and his family in Texas after the war. Baur test-flew virtually every new aircraft developed by Messerschmitt in the period 1940 to 1945. (Modlmeier)

Below: The Me 321 V1 at Leipheim prior to its first flight on 25 February 1941. There is still no mass balance on the rudder and the outer wing panels lack dihedral. (DaimlerChrysler Aerospace)

Ing. Curt Zeiler took part in the Me 321's maiden flights and most that followed. (Modlmeier)

Flugkapitän Peter Hesselbach flew the Ju 90 (KB+LA) which was used in flight trials with the first Giganten. Here he is seen while serving as copilot and navigator of a Ju 290 during the Stalingrad airlift in January 1943 (Kössler)

Below: Ju 90 KB+LA, WNr. 0002, ready to tow an Me 321 without takeoff-assist rockets, which indicates that the glider was lightly loaded. (Kössler)

Here Ju 90 KB+LA is seen towing an Me 321 using takeoff-assist rockets. (Kössler)

The takeoff was successful and the towplane-glider combination slowly gain altitude. (Schlaug)

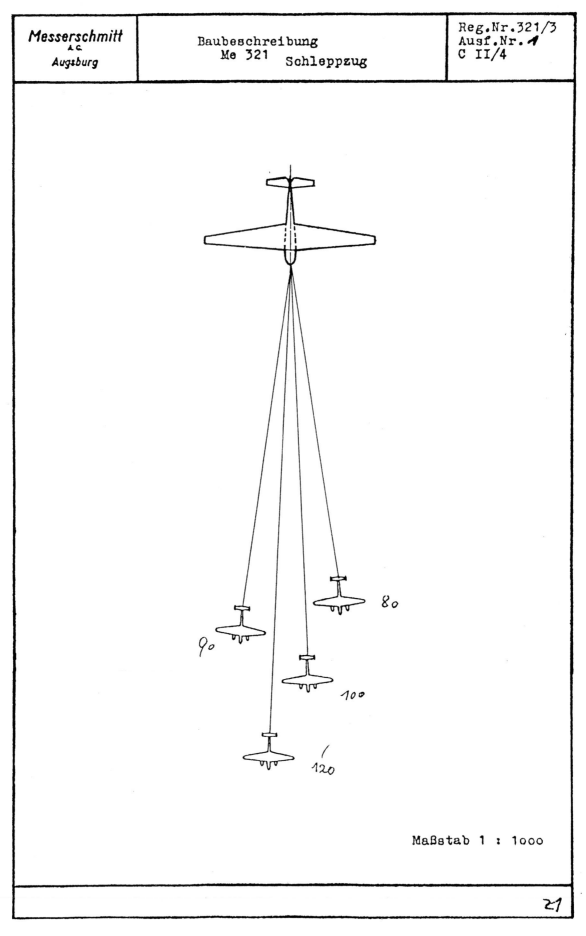

| Messerschmitt A.G. Augsburg | Baubeschreibung Me 321 Schleppzug | Reg.Nr.321/3 Ausf.Nr. 1 C II/4 |

Maßstab 1 : 1000

21

The original plan for multiple towplanes called for four Bf 110s to be used, however in practice three became standard. The numbers beside the aircraft indicate the respective tow cable lengths.

The following four photos depict a different towplane-glider combination, however they clearly illustrate the multiple towplane takeoff procedure. (1) The towplanes and glider slowly gain speed. (Petrick)

All aircraft have lifted off, however the dangerous phase (broken tow cable or engine failure by one of the towplanes) is not yet over. (Nowarra)

The main undercarriage is jettisoned. (Petrick)

Then the forward wheels are jettisoned. After this point the Gigant has a chance of making a safe landing if forced to release prematurely. (Hellwig)

A Gigant after a successful takeoff. The aircraft has yet to jettison its main undercarriage. (Nowarra)

Dangerous "Troika-Schlepp" (Triple Tow): the tow cable of the aircraft on the left has snapped and wrapped itself around the fuselage of the Bf 110. (Peter)

The Me 321 A with small cockpit designed to accommodate a single pilot. (Nowarra)

The cockpit of the Me 321 A. (Nowarra)

The two-seat cockpit of the Me 321 B. the presence of armor plates suggest that this is an operational machine. (Nowarra)

The first powered Gigant, converted from Me 321 W1+SZ. The aircraft sits on a provisional undercarriage and still has the skids of the glider. (Peter)

The Me 323 V1 in flight. The forward engine cowlings have been removed. (Petrick)

The Me 323 V1 at Leipheim. Flugkapitän Baur prepares to land the aircraft. (Petrick)

The well-known glider pilot Otto Bräutigam was killed during Me 321 flight trials while serving as a Leutnant in the Luftwaffe.

Feldwebel Bernhard M. Flinsch was another well-known glider pilot. He, too, was killed in the crash of an Me 321, on 28 May 1941.

Belehrung.

Ich wurde am 6. Okt. 1941 durch Herrn Hein, Gallas, Ref. II/13 darüber belehrt, daß von dem Vorhandensein des Lastenschleppers "Gigant" weder etwas geschrieben (Feldpostbriefe) noch gesprochen werden darf und daß das Fotografieren desselben verboten ist.

Von dem Lastenschlepper besitze ich keinerlei Licht = bilder.

Mir ist bekannt, daß Zuwiderhandelnde Landesverrat begehen und unnachsichtlich mit dem Tode bestraft werden.

Unterschrift.

Although the aircraft's size, its spectacular takeoffs and numerous forced landings made maintaining secrecy virtually impossible, in October 1941 soldiers were still being sworn to secrecy about the existence of the Giganten. (Roba)

Flugkapitän Hanna Reitsch took part in the testing of the first Me 321. By chance she was not on board during the ill-fated flight on 28 May 1941.

Below: As a result of secrecy laws, a would-be photographer literally took his life into his hands in taking a snapshot like this one. (Charles)

The Ju 90 V7, GF+GH, was also used as a towplane for Giganten. Here it is seen at Obertraubling on 27 October 1941. (Nowarra)

4

Description of the Me 321 and Me 323

Not surprisingly, the Me 321 glider and the Me 323 large-capacity transport which was derived from it were largely similar in their basic structure. Both were braced shoulder-wing monoplanes of mixed construction. The wing spar and fuselage frame were steel tube, while the wing, flaps and ailerons were made of pine, simple plywood and fabric skinning. The basic and camouflage finishes were of non-flammable paint. The wings of the Me 321 and Me 323 were identical and will be described in detail later. All control surfaces were mass- and aerodynamically-balanced, while the trim tabs (Flettner) were mass-balanced only. The horizontal stabilizer was trimmed by pivoting the entire end of the fuselage about an axis level with the top of the fuselage framework positioned at right angles to the direction of flight.

The differences between the motorized Me 323 and the Me 321 are described in detail later in this chapter.

Following the abandonment of plans to invade England, the Me 321 transport glider was assigned the role of transporting by air large or heavy items which could previously only be moved by rail or ship. Basically it was viewed as a single-use vehicle; after completing its mission the simply-built aircraft would be blown up on the spot. For this purpose a well-secured demolition charge was placed under the left pilot seat. The delayed-action charge exploded ten minutes after activation. The cargo compartment of the Me 321 was equal in capacity to an 11-meter boxcar of the German State Railway but could accept bulkier items. Its dimensions: width 3.15 meters, height 3.3 meters, sloping to 2.4 meters at the rear end. The floor of the cargo compartment was made of stout hardwood planks and was approximately 11 meters long. Longer loads could exceed this figure by approximately 1.5 meters at the front by at least 2 meters at the rear. The following loads could be accommodated: one 22-tonne or two 9-tonne tanks, vehicles of all types up to 3 meters in height, one 88-mm anti-aircraft gun with tractor and crew, military units with various small vehicles, up to 175 men with equipment or up to 22 tonnes of general cargo. For the purpose of securing loads, twenty-two tie-down lugs were affixed to the fuselage framework on the left and right sides of the cargo compartment. Access to the aircraft's cargo compartment was provided by fabric-covered clamshell doors and a loading/unloading ramp. For takeoff the Me 321 had a jettisonable, non-steerable undercarriage. It consisted of a one-piece axle with two 1650 x 500 cm mainwheels and weighed 600 kg. A rack near the undercarriage attachment point held a 5-kg sledgehammer which was used as a "mounting aid." The Me 321 had to reach a certain altitude before jettisoning the undercarriage, which usually bounced 10 to 15 meters into the air. Two smaller single wheels (650x180) in pivoting forks were located in the nose section and were likewise jettisoned on takeoff. The Me 321 landed on four sprung skids.

Four so-called "smoke generators" (Walther RI-202 b takeoff-assist rockets) could be fitted under each side of the wing center-section outboard of the strut attachment points to help the aircraft take off in overloaded condition or shorten the takeoff run,. Each rocket produced 500 kg of thrust. Use of these was controlled by four electrical switches, each of which activated one pair of rockets. Burn duration was thirty seconds. As a rule four pairs of rockets were used on operations, less on research or test flights. Created specially for the purpose of handling the takeoff-assist rockets, an airfield operations company designated *FBK (S)* fuelled each rocket with "*T-Stoff*" (96 liters) and "*Z-Stoff*" (4.3 liters) and just before a *Gigant* took off placed them on the special mounts beneath the wings and checked the installation. An operational takeoff-assist rocket weighed 325 kg. Ignition was by means of 5-liter compressed air bottles (130 atm) contained in each takeoff-assist rocket. A pressure regulator reduced the pressure to 30 atm and the compressed air forced the two fuels together. This produced a violent reaction but no flame. Once their fuel was expended, the rocket motors were jettisoned from a height of approximately 100 meters, landing by parachute. The rockets were then washed, checked and, if necessary, repaired. They could then be filled with fuel and reused.

When landing with flaps down, the Me 321 could reduce its landing run considerably by releasing a braking parachute (11 meters in diameter). In an emergency the parachute could be jettisoned.

For the pilot's protection the cockpit was armored all around with armor glass panels front and sides. Only the jettisonable cockpit roof of the Me 321 and early Me 323 was made of wooden frames and plexiglass. The cockpit was fitted with side-by-side pilot seats and dual controls. Located between the seats, in easy reach of both pilots, were the release levers for the braking chute and tow coupling. Next to the right-hand seat was the hand crank which controlled the horizontal stabilizer trim and extended the landing flaps.

A powered version of the big glider was considered early on, when towed operations continued to be dangerous and even the use of eight takeoff-assist rockets produced less than satisfactory takeoff performance. Among the methods of propulsion that were considered were pulse jets, steam turbines and the *Mistel* (piggyback) system. On 3 June 1942, Woldemar Voigt of Messerschmitt's project bureau submitted a proposal for an Me 321 powered by pulse jets. He based his proposal on the idea that because of their simple design, pulse jets could be available in sufficient numbers in a relatively short time and that the necessary modifications to the Me 321 would cost little. It was calculated that the added weight of the power plants and fuel tank system would reduce usable load to 14 metric tons for a tactically-suitable range of 300 kilometers.

The aircraft would have been fitted with twelve Argus pulse jets each producing 300 kg of thrust or twenty-four each producing 150 kg of thrust. With twelve pulse jets and maximum thrust, the aircraft would have reached a speed of 300 km/h. The pulse jets were to be mounted beneath the wing center section between the fuselage and the strut attachment points. This made it possible to retain the takeoff-assist rocket attachment points outboard of the struts attachment points. Fuel for the pulse jets would be contained in unprotected metal tanks within the lattice of the wing center section. Ignition of the pulse jets on the ground was by means of compressed air. Additional takeoff-assist rockets could be used to reduce takeoff run at maximum takeoff weight. During flight the pulse jets would be switched on and off as required to maintain the desired airspeed. A DFS 230 glider was successfully tested with pulse jets, however the project was not pursued. No experiments with the *Gigant* are known to have been carried out.

The steam turbine was also considered as a method of propulsion. Prof. Lösch and Dipl.-Ing. Pauker of the TH Wien offered to install the steam turbine they were developing in the Me 321. The proposal was submitted to the RLM's *Technische Amt* by the director of aviation research, Prof. Adolf Baeumker in April 1941, but was not pursued. It is not known if relevant calculations were made or not.

On 28 October 1942 the DFS in Darmstadt made a porposal to the RLM for a version of the Me 321 with three Bf 110s in a *Mistel* arrangement. This saw one Bf 110 attached to the top of the fuselage and one on each side of the fuselage beneath the wings. The six engines of the Bf 110s would propel the Me 321 into the air and at some point in the flight the fighters would separate from it. No trials with this arrangement are known to have taken place.

As previously stated, the Me 323 was developed from the Me 321 and was fitted with four, and later six engines. In addition, in place of the glider's skids, the Me 323 was equipped with a fixed, braked undercarriage. Because of the similarity of the airframes, the Me 321 could be converted into the powered Me 323. The addi-

tion of engines increased airframe weight greatly, resulting in a significant reduction in payload. For example, the payload of the Me 323 D was approximately 11 metric tons, while that of the Me 323 E was only about 9 metric tons. In addition to its role as transport, the aircraft could also be outfitted for specialised roles, such as flying workshop. Later several *Giganten* were ouffitted as heavily-armed escort machines, so-called *"Waffenträger"* (weapons carriers).

Specification (Me 323 D): Wingspan: 55 m, overall length: 28.15 m, maximum height: 10.20 m, wing area: 300 m², equipped weight without weapons and armor: 27 330 kg, cargo bed: 39 m², cargo area: 108 m³, maximum payload: 11,000 kg, aircraft weight: 43,000 kg, overload weight: 45,000 kg, maximum speed: 285 km/h, cruising speed: 250 km/h, range 1 100 km.

The fuselage framework consisted of a tubular steel truss (22-m lattice structure) of rectangular cross section. The entire fuselage was fabric covered. The opening at the front was covered by clamshell doors which opened outwards. Before these could be fully opened, however, the propellers of the two inboard engines (numbers 3 and 4) had to be set to prescribed positions. Each door consisted of fabric-covered tubular frames and was mounted on hinges attached to front sides of the fuselage framework. When closed they were held shut by locking latches. Halfway up each door was a gun position with a lens mount.

In the cargo compartment several plexiglas windows in each side provided the necessary light. Entry was by way of lockable outwards-opening double doors on each side at the aft end of the compartment. The cargo compartment and cockpit (referred to by the crews as the "lower house" and the "upper house") were joined by a ladder inside the fuselage on the port side.

The three-piece wing was trapezoidal in outline with a straight leading edge. It consisted of a one-piece center-section with two-part landing flaps on each side and two upswept outer sections with two-part ailerons. The wing ribs, stiffeners and leading edge skinning were made of wood, while the rest of the wing plus the flaps and ailerons were fabric-covered. The 30-meter center-section spar, which was welded to the fuselage framework, was a box-shaped structure made of steel tube. Steel tubing of varying diameters and thicknesses was welded together to form the tapered box spar. This spar absorbed the bending and torsional forces exerted on the wing. Welded to it were fishplates, to which the ribs were attached. The wing was stiffened by glued-on longitudinal and transverse strips. The plywood leading edge skinning was also glued to the ribbing. Three outriggers were attached to each side of the wing to support the trailing edge flaps and these were also supported by bracing wires. At the outer extremities of the box spar were flanges for attachment of the outer wings. The wing framework was attached to the fuselage framework by four bolts. The wing-fuselage joint was covered by a fabric-covered filet. The wing spar was braced on each side by a single strut extending to the fuselage. This in turn was braced against bending and twisting by two V-struts. All struts were covered by streamlined fairings. The pitot tube for the airspeed indicator was mounted on the port bracing strut.

An outer wing was attached to each end of the wing center-section. Here, too, the spar was a tapered box structure, 12.5 meters in length. The rib structure and attachment of the leading edge were similar to that of the wing center-section. The wingtips consisted of slightly-rounded rib boxes covered with fabric. The upper and lower girders of the center-section spar were attached to the corresponding girders of the outer wings with the aid of flanges (2 x 6 fit bolts top, 2 x 12 bottom). The joint was covered with fabric. Attached to the trailing edge of the center-section were two-part landing flaps made of wood and covered with fabric. To reduce forces, each was fitted with a compensating tab (Flettner). Those on the inner flaps had three attachment points, on the outer flaps only two. The landing flaps and tailplane incidence were now hydraulically-actuated, pressure being delivered by a pump driven by the port inner engine (number 3). A back-up hand pump was located on the starboard side of the cockpit.

A cutout in the center of the leading edge of the wing center-section was designed to accept the cockpit, which was a separate component. It was attached to the front wall of the box spar at four points. On the port side of the cockpit was the pilot's seat, with the co-pilot's seat mounted on the starboard side. Both were bolted to the floor. The seat tub and back were padded as were the arm rests on each side. In front of the pilot seats was the instrument panel in shock-absorbing mounts and a common throttle lever box. Cockpit ventilation was provided by adjustable ventilation inlets on each side. To provide crew protection against enemy fire, the cockpit was designed as an armored box: the floor and the front and rear walls, including the cabin door, consisted of 8-mm armor plates which were bolted together. A two-part superstructure covered the cockpit. It consisted of a load-bearing welded steel tube framework, part covered with *Sekuritglas* (safety glass) and part with plexiglas.

The pilots were provided with the following instrumentation: airspeed indicator with heated pitot, coarse (0 to 6,000 m) and fine (0 – 1,000 m) altimeters, vertical speed indicator, electric turn-and-bank indicator, chronometer, remote reading compass, emergency pilot compass, mechanical stabilizer incidence indicator, position indicators for all three Flettners. There were no engine monitoring instruments, however, just an ignition switch which allowed the pilot to cut each magneto independently or all simultaneously. Mounted on the port side of the cockpit was a pressure gauge (0 to 50 atm) for monitoring the compressed air pressure for the brake system.

Flight engineer positions were placed in the leading edge of the wing between the inboard engines (2 and 3, 4 and 5). These could be reached by means of crawlways inside the wing. The crawlways from the cockpit to the flight engineer positions had a clear height of about 1.3 meters. In each cabin a cushioned seat was attached to the front wall of the box spar. Several windows were incorporated into the leading edge. Above the flight engineer seats were jettisonable glazed escape hatches. The flight engineer thus had a limited view up, down and forward. In front of the seats were instrument panels with engine instruments and to the sides were control boxes with the control levers. The flight engineer's chest

parachute lay on the floor, half under his seat, and in an emergency he had to clip it onto his parachute harness.

Each flight engineer position was equipped with the following instrumentation: one rpm indicator per engine, one boost pressure gauge, two oil temperature gauges (inlet and outlet), one fuel pressure gauge, fuel and oil level gauges, one fuel flow meter (when available), one cooling gill control and indicator system (per engine), one throttle lever, one ignition switch, one injection pump, one fuel cock, fuel tank control switches and one compressed air gauge for the brake system. When variable-pitch propellers were used there was a pitch-control switch for each engine with indicators for three blade positions.

The intercom system linking the pilots, radio operator and flight engineers was part of the FuG X. Three Bosch horns were installed in the cargo compartment for signalling those crew members in the fuselage. A flare pistol and cartridges were kept in the radio operator's compartment.

On-board power was provided by 600-1,200 Watt generators (1 per engine), plus two 12 Volt batteries. Two outboard sockets were provided for connection to external power sources. Power distribution was controlled by the main switchboard located in the radio operator's compartment. In addition to individual power switches it also included a main power switch. Other main power switches were located in the two flight engineer positions.

Flight controls: two control columns with handwheels were provided for elevator and aileron control. The starboard control column could be disconnected. Rudder control was by means of two sets of rudder pedals. Those for the pilot were equipped with compressed air valves for the mainwheel brakes. All controls were operated by a system of control rods and control cables. All control surfaces and the landing flaps were equipped with Flettner tabs. One tab on each of the control surfaces (ailerons, elevators, rudder) could also be used as a trim tab. To reduce control forces, the Flettner tabs on the elevators and rudder were spring-loaded. Because of the increase in aileron forces, especially in turns, a servo-support system was built into the aileron controls. Once a certain level of force was reached and exceeded, electrically-powered servo motors took over and moved the aileron. The servos were controlled by load sensors located in a pushrod between two levers in the aileron control.

Undercarriage: The ten-wheel (initially eight-wheel) undercarriage, which consisted of three 1200 x 420 wheels aft and two 875 x 320 wheels forward on each side, was designed in such a way that it could cross uneven ground in a manner similar to a caterpillar track. Furthermore, the wheels were so arranged that the aircraft always remained in a horizontal position regardless of load. A retractable strut in the extreme rear of the fuselage prevented the aircraft from tipping backward during loading. A sprung tail skid made it possible to conduct three-point landings. In loaded condition tire pressure in all tires was 4.5 atm. In order to spread the shock of landing between several wheels, the two aft wheels acted upon the same shock absorber. Circular spring packets were used as shock absorbers. The six rear wheels were fitted with compressed-air brakes. To reduce drag, a five-piece fairing covered the undercarriage on each side. The gap between the undercarriage and fuselage was also faired.

All production Me 323 aircraft were powered by 14-cylinder air-cooled Gnôme-Rhône 14 N radial engines. The engines were installed as complete units as installed on the Bloch 175 or LeO 45. The three on the starboard side were model –48 right-hand rotation engines, while those on the port side were model –49 left-hand rotation engines. The engine cowlings consisted of the rounded cowling ring, the multi-part cowling body and the intake air duct. Each cylinder had its own short ejector exhaust. The exhausts were distributed equally over the entire extent of the engine cowling rear surface.

In order to prevent engine vibration from being transmitted to the wing structure, the engines were installed on two-piece welded steel tube mounts each consisting of a forward shock-absorbing section and an intermediate section. The latter were attached to the reinforced front box of the wing center section at four points. Even though the differences between the two engine installations were minor, they were not interchangeable. The most significant differences were:

1. The oil cooler of the "Bloch" engine was mounted beneath the engine mount, while that of the "LeO" engine was installed on the side.
2. The intermediate section of the engine mount was canted upwards one degree on the "Bloch" and six degrees down on the "LeO." Moreover, on the "Bloch" the intermediate section was braced by a diagonal strut, whereas the "LeO" was braced by a cruciform-shaped, flange-mounted support.
3. The main cowling was a three-piece structure on the "Bloch" engine and a four-piece component on the "LeO."
4. The arrangement of the engine separation points differed somewhat between the two engines.

The variants of the Me 323 were equipped with the following engines:

A Type of engine not known, two-blade Heine wooden, fixed-pitch propellers.
B and C Type of engine and propeller used are not known.
D-1 "Bloch" engines, three-blade Ratier variable-pitch propellers. Pitch control was electric, preselected by hand.
D-2 "LeO" engines, two-blade Heine wooden, fixed-pitch propellers.
D-6 "LeO" engines, three-blade Ratier variable-pitch propellers. Pitch control was electric, preselected by hand.
E-1 and E-2 as D-6.

No aircraft are known to have used a combination of Bloch engines and Heine propellers.

The two flight engineers in their wing cabins each had to operate and monitor the three engines on their side of the aircraft. The only engine controls available to the pilots were the throttle levers and ignition switches for all six engines. Using the pitch switches of the propeller pitch control system, the flight engineers could regulate engine output in flight independent of rpm and boost pressure. The engines were prone to failure in flight, however an Me 323 was capable of flying on just three engines provided all of the non-functioning engines were not on the same side.

Various pilots have also stated that the engines tended to catch fire when started after sitting idle for some time.

Fuel and oil were each contained in six self-sealing tanks located in the wing. The six fuel tanks each held 890 liters, for a total capacity of 5 340 liters. Additional fuel tanks could be installed in the fuselage, of course at the cost of reduced payload. Each of the six oil tanks held 80 liters, for a total capacity of 480 liters.

Armament: One MG 15 mounted on the roof of the armored cockpit canopy and operated by the radio operator or another crewmember, with a field of fire above and to both sides. Located behind the cockpit, between the steel wall and the wing bearer, was the radio operator's compartment. Above it was a rearwards-sliding hatch which could be used as an escape hatch or makeshift gun position.

Forward defense was provided by two MG 15 (later MG 131) machine-guns in the clamshell doors. One or two rearwards-firing MG 15s were mounted in the fuselage underside. Additional crewmembers had to be carried to man these weapons. A simple modification made it possible to mount MG 34s in the fuselage side walls, for example when the aircraft was used as a troop transport. The MG 34 was designed for use by the infantry and was not an aircraft machine-gun, however it could be installed in the above-named locations instead of the MG 15. Beginning with the E-series, MG 131s were installed in the gun positions in the center of the fuselage as standard equipment. Beginning with the E-2, defensive armament was bolstered by the addition of two EDL 151 power turrets on the upper surface of the wing center-section, each mounting one MG 151/20 cannon. These were manned by gunners or, in an emergency, the flight engineers. The *Gigant*'s armament varied from aircraft to aircraft. In some cases gun positions were not used, while in others improvized positions were added. As development of the Me 323 progressed, operational experience resulted in field modifications which were subsequently adopted as standard equipment.

Emergency Equipment

First-aid kits and medical pouches were kept in the cockpit and above the fuselage doors. The pilot seats were equipped with lap and shoulder belts, the flight engineer seats with lap belts and the gun positions with lap belts and safety harnesses. Each engine was equipped with a fire extinguisher operated by the flight engineers. There were a total of three hand-held fire extinguishers located near the flight engineer cabins and the cockpit and two in the cargo compartment.

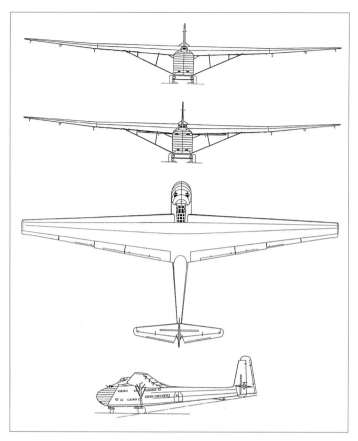

Fuselage framework and box spar produced by Mannesmann (Deutsche Aerospace)

Construction of the Me 321. The photos at the top depict the Me 321 A and those below the Me 321 B, which was flown by two pilots.

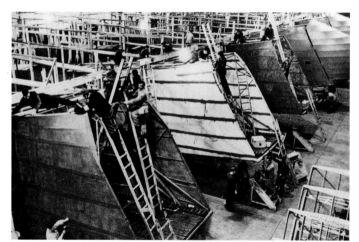

Fitting the nose doors. (Schmoll)

Left: Gigant fuselages under construction. (Schmoll)

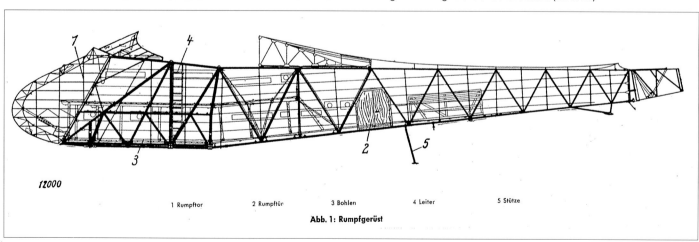

12000

| 1 Rumpftor | 2 Rumpftür | 3 Bohlen | 4 Leiter | 5 Stütze |

Abb. 1: Rumpfgerüst

The fuselage framework of a Gigant. (Handbook)

The requirement for large numbers of personnel was met through the use of a Luftwaffe punishment unit. (Schmoll)

Skinning the fuselage nose. (Schmoll)

Cutting the window openings in the fuselage fabric covering. (Griehl)

Final assembly took place outdoors at Leipheim and Obertraubling. (Radinger)

Attaching the outer wing panels. (Schmoll)

Installing the control surfaces required a great deal of work. (Griehl)

Work on the tail section has been completed. (Thiele)

This Me 321 is almost complete. In this scene the attachment points for the takeoff-assist rockets are being installed. (Schmoll)

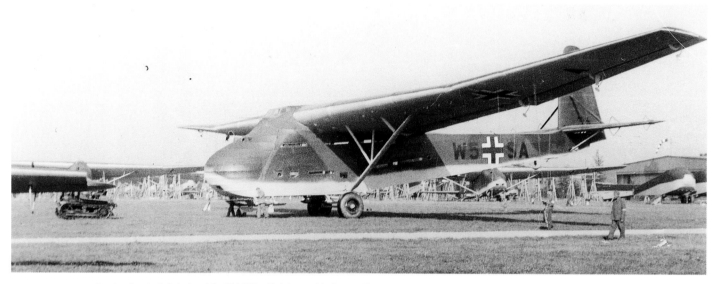

Production in Leipheim. Me 321 W5+SA is towed to the waiting area prior to being ferried to its destination. (Petrick)

Giganten sit in long rows, waiting to be picked up by the Luftwaffe. (Schlaug)

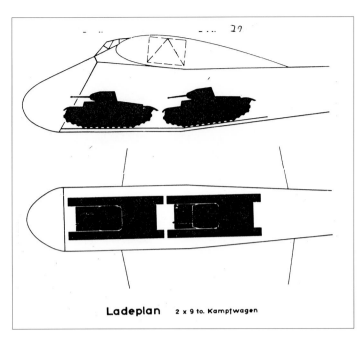

Ladeplan   2 x 9 to. Kampfwagen

With its load capacity of 22 metric tons, the Me 321 was capable of transporting two Panzer II light tanks. (Handbook)

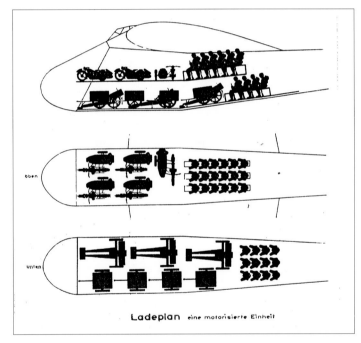

Ladeplan   eine motorisierte Einheit

Optimal utilization of an Me 321's cargo compartment by a motorized unit. (Handbook)

Right: Troop loading exercise using an uncompleted Gigant fuselage. (Peter)

Loading exercise in Leipheim using a Czech-built Panzer Skoda 38 (t) light tank weighing 9.5 metric tons. (Dabrowski)

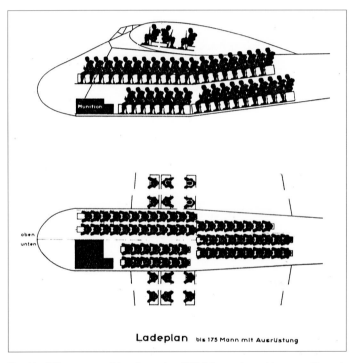

Ladeplan   bis 175 Mann mit Ausrüstung

The Me 321 was capable of carrying 175 fully-equipped troops, although this required some soldiers to sit inside the wing. (handbook)

The huge jettisonable main undercarriage of the Me 321. Tire diameter was 1.65 meters. (Petrick)

This Gigant has four tow couplings and twin nosewheels, which was unusual. (Petrick)

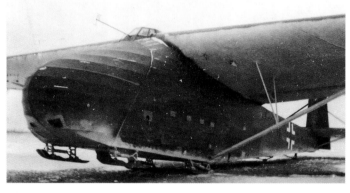

This Gigant made a smooth landing on its skids. Eastern Front, winter 1942. (Petrick)

Right: Reusable R I 500 takeoff-assist rocket. Producing 500 kg of thrust each, these rockets were used by the Me 321 in an overloaded state or to achieve a shorter takeoff run. (Peter)

Below: These takeoff-assist rockets are ready for use, having been refilled and their parachutes packed. (Borchers)

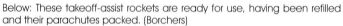

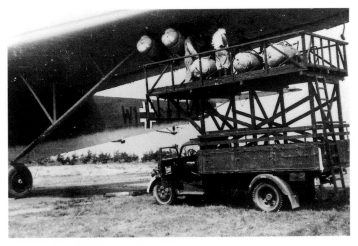

Attaching the rockets beneath the wing of a Gigant. (Borchers)

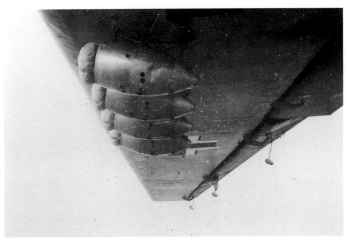

Ready to go. Takeoff-assist rockets beneath the wing of an Me 321. (Borchers)

Once their fuel was exhausted, the rockets were lowered to earth by parachute. Here they assist an Me 323 get airborne. (Peter)

Installing the armored cockpit in a Gigant fuselage. (Schmoll)

With the fabric covering burnt away, the aircraft's armored cockpit is clearly visible. (Petrick)

Even though this Gigant has exploded and burned, its armored cockpit remains relatively intact. (Hellwig)

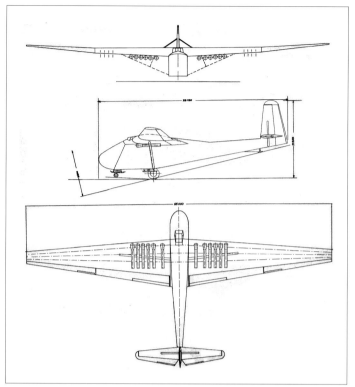

The Me 321 with pulse-jets. (Dabrowski)

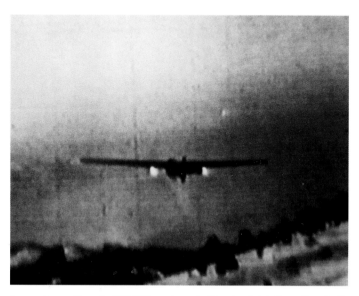

Frame from a film of a DFS 230 equipped with pulse-jets taking off under its own power.

Although trials with the DFS 230 were successful, no tests with the Me 321 are known to have taken place. (Nowarra)

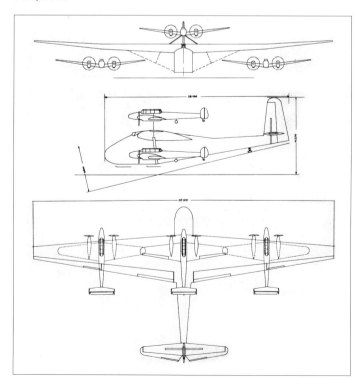

Graphic depiction of the Me 323's ability to accommodate bulky goods compared to a Reichsbahn rail car. (Handbook)

Left: DFS proposal for a Mistel-tow method which was not pursued. (Dabrowski)

Vergleiche zwischen Transportflugzeugen

	Bisherige Transportflugzeuge	Me 323
Gleiche Transport- leistung 12 to	5 Maschinen	1 Maschine
Fliegendes Personal	13 Mann	5 Mann
Fluggewichte	5 x 12,5 to = 62,5 to	1 x 45 to = 45 to
Kraftstoff- verbrauch pro Tonnenkilometer	1 ltr	0,57 ltr
Zuladung pro Maschine	2,4 to	12 to

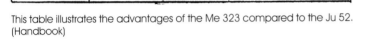

This table illustrates the advantages of the Me 323 compared to the Ju 52. (Handbook)

Right: In preparation for opening the nose doors the propellers of the two inboard engines had to be positioned as illustrated here. (Griehl)

Below: This Opel-Blitz bus also represented the limit of what the cargo compartment could accommodate. (Nowarra)

Loading this truck was precision work, as there was little room to spare. (Griehl)

Fatal consequence of an improperly secured nose door: it opened during takeoff from Pomigliano, Italy and seriously damaged the Gigant. (Hellwig)

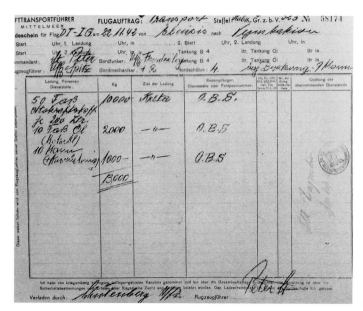

As this bill of lading shows, a load of 13 metric tons was not unusual. With such a load an Me 323, such as DT+IG on 22/11/42, was loaded to the limit. (Peter)

The few windows in the fuselage meant that soldiers flying as passengers had little light and almost no outside view. Flight engineer Storm recalled one occasion when members of an SS unit used their bayonets to cut out additional "windows." (Peter)

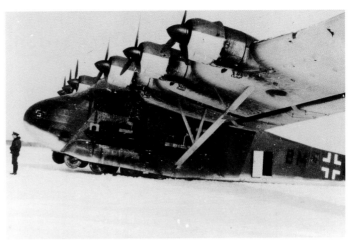

A gun secured with chains and beams inside the fuselage of an Me 323. Visible in the top center of the photo is the ladder to the "Upper House." (Nowarra)

Me 323 E-2. The airfoil-shaped strut fairing is especially obvious as part of it is missing. Also note the pitot tube on the inner vee-strut. (Hellwig)

This in-flight photo illustrates well the arrangement of the control surfaces and flaps. (Postcard)

An Me 323 on approach with landing flaps lowered. (Griehl)

Me 323 cockpit, early version. (Handbook)

Me 323 cockpit, later version. (Ott)

Exterior view of the armored cockpit. (Griehl)

Flight engineer Fw. Hermann Schladerbusch peers from his station. (Schladerbusch)

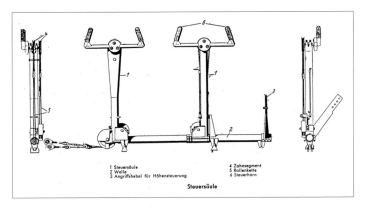

1 Steuersäule
2 Welle
3 Angriffshebel für Höhensteuerung
4 Zahnsegment
5 Rollenkette
6 Steuerhorn

Steuersäule

The Me 323's control columns. (Handbook)

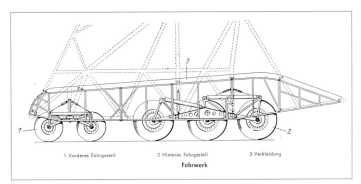

1 Vorderes Fahrgestell
2 Hinteres Fahrgestell
3 Verkleidung

Fahrwerk

Arrangement of the rough-field undercarriage. (Handbook)

The flight engineer stations were located between the two inner engines of the port and starboard wings. (Hellwig)

With the hatch removed, the flight engineer position between the engines is clearly visible. (Rößmann)

Me 323 with the lovely name "Gewitterschlitten" (Thunderstorm Sled). A hole has been dug under the rear tire of the undercarriage. This was necessary to replace the tire, as it was impossible to jack up the aircraft for such a repair. (Petrick)

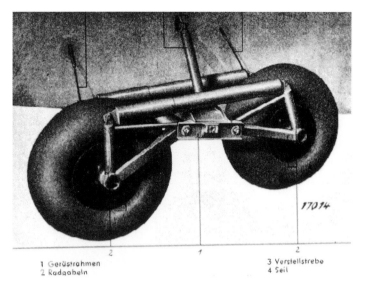

1 Gerüstrahmen
2 Radgabeln
3 Verstellstrebe
4 Seil

Forward undercarriage. (Handbook)

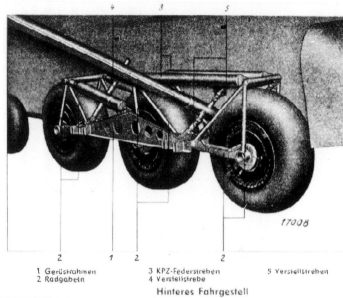

1 Gerüstrahmen
2 Radgabeln
3 KPZ-Federstreben
4 Verstellstrebe
5 Verstellstreben

Hinteres Fahrgestell

Rear undercarriage. (Handbook)

RD+QL is rolled out of the hall for final assembly. Note that the undercarriage fairings have yet to be installed. (Radinger)

The Gnôme-Rhône 14 N two-row radial engine.

The Bloch 175 bomber.

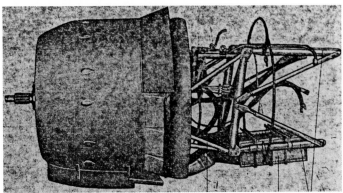

The "Bloch" power plant. (Handbook)

The "Bloch" power plant as installed in the Me 323 D-1. (Petrick)

The Lioré et Olivier LeO 45 bomber.

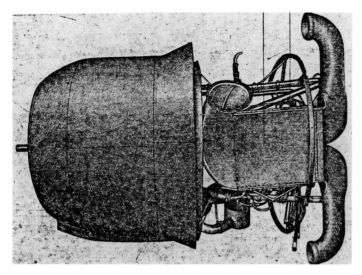

The "LeO" power plant. (Handbook)

The "LeO" power plant as installed in the Me 323 D-2, D-6 and most E-series aircraft. (Griehl)

Maintaining the engines had the highest priority. Nevertheless, the propeller pitch control mechanisms were a source of constant complaints. (Roba)

Right: Me 323 motor mount. (Handbook)

Below: With the exception of the D-2, all Me 323s powered by French engines were equipped with Ratier three-blade variable-pitch propellers. The D-2 used LeO power plants and Heine two-blade propellers. This photo depicts a D-2 at Castelvetrano, Sicily of a Sd.Kfz. 263 heavy armored radio car. (Petrick)

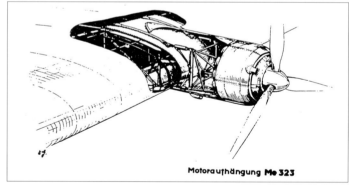

Motoraufhängung **Me 323**

Interesting details: the gun position above the cockpit, first improvised at the unit level, then installed on the production line. Behind it is the window of the radio operator's compartment. It could be opened and used as a makeshift gun position. On the wings the two EDL 151/20 turrets of the E-2, but no gun positions in the rear fuselage. Interestingly, both turrets lack fairings. (Obermaier)

The Gnôme-Rhône engines tended to catch fire when started, therefore a fire-extinguisher was always kept ready. Damage resulting from such fires was rare. (Giesecke)

The EDL 151 turret of an E-2. In this case the turret fairing is present. An air raid is taking place in the background. (Petrick)

This EDL 151 is not operational. Possibly the MG 151 is being serviced. In an emergency the flight engineers had to man the turrets. (Nowarra)

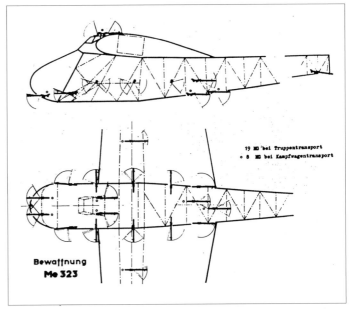

According to the handbook, up to 19 machine-guns could be used to defend the Me 323. In most cases these would have been small-caliber army machine-guns. Kurt Schnittke (1943-45 pilot for Generalingenieur Roluf Lucht, the director of Messerschmitt Regensburg) recalled an incident where soldiers on board an Me 323 panicked when the aircraft came under attack and simply fired their machine-guns through the side of the fuselage. (Handbook)

Me 323 DT+IG, seen here preparing to depart Pomigliano for Leipheim for its 250-hour inspection, has an improvised gun position in the area of the fuselage Balkenkreuz. (Peter)

The Me 323 E introduced stronger armament mounted in the fuselage sides. (Radinger)

Left: Production type gun position. (Griehl)

Below: This Me 323 D-1 has been retrofitted with guns in the nose doors. (Nowarra)

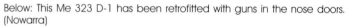

5

Decentralized Production

Oberingenieur Josef Fröhlich, the leader of the design team which produced the Me 321 and Me 323, stated in his "Leipheim Report" that the *Giganten* would be assembled in Leipheim and Obertraubling but not entirely built there. In addition to specialized equipment built by other manufacturers, aircraft components and sub-assemblies would be built by subcontractors and delivered to Messerschmitt for final assembly. Subcontractors varied in size from family businesses to major concerns. For example, the fuselage framework and wing spars were made by Mannesmann-Röhrenwerke, a well-known company, in Düsseldorf-Rath and at its Komotau branch plant in the Sudetenland. Because of their similarity to the transmission towers of overland power transmission lines, these were always designated "Lattice Masts." Engineer Hilmar Stumm, a member of the Me 321-Me 323 production team in Obertraubling, recalled the following incident: The driver of an automobile mistook the fuselage framework, which was lying on the ground, for a bridge and drove his vehicle into it. Before he realized that the "bridge" was narrowing rapidly, he was stuck fast.

The wing leading edges and the wing ribs were manufactured by the May Furniture Company of Stuttgart. The undercarriage framework and wheel forks of the *Gigant* were made by Skoda in Pilsen. Production of the aircraft's tail surfaces was assigned to Wolf Hirth in Nabern. Hirth had its own production facility for light aircraft and gliders, however for larger contracts, for example the production of wooden tails for the Bf 109, it always worked with Schempp of Kirchheim. The relationship between the two was so close that personnel from each company worked with the other. Production of the *Gigant* tail units was such a major undertaking that Wolf Hirth organized a production group which included several woodworking companies in southern Germany. Basic design work on the *Gigant*'s tail surfaces was done by Josef Fröhlich, however the detail work was left up to Hirth. The task was carried out by a design team consisting of Wolfgang Hütter, Johann Kout, Peter Theyer and Hubert Clompe. The two companies produced a prototype tail unit for the Me 321 made entirely of wood. This was accepted by Messerschmitt and a contract for quantity production was issued on 6 November 1940. Wolfgang Hütter made regular trips to Augsburg to consult with Messerschmitt on details well into December. The tail section for the Me 321 V1 was completed in time for the aircraft's maiden flight on 25 February 1941, even though the Schempp-Hirth facility in Kirchheimer had sustained major damage in a fire on 1 December 1940. It was not until after the war that it was learned that the fire had been the result of sabotage. A Norwegian worker had set the fire on behalf of the British Secret Service. The contract was retained nevertheless, as a result of transferring production and administration to the facilities of the production group. By October 1941 most of the facilities destroyed by the fire had been rebuilt and work was transferred back. Many drawings had been destroyed in the fire and some had to be recreated from memory. In most cases these concerned the company's own aircraft. The work was done by Reinhold Seeger, who remembers well the many changes made to the *Gigant* tails and the associated paperwork.

Hirth set aside most work on its own designs and most production in Kirchheim was devoted to Me 321 tails until 1942 and then Me 323 tail sections. Apart from the changes mentioned, the two were largely similar. There were production delays in Leipheim and Obertraubling during the course of the year, however these were due to a shortage of workers at Messerschmitt. On 30 September 1942 980 workers at Leipheim were drafted and were not replaced until 1943, and then by unqualified personnel.

At first Schempp-Hirth continued to deliver the same number of tail units as before, but then this had to be adjusted to meet the changing requirements of other members of the production group. The latter were required to increase production of Ju 87 components, for example. Schempp-Hirth built approximately 250 *Gigant* tail sections in 1941 but only about 50 in 1942, a noticeable difference. Only 200 Me 321s had been built when production ceased on 30 June 1942, which suggests that some of the excess Me 321 tail sections may have been converted for use on the Me 323.

At the beginning of 1943 all activities relating to the *Giganten* were transferred to the Luftschiffbau Zeppelin GmbH's aircraft department in Friedrichshafen. Only series production continued in Leipheim and Obertraubling.

Zeppelin worked on the Z-Me 323 development with Jumo 211 F engines and revised tail surfaces. Plans were made to produce 200 examples of this variant, however it proceeded no further than the prototype phase, having been superseded by the Z-Me 323 G. On 10 March 1944 the RLM put an end to the entire Me 323 program. On 30 April 1944 the Me 323 delivery plan was reported completed and the last aircraft delivered. Schempp-Hirth delivered approximately twenty completed tail sections in 1944, raising its total to approximately 415 tail sections for the Me 321 and Me 323.

June 1943: Ceremony for operations manager Karl Schmid in the big factory hall in Obertraubling on the day he was awarded the Knight's Cross of the War Merit Cross. (Schmoll)

The core of the Gigant team in Leipheim. Each was responsible for a certain area of decentralized component production. On the far left is the director of the Gigant program, Obering. Fröhlich. (Stumm)

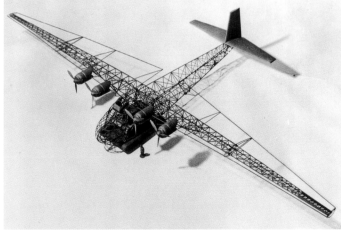

The fuselage framework and box spar, seen here in model form, were manufactured by the Mannesmann Company. The "Organisation Todt" (named after its founder Fritz Todt, Reich Minister for Armaments and Munitions until his death in a plane crash on 8 February 1942) organized transport of the bulky components. (Dabrowski)

Left: They brought the threads together: left Obering. Josef Fröhlich, right Hans Spieß, director of the Leipheim facility. In the background Me 323 D-1 RD+QI. (Vogel)

Head of production in Obertraubling was Karl Schmid (with hat), seen here talking with a co-worker. (Schmoll)

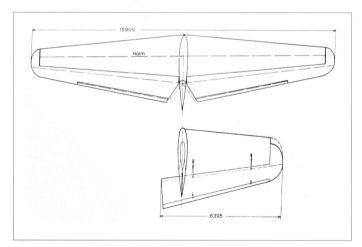

Production tail as installed on the Me 321 and Me 323. Manufacturer Wolf Hirth of Nabern. The unit's dimensions were impressive: the horizontal stabilizer had a span of 15.9 meters, significantly greater than the 9.92 meters of the Bf 109's wing! Hirth, together with Schempp of Kirchheim, built more than 400 Gigant tails. (P.F. Selinger)

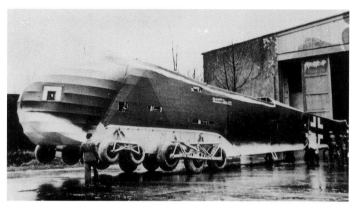

Components of the rough-field undercarriage were built by the Skoda Company. (Radinger)

Here undercarriage components are being assembled into complete units. The photo was taken on 2 February 1944, toward the end of Me 323 production. Horst Lattke, Edmund Eisele and Hilmar Stumm (left to right) are seen examining a torque plate. (Stumm)

Right: A Gigant vertical stabilizer under construction. (P.F. Selinger)

Three vertical stabilizers ready for delivery in Kirchheim on 5 March 1943. (P.F. Selinger)

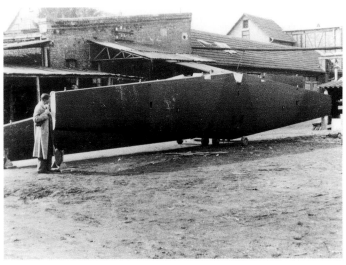

Kirchheim on 5 March 1943, delivery day. Standing next to the horizontal stabilizer is Johann Kout. (P.F. Selinger)

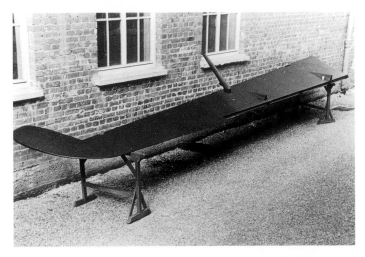

An Me 323 elevator built by Schemmp-Hirth in Kirchheim. (P.F. Selinger)

Repair work on the horizontal stabilizer of X1B. Serious damage resulted in the replacement of the entire tail. Provision of sufficient spares had to be taken into consideration when drawing up production plans. (Hellwig)

Left: Non-standard tail sections were also designed and built in Kirchheim, such as this example on VM+IK which does not have horn balances on the rudder. In addition, the tail is braced with wires only. This variant was most likely used by the Luftschiffbau Zeppelin for flutter tests. (Kuettner)

Installing a brand-new tail section. The man on the crane gives some idea of the imposing height of his workplace. (Petrick)

Below: The revised tail section for the planned Me 323 F and subsequent variants was also designed by Schemmp-Hirth. (P.F. Selinger)

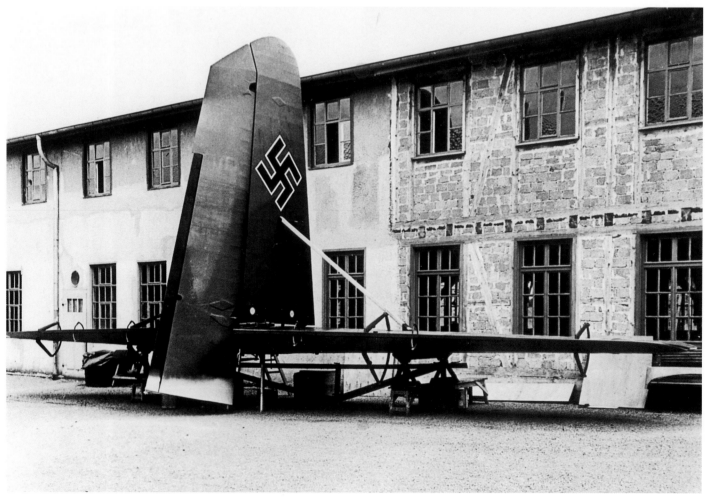

6

The Leipheim and Obertraubling Production Sites

The Leipheim (near Ulm) and Obertraubling (near Regensburg) airfields are inextricably linked to the story of the *Giganten*. It was there that the Me 321 and Me 323 were built, even after the program was transferred to the Luftschiffbau Zeppelin. German specialists, military convicts and foreign workers all helped build the aircraft. Production numbers for the Me 321 and Me 323 are split fairly equally between Leipheim and Obertraubling.

Leipheim: In the autumn of 1935 the Army Administration purchased land south of Leipheim. Planning was immediately begun to build an airfield there. Construction of aircraft hangars and quarters began in the spring of 1936. The requirement for thousands of workers resulted in an economic upswing in the area, almost eliminating unemployment. The first military personnel for a new *Kampfgeschwader* (bomber wing) arrived on 12 March 1937. The first base commander was *Oberstleutnant* Dr. Fisser. The new *Geschwader* was *KG 255 ("Alpengeschwader")*, formed from elements of *KG 153*, which had been transferred to southern Germany on 1 April 1937. The unit's *II. Gruppe* was assigned to Leipheim (*4.* and *5. Staffel* plus the *Stabskompanie*, under *Major* Petzold, *Hauptmann* Pilger and *Hauptmann* Mitzeck). The unit flew the Do 17 E, the so-called "Flying Pencil", and the Do 17 Z. The *6. Staffel* was formed on 1 July 1937 (Oblt. von Schroetter). In 1938 the *Alpengeschwader* received *Gruppe* emblems, all featuring plants native to the Alpine region. The *Gruppe* at Leipheim was identified by the gentian. Dr. Fisser was promoted to the rank of *Oberst* and made *Geschwaderkommodore*. *Oberst* von Stutterheim assumed command of *II. Gruppe* in Leipheim. On 1 May 1939 *II. Gruppe* was disbanded in order to form the basis of the new KG 77 being formed in Königgrätz. On 12 August 1940 *Oberst* Dr. Fisser was shot down by anti-aircraft fire and killed during an attack on a radar station on the Isle of Wight. He was succeeded by *Major* Dr. Moser. In 1942 Leipheim became a test airfield for the Messerschmitt factories in Augsburg. This was to be the home base for the *Gigant Geschwader* until its disbandment in August 1944. The *Giganten* made their first flights and underwent flight trials there and flight personnel were also trained to fly the *Gigant* there.

At Leipheim the *Giganten* also underwent inspections, overhauls and repairs which could not be completed in the field.

On 18 July 1942 at Leipheim Fritz Wendel made the first flight in a Me 262 on jet power alone. The flight in the Me 262 V3 lasted twelve minutes. Leipheim had been selected for the flight on account of its long paved runway. Assembly of the Me 262 began at Leipheim in April 1944 after production of the Me 323 ended. The technical personnel of *8./ZG 26*, which was to equip with the new fighter, were also sent to Leipheim. The *Staffel* was part of the *III. Gruppe* of *ZG 26* comamnded by *Major* Kobler, who in March 1944 was ordered to move his *Gruppe* to southern Germany. At Leipheim and Schwäbisch Hall (*9. Staffel*) the unit's ground personnel would be trained to handle the new fighter. The aircraft would take off from the nearby autobahn and land on the airfield. The command post was situated in the Leipheim autobahn rest stop. *III./ZG 26* began Me 262 conversion training on 10 May 1944. Earlier, on 24 April, Leipheim had been attacked by Allied bombers for the first time. Approximately 230 tons of bombs fell on the airfield and the surrounding area. The airfield and hangars were badly damaged and several *Waffenträger* which were sitting in the open were destroyed. Production of the Me 262, which took place in a so-called "Forest Factory" at the edge of the airfield was less affected. Concealed by nets and tarpaulins, the jet fighters were assembled among the trees, virtually in the open. By 10 August 1944 a total of ten prototypes and 112 production aircraft had been completed at Leipheim, with just 21 destroyed in air attacks. This would suggest that while some damage was inflicted, production of the Me 262 was not stopped. At times in 1944 the situation was rather chaotic. Typical of this is the fact that both *Major* Barth and *Oberstleutnant* von Halensleben had papers identifying them as *Kommodore* of the *Geschwader*. *Major* Barth led the unit until the end of the war after von Halensleben and three others were killed by an American fighter-bomber.

From July 1945 until 1948 the Leipheim airbase served as a Polish refugee camp. Jewish refugees were housed there from 1948 to 1951. American units occupied the base from 1951 to 1956. A repair battalion, an engineer battalion, a heavy bridging unit and finally an armored battalion were stationed there. From 1953 to 1956 the runway, taxiways and hangars were repaired and expanded. F-86D Sabres from Bitburg were stationed at the airfield from 14 February to 30 September 1957.

On 16 March 1959 the *Bundeswehr*'s *Ausbildungsregiment 4* (4th Training Regiment) took over the airfield. *Jagdgeschwader 75*, an all-weather fighter unit, was formed on 1 October 1940 under its commander *Major* Wegener. The unit was equipped with the F-86K Sabre. At the end of 1961 the unit was transferred to Neuburg and renamed *JG 74*. From then on Leipheim was home to the *Luftwaffen-POL-Depot* and the *Feldwerft G-91* of *Luftwaffen-Versorgungsregiment 3*. The airfield continues to be used by the *Bundes-Luftwaffe* to the present day.

Obertraubling: Constructed in the period 1936 to 1938, after which it was one of Germany's most modern airfields. The first air units were stationed at Obertraubling in October 1938 during *"Fall Grün"* (Case Green, the occupation of the Sudetenland). The airfield was always used for training, no combat missions were flown from there. In 1940 some of the buildings were made available to the Messerschmitt GmbH Regensburg. Obertraubling became a training, company and testing airfield. Messerschmitt built the Bf 109, Bf 110, Me 321, Me 323, Me 163 (70 prototypes) and, from September 1944, the Me 262 (a total of 103 examples, also in a "Forest Factory" similar to the one at Leipheim). The first air raid alarm in the area was sounded on 16-17 April 1943, although until August of that year only a few bombs fell in the surrounding fields. On 22 February 1944, during the "Big Week" raids against German aircraft production facilities, the Allies delivered their first direct attack against Obertraubling airfield. Thanks to the field's heavy anti-aircraft defenses little damage was inflicted. A second attack was made on 25 February, by 220 American bombers in five waves. Seventy percent of the airfield and production facilities were destroyed. Anti-aircraft fire shot down 12 to 15 enemy bombers and the attackers suffered further casualties during the return flight to Sicily. Nevertheless, the anti-aircraft gun crews lost about 95 killed. On 21 July 1944 American bombers dropped approximately 6,000 phosphorous bombs and incendiaries over the airfield. Fires burned all day. Further raids took place in autumn 1944 and spring 1945. On 4 February 1945 the nearby rail line to Munich was bombed. The Obertraubling airfield's anti-aircraft defenses consisted of a ring of flak positions which also encircled Regensburg. The guns were manned mainly by 16- and 17-year-old students from local schools. In most cases the guns were commanded by non-commissioned officers who had been wounde din action and were no longer fit for combat. On 22-23 April 1945 the alarm was sounded, the American army was "at the gates." On 25-26 April all Messerschmitt aircraft and materiel on the airfield was set on fire. The next day the American 21st Infantry Division occupied the airfield, 80% of which had been destroyed. On 7 November 1946 it was released to provide housing for refugees. Gradually, housing developments encroached upon the airfield grounds and businesses resumed operation on a modest scale. On 1 April 1951 the town of Neutraubling was officially founded on the site of the former airfield.

Produced at Leipheim and Obertraubling: the Me 321, the largest glider in the world. (Nowarra)

The Me 323 was also produced at Leipheim and Obertraubling. Here the V2, W9+SA, about to land. (Radinger)

The Gigant program resulted in visits by all kinds of senior military officers, especially to Leipheim, in this case a Japanese military delegation in 1942. The German officer in the center is Major Dr. Moser, who became base commander of Leipheim following the death of Oberst Dr. Fisser. (Vogel)

Obering. Josef Frölich with a Japanese designer. (Vogel)

Japanese officials prior to flight demonstrations. Persons whose identities are known: (1) Obering. Josef Fröhlich, (2) Oblt. Waldemar Kost, adjutant to Major Mauß, (3) Hptm. Mehring, (4) Oblt. Rudnik, (5) Oblt. Radler. (Vogel)

German-Japanese group photo in Leipheim. Far left the base commander Dr. Moser, beside him Oblt. "Sepp" Stangl, behind Oblt. Radler and Obering. Fröhlich. In the center of the photo, behind the Japanese, are plant manager Spiess, Major Mauss and his adjutant Oblt. Kost. On the extreme right is Oblt. Seidel. The Japanese obviously reached an agreement with Messerschmitt, for several Messerschmitt engineers and technicians accompanied them on their return. They never reached Japan, however, as their ship was sunk by an American submarine.

Me 321 production in the manufacturing halls. Here the wing of an E-2 is being assembled. (Deutsche Aerospace)

Final assembly of Giganten at Leipheim took place in the open. (Griehl)

Completed Me 323 at Leipheim. (Radinger)

Waiting to be collected by the Luftwaffe. (Nowarra)

Only possible in Leipheim – three Gigant variants in one photo: in the foreground one of the few four-engined Me 323 Cs, behind it a six-engined Me 323 D, and an Me 321 glider. (Lange)

Leipheim was the site of Gigant acceptance flights as well as a range of tests. Here may be seen the tail of the Me 323 V12, DT+DU. (Radinger)

Waiting for takeoff – in the background the Me 323 V12, DT+DU. (Radinger)

Lively discussion during a break. On the far left is test pilot Hans Krauss. (Radinger)

Series of photographs taken after a failed takeoff by Me 323 D-1, RD+QA, at Leipheim in 1943. The crash was caused by improperly installed ailerons. (Kuettner)

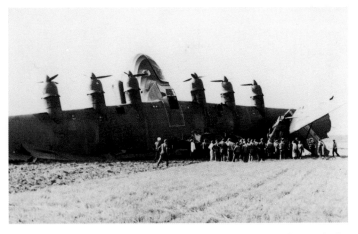

Ground personnel rushed to the scene. Here they examine the crash site up close. (Kuettner)

The Gigant was literally torn apart. No details of casualties are known. (Kuettner)

Coffee break in Leipheim. From left to right: unidentified, Oblt. Willy Seidel (trained pilots on the Gigant), Hans Spieß (director of the Messerschmitt factory in Leipheim), Josef Fröhlich, head of the Gigant design team. (Vogel)

Paratrooper General Kurt Student also visited Leipheim. (Vogel)

General Student on his arrival in Leipheim. Standing opposite him is Obering. Fröhlich, to his left Messerschmitt factory director Croneiß. On the far left is Major Dr. Moser, the commander of Leipheim Airbase, in conversation with Oblt. Kost. (Radinger)

General Student speaks to the soldiers. The purpose of his visit to Leipheim was obviously to determine the Me 323's suitability for paratrooper operations. (Peter)

Subsequent inspection of the Me 323 production line by the general. The soldiers have fallen in. The aircraft in the background is believed to be the Me 323 V14. (Peter)

Since their successful actions in the Western Campaign the paratroopers had been acknowledged as an elite corps. Here members of the attack force which took the Belgian fortress of Eben Emael are presented with the Knight's Cross: from left to right, rear row: Oblt. Witzig, Oblt. Zierach, Lt. Ringler, Oblt. Kiess, Oberarzt Dr. Jäger. Front row: Lt. Delica, Hptm. Koch, Hitler, Lt. Meissner, Oblt. Altmann. (Nowarra)

A group of prominent people in Leipheim, apparently before the formation of K.Gr.z.b.V. 323. Third from the left is Ing. Stumm, next to him Obering. Fröhlich (both of Messerschmitt), then Generalfeldmarschall Milch, Messerschmitt director Croneiß, behind him on the right Major Mauß and Major Unruh (both of K.Gr.z.b.V. 323). (Radinger)

Civilians involved in the Gigant program on the airfield in Leipheim. The photographers set up prior to this Me 323 D-1's takeoff for Pomigliano. From left to right: Ing. Kurt Brandt (drawings supervisor), Hans Spieß (factory director Leipheim), Müller (statistician), Frl. Erna Nied (Fröhlich's secretary), Ing. Petri (Fröhlich's deputy). (Vogel)

Hptm. Zierach was surely supposed to examine the details following Student's visit to Leipheim. It is presumable that the paratroopers were interested in the Me 323 as a jump aircraft, and test jumps were made. There is, however, no evidence that the Me 323 was ever used by paratroopers in an operational role. Here Hptm. Zierach is seen with Hans Spieß (left) and Josef Fröhlich (right). (Vogel)

Below: The flight of the Me 262 V3 at Leipheim marked the beginning of a new era in aviation. Messerschmitt transferred its Gigant program to the Luftschiffbau Zeppelin in Friedrichshafen. (Radinger)

Flugkapitän Fritz Wendel made the first flight in the Me 262 V3 (PC+UC) on turbojet power alone at Leipheim on 18 July 1942. In the background is an Me 321 awaiting delivery. (Radinger)

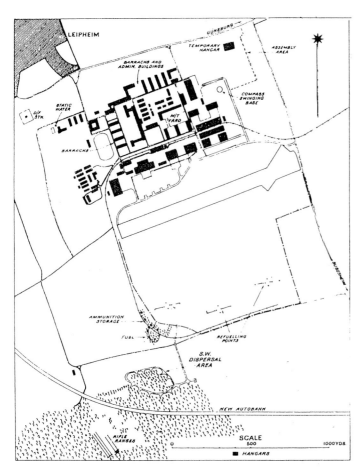

A B-17 Flying Fortress drops its deadly load. (Nowarra)

Allied aerial reconnaissance provided detailed information on the activities at Leipheim. There were similar sketches of almost every German airfield, which were used to brief pilots before attacks. (USAF)

The Leipheim airbase was bombed several times, but the first time it sustained serious damage was on 24 April 1944. After the inferno: wrecked hangars and shattered aircraft. Visible in the background are parts of Giganten, in the foreground the remains of a Bf 110. (Schmoll)

Obertraubling airbase belonged to the Messerschmitt GmbH, Regensburg and was used mainly for Gigant production and acceptance flights. After the death of Theo Croneiß, Roluf Lucht, chief engineer of the RLM's Technische Amt, took over as director of the Obertraubling operation. Here Lucht gives Nazi dignitaries a tour of the Me 323 production line at Obertraubling. (Schmoll)

Three aerial photos of Obertraubling airbase. This photo was taken on 18 February 1943. Numerous Me 323s are visible, but only a few Me 321s. (Vilsmeier)

This photo was taken a short time later, by which time a number of slit trenches had been dug. With the Giganten is an He 111 Z, while one Me 321 has a winter camouflage finish. This suggests that a number of the gliders were towed back to Obertraubling from the Eastern Front. (Schmoll)

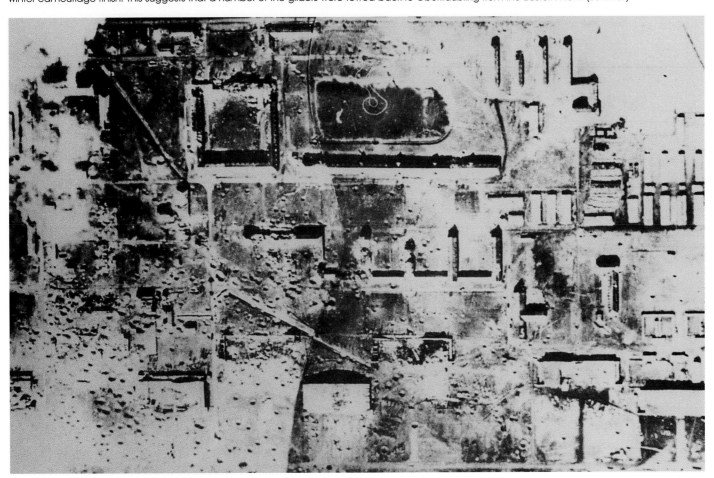

The former Gigant production site at the Obertraubling airbase was heavily bombed on 22 and 25 May 1944 and 70% destroyed. (Schmoll)

7

The Me 321 *Staffeln*: Establishment and Operations

It was intended that the Me 321 would see its first action with the start of the German invasion of the Soviet Union in June 1941. In preparation for this, four *Großraumsegler-Staffeln* (G.S.) were formed at Leipheim and Obertraubling. Each had an authorized strength of six Me 321s and several towplane flights of Bf 110s or He 111s. G.S. 1 under Oblt. Melzer was destined for the northern sector, while G.S. 2 under Oblt. Baumann was to serve as supply and ferry *Staffel* for all the other *Großraumsegler-Staffeln*. G.S. 22 under Oblt. Schäfer was to see action in the central sector and G.S. 4 under Oblt. Pohl in the southern sector. The existing training *Gruppe* in Langensalza was split up to assist in the formation of these four *Staffeln* with a remnant detachment assigned to Merseburg airfield, which was the designated staging point.

In July 1941 the Me 321s of G.S. 1 and their towplane flights left Leipheim and Obertraubling for the northern sector of the Eastern Front. By August 1941 most of the glider-towplane combinations (Me 321/Bf 110) had arrived in Riga by way of Schroda and Powehren. There were several unplanned landings en route, mainly due to severed towlines, however thanks to the tireless efforts of Junkers pilot Hesselbach and his Ju 90 (KB+LA, WNr. 0002) the gliders were all towed out of their improivised landing fields.

The first live missions – supplying German troops occupying the island of Ösel – were flown from Riga. On 21 September 1941 a Bf 110-Me 321 combination delivered 20,000 liters of gasoline and 4 tons of ammunition. One day later another towplane-glider combination delivered more fuel and ammunition to the island. During a similar operation on 27 September two Bf 110 towplanes were shot down by Russian flak. A total of four *Giganten* saw action. These were very likely one-way operations with none of the gliders being recovered. They were either stripped and scrapped or destroyed. These were obviously G.S. 1's only missions, because in November it and G.S. 2 were withdrawn from the Eastern Front to Merseburg where the units were subsequently disbanded. Most of the personnel of the two units were probably used in the formation of *1.* and *2. Staffel KGr.z.b.V. 323* at Leipheim in May 1942.

G.S. 22 flew via Schroda and Terespol to Orsha. Once again the transfer was anything but smooth, as there were several forced landings. In most cases a makeshift runway had to be created and the Me 321 placed onto a takeoff trolley and fitted with takeoff-assist rockets by members of the FBK before the Ju 90 could tow the big glider. The Ju 90 was flown by *Flugkapitän* Alfred Gymnich with Paul Heerling as flight engineer and Fritz-Hermann Reinhardt as radio operator.

Beginning in early August G.S. 22 flew transport missions into the central sector of the Eastern Front, mainly carrying drums of fuel to Shatalovka (150 kilometers distant). In October 1941 the unit transported fuel for panzer units located approximately 240 kilometers southeast of Orsha (Rudakovo, Vyazma-Briansk, etc.). These missions, on which the gliders usually carried about 18 metric tons of fuel, could be termed "flammable" in the truest sense of the word. In one case, the crew of a Me 321 counted more than 100 holes in their aircraft after a mission. Miraculously, none of the fuel drums was hit. At the end of October the weather worsened to the point that further missions from Orsha were impossible.

In mid-July 1941 G.S. 4 moved from Merseburg via Jasionka to Vinnitsa in the southern sector of the Eastern Front. From mid-September to October the unit flew supply missions (fuel and bombs for Stuka units) from Vinnitsa to Kirovograd and Nikolayev.

In November 1941 all of the *Großraumsegler* units and their Me 321s were withdrawn from the Soviet Union. G.S. 22 and G.S. 4 went to Leipheim, where in late 1941 they were renamed *3.* and *4./KG.z.b.V. 2*. At a later date the Bf 110 and He 111 towplanes were replaced by the He 111 Z. On 13 January 1942 an order was issued for all the *Großraumsegler-Staffeln* to be disbanded, however this order was rescinded on 27 January.

What had led to the development of the He 111 Z and its operational use? Heinkel developed the He 111 Z as the result of a proposal by the RLM for a towplane which could safely tow a fully-loaded Me 321. Supposedly it was Ernst Udet himself who came up with the idea for the new towplane, having reached the conclusion that the *Troika-Schlepp* method was too dangerous. In fact, numerous *Troika-Schlepp* aircraft had made forced landings in the area around Leipheim and Obertraubling. This method of towing had resulted in many accidents and forced landings en route to the front, and the introduction of the new towplane was supposed to address the problem. The aircraft was the result of combining two He 111 H-2 or H-6 bombers through the addition of a new wing center-section complete with a fifth Jumo 211 F-2 engine. The five-engines had a combined output of 6,700 H.P. The complete fuselages with tail surfaces could be used without modification. The port fuselage was from ongoing production and was equipped with all instrumentation and controls. An older repaired machine was used for the starboard fuselage. It was equipped with only the most important components so that the aircraft could be controlled from there in an emergency. The factory code (*Stammkennzeichen*) and serial number (*Werknummer*) were always determined by the new construction fuselage, as was the year of construction. The He 111 Z had a wingspan of 25.4 meters and was 16.69 meters long. The aircraft's empty weight was 15,000 kg and takeoff weight, including fuel, was 21 400 to 28 400 kg. Maximum speed was 480 km/h. The towplane was built by the Mitteldeutschen Metallwerken in Erfurt. Following two prototypes the RLM ordered a small batch of ten machines. Completion of these was slowed by ongoing He 177 production. The two prototypes were delivered in November 1941, followed by one aircraft in August, one in September, two in October, three in November and three in December 1942. It is very likely that more than twelve examples of the He 111 Z were built, however it is no longer possible to say how many. Plans to modify the He 111 Z for the strategic reconnaissance and bomber roles were not realized.

On 31 August 1942 *3.(G.S.)/KG.z.b.V. 2* and *4.(G.S.)/KG.z.b.V. 2* each had one "*Zwilling*" (Twin) on strength. The *3. Staffel* had 17 gliders, of which just one was serviceable, while *4. Staffel* had eleven Me 321s, all of them serviceable. Two months later *3. Staffel* had three "*Zwillinge*", one of which was unserviceable, while *4. Staffel* had two of the towplanes on strength. The two units had just two of nineteen and one of twelve *Giganten* serviceable, respectively. In November 1942 the units were transferred to Obertraubling and were renamed *G.S.Kdo. 1* and *G.S.Kdo. 2* respectively (large-capacity glider detachments). The two detachments were supposed to take part in the airlift designed to supply the beleaguered 6th Army at Stalingrad together with *I./LLG 2* and *LLG 1* based at Lechfeld. Twelve glider-towplane combinations departed for Russia, however as a result of bad weather and organizational problems only two managed to struggle through to Makeyevka by mid-January 1943. By that time towed flights to Stalingrad were out of the question since no suitable airfields remained in German hands. Given the general chaos that existed, it is unlikely that such flights would have been possible anyway. *Generalfeldmarschall* Milch, whose job it had been to organize and direct the effort to supply the 6th Army from the air, had failed. When even supply drops by the He 111 towplanes became impossible, on 25 January 1943 Milch released the transport gliders from his special headquarters' area of command. G.S.Kdo. 2 moved to Bagerovo in the Crimea. During all of January 1943 a total of 12 Me 321 glider-towplane combinations tried to reach the Crimea from Obertraubling, however only a few succeeded. Many were obliged to make forced landings for various reasons and not all could be recovered.

At the beginning of March there was a daily average of 45 G 242 and 110 DFS 230 gliders, plus three Me 321s, available for operations from the Bitter Salt Lake, Zokur and "Molkerei" airfields in support of the 17th Army in the Kuban bridgehead. The transport gliders were iused to fly in supplys and fly out troops, especially the wounded. The few *Giganten* were each capable of carrying 90 troops. The flights must have been uncomfortable, as the troops had to stand with only transverse safety straps to hold onto. Because of the lengthy preflight preparations and poor airfield conditions, the number of sorties flown by the *Giganten* was low, for the huge gliders were quickly damaged in the rough conditions and rendered unserviceable. Only one of the Me 321s returned to Obertraubling after these Eastern Front operations, the rest having been "used up" in the effort to supply the Kuban bridgehead (31 January to 9 October 1943).

On 10 March 1943 *G.S.Kdo. 1* at Obertraubling had eighteen Me 321s, of which just one was serviceable, and six He 111 Z (none serviceable). *G.S.Kdo. 2* had twenty Me 321s (7 serviceable) and six He 111 Z (one serviceable) on strength. At the end of May 1943 *G.S.Kdos. 1* and 2, under the combined designation "*Arbeitsstab Hptm. Pohl*", moved to Reims and Istres in southern France with a combined total of eleven He 111 Z and twenty Me 321s. The remaining aircraft stayed behind in Obertraubling. Following the Allied landings on Sicily on 10 July 1943 it was intended to use the He 111 Z-Me 321 combinations to transport paratroopers to the island, however in the general chaos this did not happen. Instead, in the days that followed, the He 111 Z towplanes flew numerous Go 242 gliders to Naples-Pomigliano. The enormous engine power of the "*Zwilling*" enabled it to easily tow two Go 242s at the same time. Pomigliano airfield was subjected to an air raid at 0100 hours on 15 July 1943. Of the ten He 111 Z towplanes there, one was totally destroyed while the others sustained only minor damage. Two Heinkels were able to fly back to Istres with Go 242s in tow and the remaining machines flew back alone at 0900 hours. In the days that followed, eight He 111 Z flew tow missions (with Go 242s) from Istres to Pomigliano and from there to Sicily.

On 17 August 1943 the Allies carried out a devastating air raid against the huge airfield at Istres, destroying 180 powered aircraft and gliders and killing 40 to 50 members of the transport glider units. The "*Arbeitsstab Hptm. Pohl*" lost one He 111 Z and five Me 321s, while two He 111 Z and two Me 321s were damaged. A few days later G.S.Kdo. 1 moved to Reims. On 20 October 1943 all ten of the surviving He 111 Z towplanes were there. Then "*Arbeitsstab Hptm. Pohl*" transferred to Dijon. The last surviving report concerning the complement of Me 321s is dated 20 December 1943: 21 *Giganten* in Dijon and 16 with the "*Wartungsstab*", location unknown.

Since the "*Arbeitsstab Hptm. Pohl*" was subsequently disbanded and the Me 321s do not appear in later reports by *XI Fliegerkorps*, it is likely that the remaining transport gliders, most of which were no longer serviceable anyway, were scrapped.

Eight He 111 Z went to I./LLG 2 in Hagenau. There were four of these aircraft there on 10 June 1944, when they assigned to *Ergänzungsgruppe (S) 2* in Posen. After the disbandment of the

Gruppe the four He 111 Z returned to I./LLG 2, but in September 1944 this *Gruppe*, too, was disbanded in Fürstenfeldbruck. At the end of November 1944 four He 111 Z were on the strength of IV./KG 200. These were probably the four aircraft mentioned above.

In December 1944, however, they no longer appear in IV./KG 200's strength returns. What happened to the four Heinkel towplanes during that time is not known, perhaps they were destroyed or scrapped.

A portside "Kettenhund" (wingman) with a tow cable attachment as developed by the DFS in Ainring on the wingroot. The Bf 110 belonged to GS 1, whose Staffel emblem consisted of a Dachshund sitting on a British steel helmet. (Petrick)

Me 321 W1+SR of GS 1 bore the same Staffel emblem as the towplanes. (Petrick)

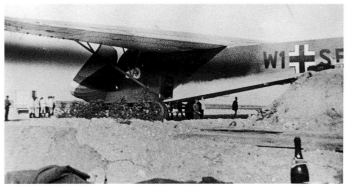

Me 321 W1+SF of GS 2 wears the same emblem as Oblt. Auer's towplane, but with an oval background. The emblem was designed by Fw. Rudolf Knecht. (Nowarra)

Oblt. Edmund Auer in his Bf 110. The emblem, which consists of a Baron Münchhausen figure riding a cannonball pulled by three geese, identifies it as a towplane of GS 2. (Auer)

The emblem on this Bf 110 identifies it as a towplane of GS 22, which in November 1941 became 3.(GS)/K.Gr.z.b.V. 2. (Nowarra)

Left: The Staffel emblem of GS 22 consisted of an heraldic shield with a stylized eagle pulled by three smaller eagles, and beneath the British Isles in crosshairs. (Nowarra)

An He 111 Z towplane of GS 4. The Staffel emblem consists of a three-headed eagle. (Schlaug)

After landing on the island of Ösel. (Petrick)

Since most Me 321s made the flight to the front fully loaded, takeoffs from en route airfields required the use of takeoff-assist rockets. (Hellwig)

Below: Me 321 W2+SC of GS 1 during transfer to Riga. Here it is seen being raised onto a takeoff trolley at an airfield en route (probably Schroda). (Petrick)

Ju 90 KB+LA, WNr. 0002. Wingspan 35.27 m, length 26.45 m, powered by four Pratt and Whitney Twin Wasp radials each producing 1,200 H.P. for takeoff. The aircraft reached a maximum speed of 385 km/h and made its maiden flight on 21 July 1939. (Nowarra)

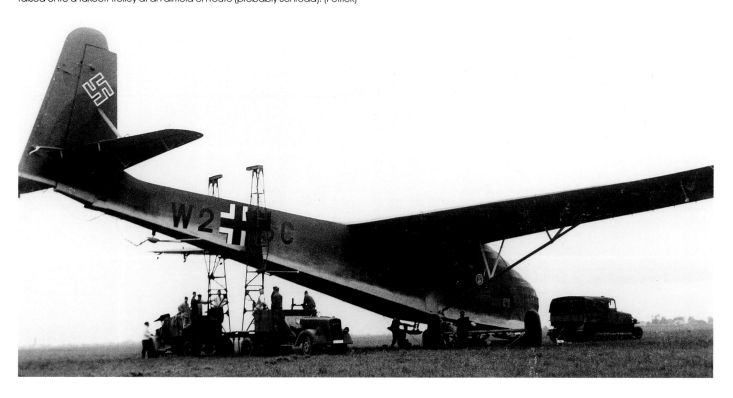

W2+SM ready for takeoff. (Koos)

The rocket-assisted takeoff is a success. On the ground, the next Me 321 waits to depart. (Koos)

One of the Troika-Schlepp flights to Ösel during the period 21 to 26 September 1941. (Petrick)

This badly-damaged Me 321 was obviously unable to jettison its main undercarriage and landed hard on Ösel. (Petrick)

Everything that was salvageable was removed from the aircraft, which was then set on fire. The main undercarriage was not saved. (Petrick)

Hptm. Alfred Gymnich (former DLH captain), to his right wearing the Junkers cap flight engineer Paul Heerling, left radio operator Fritz-Hermann Reinhardt. The man on the far right is not known. (Kössler)

Ju 90 KB+LA often succeeded in getting stranded Me 321s back into the air. In this case it would appear to be a transfer flight, as the Me 321 had not jettisoned its undercarriage. (Griehl)

The large main undercarriage was the main problem in getting a stranded Me 321 back into the air. If there was no airfield operating company with specialized equipment, the Gigant could not be recovered. (Griehl)

Smooth landing by W2+SH on the Eastern Front in 1942. Retrieval would have been possible. (Petrick)

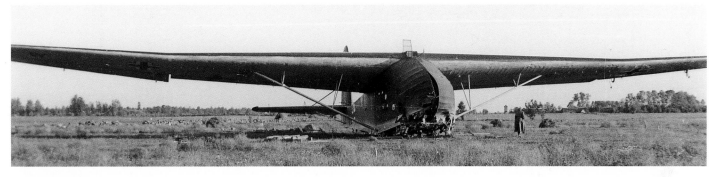

Crash-landing with serious damage in the nose area. In such cases the Me 321 was almost always cannibalized, or if there was no time, blown up or burned. (Petrick)

Crash-landings were especially dangerous when the Giganten were loaded with fuel. If a fire broke out, saving the Me 321 was impossible. (Petrick)

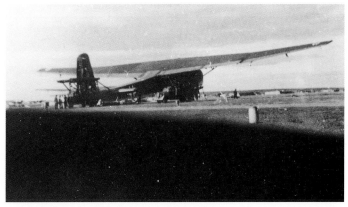

Orsha airfield served as a Gigant support base and many supply flights were made from there to the front. The equipment necessary to prepare a Gigant for flight was available there. (Nowarra)

After a fire, usually all that was left was the steel framework. (Thiele)

A fully-loaded Me 321 waits for a triple-tow takeoff. (Radinger)

Things did not always go smoothly at Orsha. This attempted takeoff on 3 October 1941 obviously failed because the takeoff-assist rockets did not fire. One Bf 110 has already crashed, the others have released the tow cables. (Petrick)

Me 321 W2+SA glided a few meters and then landed on the edge of the airfield. (Nowarra)

The Gigant was seriously damaged in the forced landing. Soldiers rushed to the scene to see the crashed giant up close. (Petrick)

Since Me 321 W2+SA could not be saved, it was cannibalized. Here the tail has already been removed. (Nowarra)

In keeping with the season, this Me 321 W8+5K was given a coat of white camouflage paint on its tail and upper surfaces. (Petrick)

The cause of this serious damage is known: on 24 April 1942 Ju 90 KB+LA collided in Leipheim with Me 321 W7+SH during takeoff. The Ju 90 developed engine trouble, whereupon the Me 321 pilot released the tow cable. (Ott)

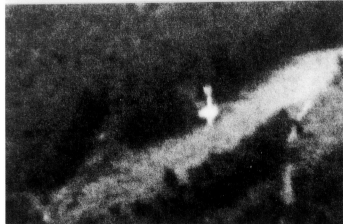

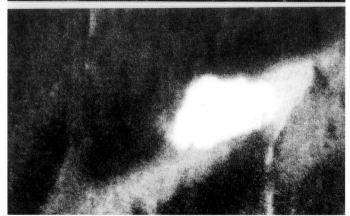

A number of Giganten were lost over Russian territory. This crash was probably the result of ground fire. The explosion suggests that the Me 321 was carrying fuel.

There were also casualties at home before transfer to the front. Storms posed a serious threat to unloaded Giganten with their wingspan of 55 meters. It was therefore very important to tie them down carefully. (Petrick)

The Ju 90 veered right and struck the rolling Me 321. Both aircraft were damaged. The Ju 90 was out of service for some time and the Me 321 fuselage was beyond repair. (Ott)

Ernst Udet had been a successful fighter pilot in the First World War and later a daring stunt pilot. He therefore knew what he was talking about when he described the Troika-Schlepp as "aerobatics." The He 111 Z was designed at his suggestion. (Schnittke)

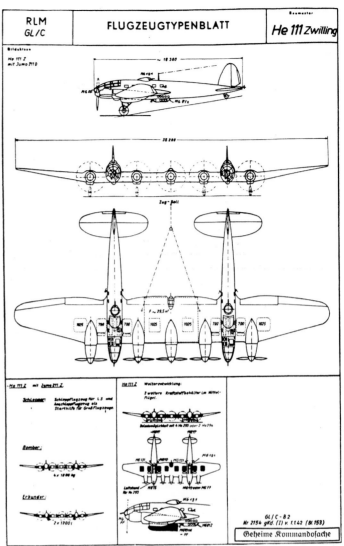

The original type sheet for the "Zwilling" (Twin). The gun position in the newly-designed wing center section never got past the design stage. (Koos)

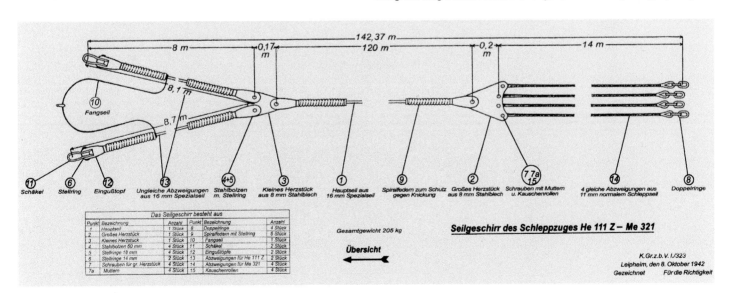

A specially-designed cable harness was required to tow the cumbersome Gigant with the He 111 Z. (Fricke)

The cable harness attachment on the He 111 Z. The safety wire lies loosely on the wing center section. (ECPA)

View of the cable harness of He 111 Z DG+RU. The tow cable was 120 meters long. (Nowarra)

Another view of the cable attachment, here on He 111 Z TM+KU, photographed at Istres airfield. (Petrick)

Preparations for an Me 321 flight with He 111 Z towplane. (Nowarra)

Right: A familiar sight to the residents of Leipheim and Obertraubling. (Schlaug)

The He 111 Z V1, DS+EQ, was used for various trials at Lärz, Obertraubling and Leipheim in April and June 1942. One of the aircraft's pilots during the trials was Fl.Ing. Werner Altrogge. (Nowarra)

Crews had to practice flying the Me 321 / He 111 Z glider-tug combination before taking it into action. (Nowarra)

An He 111 Z with an Me 321 safely in tow. (Nowarra)

An He 111 Z / Me 321 (in winter camouflage) combination. Two such combinations made it to Makeyevka in spite of adverse weather conditions. (Schlaug)

Glider-tug missions to Stalingrad would have been possible for a short time had the He 111 Z been equipped with auxiliary fuel tanks as illustrated here. (Schlaug)

Gigant missions on the Eastern Front. A few of the giant gliders remained in service after the end of the 6th Army. When conditions permitted, they were capable of transporting about 90 soldiers without special modifications. (Kössler)

For an Me 321 such as this one, recovery was almost impossible. A hard landing damaged the fuselage framework in the middle, as revealed by the wrinkled fabric skinning. (Petrick)

Often the last hope: an Me 321 on the Eastern Front after a smooth landing with urgently needed supplies. (Kössler)

Taken in Russia in March 1943, this photo depicts part of the crew of He 111 Z DG+DZ: left Obfw. Willi Kirschner, right Obfw. Willi Schröer. The identity of the Oberfeldwebel in the center is not known. (Schlaug)

After the frost came the mud – as here on a Russian airfield. (Creek)

In spring 1943 there was sometimes a large number of He 111 Z aircraft on Luftwaffe airfields in the Mediterranean area. (Nowarra)

The Go 242 was much used by the Luftwaffe. The He 111 Z also served as towplane for this type. (Nowarra)

Allied air raid on Istres on 17 August 1943 which turned the huge complex into an inferno. (Storm)

Designed to tow the huge Me 321, the He 111 Z was easily capable of towing two Go 242 gliders at a time. (Nowarra)

From the airfield perimeter German soldiers watch the work of destruction. (Storm)

With the bombers gone, the soldiers leave cover. (Storm)

The many aircraft casualties included one He 111 Z completely destroyed and three others damaged. (Koos)

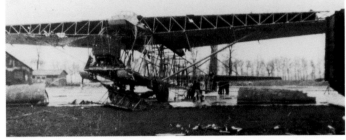

Below: By the beginning of 1944 the He 111 Z's days as a towplane appeared to be over. (Hellwig)

Fate of a giant: no longer required and scrapped. Some met this fate soon after they entered servic. (Petrick)

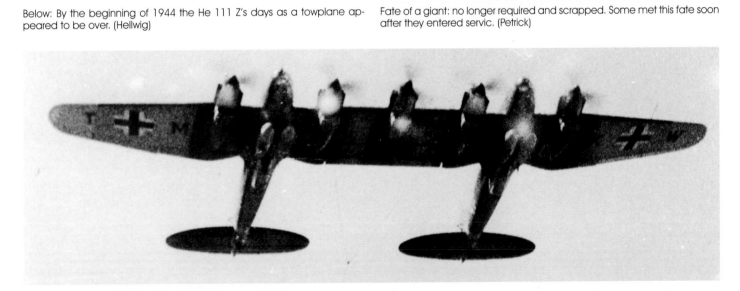

The fate of the remaining serviceable He 111 Zs at the end of 1944 remains unclear. Did they remain on the ground or were they used by KG 200? (Aders)

8

Formation of the Me 323 *Gruppen*
and Operations until Transfer to the East

Development of the Me 323 began soon after design work on the Me 321 was completed and thus proceeded almost in parallel with it. In June 1941 the RLM issued a contract for the construction of fourteen *V-Muster* (prototypes) of the Me 323, seven in four-engined configuration and seven with six engines. By July 1941 Karl Baur had already made several flights in four-engined *Giganten* and in August flew the first six-engined Me 323 (see chapter: "*The First Giants*"). Though its load capacity was 9 metric tons less than that of the Me 321 glider, the Me 323 was preferred because of its ability to take off under its own power. This eliminated the lengthy pre-takeoff preparations and the risks associated with towed operations. Just nine months later preparations began for the first operational use of the new large-capacity transport.

I. Gruppe

The formation order for a *Kampfgruppe z.b.V. 323* was issued on 1 April 1942. *G.S. 1* and *2* had previously been withdrawn from the Eastern Front in November 1941 and transferred to Merseburg and then Leipheim. There they were redesignated *1.* and *2./KG.z.b.V. 2*. Under their *Kommandeur Major* Günther Mauß they formed the basis for *1.* and *2. Staffel* of *KGr.z.b.V. 323*, which were formed on 1 May 1942. Initially the units trained pilots, however on 27 May the *Ausb.Kdo. 323* (Training Detachment 323) was also formed. More on this at the conclusion of the chapter.

On 1 November 1942 the *1. Staffel* of the new *KGr.z.b.V.* 323 moved to the Mediterranean, soon followed by the *2. Staffel*. Soon afterwards the *Gruppe* was renamed *I./KG.z.b.V. 323*. The following description of the unit's transfer and subsequent operations is based on the writings of Uffz. Spitzer of *1. Staffel*.

On 1 November the first Me 323s took off from Leipheim bound for Eleusis, Greece by way of Vienna, Belgrade and Sofia. One day later the ground personnel left by train for Athens, where they arrived on 12 November. By then the *Giganten* had already flown several supply flights to Crete, and when the ground personnel arrived in Eleusis they learned that the aircraft had been transferred to Lecce, Italy. On 8 November 1942 the Allies began "Operation

Torch", landing troops near Oran in West Africa. Paratroopers were dropped, after which approximately 850 landing craft put ashore about 140,000 soldiers. In response, one day later German troops landed at the El Aouina airport and occupied Tunis. One day later the airfield was attacked by RAF Beaufighters which destroyed or damaged a large number of aircraft. Among the aircraft destroyed was a *Gigant*. The *Giganten* flew from Lecce for three weeks, then the entire *Gruppe* moved to Pomigliano d'Arco near Naples to the Alfa Romeo company airfield which had a paved runway 1 200 meters long. Naples' commercial airfield at Capodichino served as the *Gruppe*'s alternate airfield. On 26 November 1942 Me 323 WNr. 1207 (DT+IG) took off for Africa piloted by Oblt. Ernst Peter. The aircraft was carrying the first armored vehicle to be transported to Africa by air, a *Marder* tank-destroyer armed with a 75-mm gun and weighing 11.6 metric tons. After a flight of three hours and 25 minutes the *Gigant* landed at Bizerta. At this point it should be mentioned that front-line operations by the Me 323 were being evaluated at that time. Fl.Hpt.Ing. Kurt Müller of the *E-Stelle Rechlin* had been seconded to *I./KG.z.b.V. 323* for the purpose of examining and documenting the results. He summarized his findings in a report titled "Me 323 Front-Line Experience Report" which was co-signed by Gruppenkommandeur Major Mauß. In it he wrote:

"At this time I./*KG.z.b.V.* has on strength 13 aircraft, of which nine saw action yesterday. The aircraft took off at one-minute intervals. The level of operational readiness may be derived from this fact. In the period from 1 November to 10 December 1942 the *Gruppe* flew 82 sorties, delivering 865 tonnes. The number of available aircraft was six in the beginning, later fourteen. Of these 40 to 60 percent were serviceable. Maintenance was hampered by several moves.

Missions by the Me 323s to date have taken place under the following conditions: weather: good visibility, dry, little turbulence and temperatures around 10 to 25° C, or generally favorable. Loadings: payload of 9 tonnes, maximum 10 tonnes, plus 2.4 tonnes of fuel in tanks for range, all-up weight approximately 43 to 44.5 tonnes (previous allowable 43 tonnes). Flight distances: 600 km with payload (fuel at takeoff 5 400 + 2 400 l), 700 km empty or with minimal payload (equipment, wounded), refueling stop half way. Fuel consumption: approximately 9 300 l for the entire flying distance of 1 300 km. On average 35% of the aircraft were serviceable in the beginning, later 65%. Maintenance was concentrated mainly on the engines. The propellers were a constant source of complaint. Pitch motors failed, and propeller spinners often could not stand the stress.

The airframe proved very acceptable, maintenance requirements were within normal limits. Loading and unloading was admirably quick and simple and the process was kept as short as possible due to the threat of attack at destination airfields (significantly shorter than the Ju 52).

The problem of load distribution proved much simpler than expected. The crews, who had received sufficient instruction during their conversion courses, stowed the payload with and without aids (slide rules) and the trim was always correct. Even the majority of those personnel who had received intensive instruction in Dornstadt in calculating the center of gravity eventually adopted the "seesaw" method, which meant that they made their way to the rear of the fuselage and checked whether or not the fuselage dropped. In spite of this, ground personnel must continue to receive thorough instruction in load distribution. Securing of the payload with the standard tie-down materials created for that purpose also worked flawlessly. The undercarriage is deserving of praise as it provides the aircraft with excellent maneuverability even when fully loaded.

Handling characteristics: demands on handling characteristics have been minimal on account of the favorable weather, and they are therefore still adequate. Negative aspects are the type's marginal longitudinal stability in cruising flight and its heavy control forces, especially on takeoff. The aircraft also demonstrates inadequate aileron effectiveness when it encounters downwash from a preceding aircraft. Low-level flight is extremely uncomfortable. Occasional dusk and night landings proved difficult on account of poor controllability and the poor view from the cockpit.

The aircraft's main shortcomings in its present role: so far the engines have not given significant cause for complaint. There are constant problems with the Ratier variable-pitch propellers. Airframe: fuel tankage is inadequate, refueling the aircraft takes too long, the fuel chart for added range is unobtainable (according to Messerschmitt this is being remedied). The armament is practically unusable and is already being improved in the field through the improvised installation of the *B-Stand* (dorsal turret) from the He 111 (the *E-Stelle Tarnewitz* will have to intervene energetically with the Messerschmitt company). The entire arrangement of the pilot's seat, particularly in respect to view from the cockpit during formation flying and formation approaches for landing (according to Messerschmitt this will not be changed on the production line). Inaccessible emergency exits for the pilots and radio operator, the lack of precautionary measures for ditching. The inability of the pilot to communicate with the gunners, the absence of direction-finding equipment (a proposal for this by Messerschmitt was supposedly rejected by the *LC-Amt*).

To date aircraft have been written off on the ground as a result of enemy action or because of pilot error. It is likely that the three accidents during ferrying were in part due to inadequate instruction on the type and/or pilot error (the information in brackets was added by the author).

1. (10/11/42, WNr. 1107, RD+QG), El Aouina)
Aircraft destroyed by fire on ground after strafing attack. The crew under pilot Lt. Krüger was lucky, no one was injured.

2. (23/11/42, WNr. 1110, RD+QJ), Bizerta)
Aircraft destroyed (80%) on ground in bombing raid. No injuries to personnel.

3. (22/11/42, WNr. 1203, DT+IC), Piacenca)
Heavy landing during ferry flight, airframe destroyed (60%). No injuries.

4. (02/12/32, WNr. 1204, DT+ID, southwest of Termoli)
Aircraft ditched as a result of engine failure and overturned. 3 killed, 5 injured.

5. (19/12/42, WNr. 1108, RD+QH)
Aircraft flew into the ground (hill near Rimini) during ferry flight (probably while on instruments) and exploded. 9 killed (pilot Lt. Hoffmann and crew).

Overall, valuable experience has been gained which must be immediately incorporated into the further development of the Me 323."

I. Gruppe's losses continued when 1943 began. The following are several examples: 15/01/43 Grid Square 2811 (coast of Tunisia): attack by 15-20 enemy fighters, P-38 Lightnings of the 14th Fighter Group. WNr. 1111, RD+QK, which was outside the main formation, was shot down. All nine crewmembers and 16 passengers were killed. The aircraft's pilot was *Leutnant* Krüger, who had survived the destruction of his first *Gigant* in the attack on El Aouina airfield. 1st Lt. William Paul Moore, who claimed the victory, misidentified the *Gigant* as a "six-engined Italian seaplane." On the return flight the *Giganten* were attacked by eight American fighters, and WNr. 1211, DT+IK, was shot down. Nine crewmembers and three passengers were killed. 2nd Lt. Soren E. Anton also described his victim as a "six-engined seaplane." Obviously the Allied forces in the Mediterranean were unaware of the *Gigant*'s existence at that time. Another *Gigant* landed safely at Palermo in spite of having been hit 100 times.

The dangerous and costly supply flights across the Mediterranean continued, even though growing numbers of Allied aircraft were scouring the area for transport vessels and aircraft. Vastly outnumbering the German fighter escort, they shot down many of the transport aircraft they discovered. The transport units, especially those flying the Ju 52, the most widely-used type, suffered grievous losses until the end of the effort to supply the *Afrika-Korps* and the surrender of *Armeegruppe Tunis*. Slow, cumbersome and, because of their huge size, easily sighted from a great distance, the

Giganten were easy prey in spite of their defensive armament. Shooting down a Lightning was a notable feat and successful gunners were usually awarded the Iron Cross, Second Class, however such successes were rare.

In spite of all the setbacks and dangers, in the spring of 1943 the crew of Obfw. Eitel were able to celebrate the delivery of their 5,000th metric ton of goods to Africa in their aircraft WNr. 1202, DT+IB.

But life for the *Gigant* crews continued to be dangerous. An example: while on patrol for enemy shipping, on 14/02/43 a group of P-38 Lightnings and B-25 Mitchells happened upon a group of transport aircraft, fifty Ju 52s and several Me 323s. The American aircraft attacked immediately and shot down four Ju 52s and one Me 323.

On 9 March 1943 *Generalfeldmarschall* Erwin Rommel left Africa on account of illness. When he had recovered, Hitler sent him around the Reich as a sort of "touring war hero", then made him commander of Army Group B in France. Rommel's successor in Africa was *Generaloberst* Hans-Jürgen von Arnim. The costly effort to supply the *Afrika-Korps*, or *Heeresgruppe Afrika*, as it was now called, went on. Pilot Oblt. Ernst Peter summed up the grim situation: "A transport pilot faced three possibilities: first, be shot down over the sea, second, be hit during landing, loading or takeoff and eventually be killed by one's own fuel or ammunition, or third, escape once again and wait for the next day." The crews also faced hazards posed by mechanical defect or human failure, which because of the constant stress – or more accurately overstress – was all too common.

For the Ju 52 transport units 18 April 1943 was an especially black day, because of an incident which the Allies dubbed the "Palm Sunday Massacre." At about 1730 hours approximately 80 Tomahawks and Spitfires intercepted 65 Ju 52s flying from Tunis to Sicily. The transports were flying off Cape Bon, abeam Ras el Ahmar, in a ten-kilometer-stream which made effective fighter protection impossible. German losses were one Bf 110, nine Bf 109s and 24 Ju 52s. Another 35 Ju 52s were badly damaged and most had to make forced landings on the coast. Only six Ju 52s made it through in one piece. It should be noted that there was often a wide disparity between the number of kills claimed by the Allies and the losses reported by the Germans and Italians. One reason for this was the Allied practice of sharing victories and counting "probable" kills, while another was that Allied pilots frequently misidentified the type of aircraft they had attacked. The entry in the war diary of *KG.z.b.V. "N"* (N = Naples), under whose command were *I.* and *II./KG.z.b.V. 323* (the latter having arrived in mid-January) and the Ju 52 units, for 18 April 1943 read: "The two formations took off at 1425 hours under the command of *Hauptmann* Dudek. Formation strength: (no entry). Return takeoff from Tunis took place at 1845 hours. At 1900 hours abeam Cape Bon approximately 80 British and Canadian fighters attacked the formation, which was carrying German soldiers plus Italian and French civilians. Flying in close formation, the air group was almost defenseless after its weak fighter cover of seven aircraft was attacked and driven off. The formation

then made a hard right turn toward the Cape Bon Peninsula, resulting in several collisions. Those aircraft which force-landed in favorable terrain were strafed, resulting in additional casualties. During the night, night fighters circled over the field, dropping bombs and strafing aircraft which were clearly visible in the moonlight. *Hauptmann* Dudek immediately contacted the Air Transport Commander Mediterranean, Tunis Detachment to organize a recovery effort for the wounded. Crew losses: 9 dead, 31 missing, 7 seriously wounded, 7 slightly wounded. Aircraft losses: 13 total losses, 5 aircraft missing. Operational *Geschwader* aircraft: 14 Ju 52s. Subsequently the order was issued: henceforth formation missions to Tunis by Me 323s only.

In April 1943 the Allied air forces in Tunisia were flying approximately 2,500 sorties daily. *Luftwaffe* units were bombed and strafed constantly, resulting in losses which could not be made good. It also meant losses in aircraft and pilots day after day. Although this part of the chapter is dedicated to *I. Gruppe*, by this points its experiences were intermeshed with those of *II. Gruppe*, whose story will be covered in depth later in the chapter.

19/04/43: No missions by Ju 52s to Bizerta, however a formation of sixteen Me 323s (among them X1U, C8+BP) made an uneventful crossing. Not so fortunate was a formation of sixteen Italian trimotor transports, which was intercepted by Spitfires near Pantelleria at 0725 hours while flying to Tunis. Twenty-five minutes later the Spitfires were joined by fighters of No. 7 Squadron, SAAF, off Cape Bon. The Allied fighters shot down eight transports and probably four escort fighters.

The blackest day for *KG.z.b.V. 323* was undoubtedly 22 April 1943, when *I.* and *II. Gruppe* lost fourteen *Giganten* and 119 crewmembers, to say nothing of a huge quantity of fuel and ammunition (this incident will be described in a subsequent chapter).

The unit's losses were detailed in one of its final diary entries dated 30 April 1943: personnel: killed 42, missing 204, seriously wounded 28, slightly wounded 52. Aircraft (Me 323): destroyed 39 (6), missing 29 (13), badly damaged 21 (6), slightly damaged 12 (2).

1 May 1943 saw the start of a general reorganization of all German transport units. The various *K.Gr.z.b.V.* were combined to form five so-called "*Transportfliegergeschwader.*" By order of Headquarters, XIV Air Corps the *Stab K.Gr.z.b.V. (N)* was also transformed, becoming *Stab Transportfliegergeschwader 5*. *Oberstleutnant* Damm remained as Kommodore. The *Gruppen* of *K.Gr.z.b.V. 323* were now part of *TG 5*.

13 May 1943: Capitulation of the German-Italian *Heeresgruppe Afrika*, surrender of the last Axis forces in Africa. *Generaloberst* von Arnim was captured by the Americans along with another fourteen German and seven Italian generals. 50,000 soldiers had been killed, and the 43,000 previously taken prisoner were joined by another 248,000. Just 638 soldiers managed to escape to Europe (most by aircraft). The British and Americans now had a free hand and 3,700 aircraft with which to prosecute the air war in the Mediterranean area. Heavy bombers struck German airfields almost every day. Allied fighters destroyed German transport aircraft over

the sea wherever they found them. German fighter cover was weak and ineffectual, and consequently the transport units suffered losses almost daily.

20 May 1943: Me 323s WNr. 1128 and 1240 of *I. Gruppe* were shot down by fighters of the 325th Fighter Group near Villacidro, Sardinia. WNr. 1128: 1 killed, 4 wounded, WNr. 1240: 3 killed, 2 wounded. The pilot of WNr. 1240, *Oberleutnant* Peter of the *Stabsstaffel I./TG 5* wrote an account of the incident, which is reproduced here as typical of such incidents:

"On 20 May 1943 I was assigned to lead a group of four aircraft carrying supplies to Sardinia. We took off from Pomigliano at 0935 hours and headed west. After reaching the coast we turned south to C. Comino. We flew over Nuoro, Lago-Omodeo and from there on a heading of 180° to Villacidro.

I had to fly to Decimomannu, whereas the other three machines were supposed to land at Villacidro. At 1230 hours I waggled my wings, the signal to the other aircraft to break formation. The three aircraft bound for Villacidro turned away to the right. Five minutes later I saw muzzle flashes from anti-aircraft guns and soon afterwards mushroom clouds of smoke from bombs exploding on Villacidro airfield. One of the other aircraft was still close to me and together we descended and sought cover among some nearby hills. The other two machines followed at a distance. We also saw bombs falling on Decimomannu. We remained in the holding area for about fifteen minutes. Then, all of a sudden, radio operator Obfw. Moldehn and gunner Fw. Schröder reported that about 27 enemy machines were diving on us from astern from a height of 2 500 meters. The gunners opened fire at the same time. The radio operator, who continued to observe the enemy aircraft, instructed me to evade them by turning right, which I did. Several seconds later I felt the machine being hit and tracers struck the instrument panel. At that moment I was at a height of about 100 meters. I noticed that we were smoking heavily. Immediately afterwards we were attacked from behind again. I heard a scream and saw the radio operator rush into the cockpit and continue firing. The gunner, Fw. Schröder, had been badly wounded.

The machine was burning fiercely, especially in the aft section, and I began preparing for a forced landing. I was able to put the aircraft down on a rocky flat at the base of a hill without flipping over. In the process I had to avoid several tall obstacles. Uffz. Freudenberg and the driver of the fuel truck we were carrying leapt out as soon as the machine touched down and were killed. Flight engineer Uffz. Korzeniewsky must have been so badly wounded or burned that he was unable to get out and died in the machine. I and the following members of the crew escaped the machine with minor injuries:

Radio operator Obfw. Moldehn, second pilot Fw. Spitz, gunners Obgefr. Dennerlein and Krüger, gunner Fw. Schröder (seriously wounded in the chest and arm), flight engineer Uffz. Seitz (serious burns on the right arm) and the second driver of the fuel truck.

I know that two of the other machines were attacked and damaged to some degree. One of them did not burn and its cargo of one truck, one car and 22 drums of field telephone cable was recovered. The last we saw of the second machine was a large cloud of black smoke about ten kilometers away. The last machine flew away to the north and I do not know what became of it. *Hauptmann* Jochen and Fw. Karallus conducted the investigation, which was hampered by the destruction of all the telephone lines. About three hours later I and three members of my crew flew back to Villacidro in aircraft X 1 A to report to the *Gruppe* on the incident. The injured crewmembers were immediately taken to hospital. According to Fw. Karallus a Lockheed Lightning was shot down by his machine.

The formation had consisted of the following aircraft:

X 1 R Cargo: 1 88-mm anti-aircraft gun, 2 lots of ammunition, 5 bicycles and one man,
X 1 P Cargo: 1 truck, 75 drums of field telephone cable and one man,
X 1 C Cargo: 1 fuel truck, 1 standard truck and 2 men,
Y 1 N Cargo: 1 truck, 1 car, 22 drums of field telephone cable and 2 men."

Obergefreiter Walter Krüger, also of the Stabsstaffel I./TG 5, described the incident from a gunner's point of view:

"On 20 May 1943 I was a gunner on Me 323 X 1 C on a flight to Sardinia. While we were approaching the Villacidro airfield the anti-aircraft guns opened up and I saw bombs exploding on the airfield. We subsequently descended and flew into the holding area. All of a sudden I heard over the intercom that about 25 to 30 enemy fighters were diving on us. At that moment I was in the machine-gun position in the nose of the aircraft and therefore could not see the enemy fighters as they were attacking from above and behind. Soon enemy fire began striking our machine, which caught fire immediately. I saw the pilot preparing for a forced landing. I immediately rushed to the door so as to be able to get out quickly. I saw gunner Uffz. Freudenberg jump out as soon as the machine touched down. I was thrown forward on impact and ended up lying under the auxiliary tank. When the machine came to a stop I was able to free myself from the auxiliary tank and leave the aircraft, which was blazing fiercely."

From 1 June to 15 October 1943 *TG 5* was under the command of the *Transportfliegerführer (TFF) Rom* (Air Transport Commander Rome), later Viareggio. Missions were flown from Pomigliano d'Arco (*I./TG 5*) and Pratica di Mare and Pistoia (attached *III./TG 1*). Until 22 September 1943 the attached *IV./TG 3* flew missions from Metato (in the Lucca – Pisa – Viareggio triangle) and Siena-South. Note: Entries in the *Gruppe* war diary continue only as far as 15 October 1943; the *Gruppen* may have remained at their bases longer.

I./TG 5's accomplishments in June 1943: 123 sorties, 111,090 kilometers flown, 81,440 metric tons of ammunition, 302,400 metric tons of fuel, total transport: 1,245,825 metric tons, passengers delivered 672, non-wounded brought back 1,331, wounded brought back 113, materiel brought back 93,302 metric tons, fuel consumed 768,435 metric tons. The *Gruppe* continued to suffer losses, several examples of which are detailed here.

On 10 July 1943 Allied forces landed on Sicily. On 18 July *I./ TG 5* had transferred to Pistoia. Me 323 WNr. 1249 of *I. Gruppe* sustained 60% damage in a landing accident at Pistoia. Pilot Franz Müller described how this happened on 11 May 1998, fifty-five years after the incident: "On 17 July 1943 we took off from Grosseto for Corsica. Over the sea we were suddenly attacked by a fighter from ahead. Number five engine and the wing main spar were hit. When the fighter attacked again it was shot down by my gunners. We landed safely in Bastia. Toward evening the next day (18 July) I took off on four engines. Unbeknownst to me they had filled the aft reserve tanks. This made the machine tail-heavy, which caused a crash-landing at Pistoia and considerable damage. I remember this incident vividly because it was my only crash-landing of the entire war."

21 July 1943: Me 323 RF+XP, WNr. 1132 of *I. Gruppe* sustained 50% damage in a landing accident at Pistoia. This *Gigant* had departed Leipheim on 24 June, flying to Pomigliano by way of Wiener-Neustadt, Belgrade-Semlin, Saloniki, Athens-Eleusis and Grotaglio. The aircraft, which arrived at its destination on 6 July was flown by Fw. Karl Blanke of *II. Gruppe*. Blanke subsequently returned to Leipheim by train.

25 July 1943: On this date a cease-fire was declared between the Allies and Italy. Mussolini was removed and arrested.

The withdrawal from Italy of *TG 5* began with the transfer of *1. Staffel* by rail to Leipheim on 6 August. On 19 August Hptm. Sepp Stangl, technical officer of *I./TG 5*, took over the duties of the *Geschwader* technical officer *Major* Oskar Unruh, who had left the service.

8 September 1943: Allied landing in Calabria. Announcement by the Americans of the cease-fire with Italy, followed by German countermeasures. Italian troops were disarmed, some taken prisoner, some released. On 9 September American troops landed near Salerno. 12 September: Mussolini, who was being held prisoner on the Gran Sasso d'Italia, was freed by German paratroopers. Me 323 WNr. 1106 made a crash-landing near Tula on the island of Sardinia, killing one man and injuring two others. The aircraft was en route to Germany, having been one of the last to leave.

11 October 1943: The *TFF 1*, *Generalmajor* Ulrich Buchholz, released *TG 5* from his area of command (Mediterranean). Before doing so he expressed his appreciation for the extraordinary accomplishments by the *Geschwader* in the transport role under its *Kommodore* Gustav Damm.

II. Gruppe

The *II./KG.z.b.V. 323* was created from the *K.Gr.z.b.V. 104*. Equipped with Ju 52s, the *Gruppe* had seen action in Holland, Norway, Greece and the Eastern Front. Then, in March 1942, the unit reequipped on the Go 244 (twin-engined version of the Go 242 transport glider).

With this less than completely satisfactory type, it returned to action in the southern sector of the Eastern Front (Poltava, Rostov). In October 1942 it returned to Germany. On 15 December 1942 the four *Staffeln* of the *Gruppe* moved back to Leipheim where they underwent training on the Me 323. Retrained and reequipped, on 13 January 1943 the *Gruppe* was renamed *II./KG.z.b.V. 323* under *Gruppenkommandeur Oberstleutnant* Werner Stephan. At the very same time a special headquarters under *Generalfeldmarschall* Erhard Milch was trying to amass as many transport aircraft as possible quickly as possible for an airlift to supply the German 6th Army surrounded at Stalingrad. The "*Sonderstab GFM Milch*" gathered together transport gliders and transport aircraft of every type. In addition to He 111 Z / Me 321 towplane-glider combinations, consideration was also given to employing the Me 323s of the newly-formed *II./KG.z.b.V. 323* in the Stalingrad airlift. The *Gruppe* had been assigned eleven brand-new Me 323s, plus five *Giganten* specially equipped for winter operations and one Me 323 training aircraft. The *Sonderstab* claimed a total of 15 aircraft of this type. Since the transport capabilities of the Me 323 were also urgently required in the Mediterranean theater to supply the Afrika-Korps, *II./KG.z.b.V. 323* was only considered for a single mission from Makeyevka to Stalingrad. It is worthy to note that on 29 January 1943 the Me 323, which had been considered unsuited to night flying, was cleared for night flight under simple conditions (six days before and six days after the full moon with a visible horizon) effective immediately. Moreover, while the efficacy of the He 177 for winter operations was at least questioned, it was simply assumed that the Me 323 was suitable for winter operations even though there was no experience to draw upon. On 31 January 1943 the Me 323s were still included in mission planning. They were not on standby, however, instead making transport flights to Wiener-Neustadt, Belgrade-Semlin, Saloniki, Athens-Eleusis and other destinations.

The *II./KG.z.b.V. 323* did not see action at Stalingrad as the 6th Army under *Generalfeldmarschall* Paulus was forced to surrender on 2 February 1943. By the end of its relatively ineffective existence the *Sonderstab GFM Milch* had lost a total of 256 aircraft – Ju 52s, He 111s, Ju 86s, He 177s, Fw 200s and Ju 290s. An additional 179 aircraft suffered varying degrees of damage. On the other hand the Me 321 and Me 323 were spared the flight to Stalingrad. The loss of suitable airfields as the Red Army advanced, the stresses placed on men and machines by terrible weather conditions, chaotic organization and contradictory orders, plus almost unlimited resources on the other side eventually doomed the airlift to failure.

And so, on 8 February 1943, the *Giganten* of *1.* and *2. Staffel* of *II./KG.z.b.V. 323* flew from Leipheim to Istres, followed on 12 February by the machines of *3.* and *4. Staffel*. From Istres the transports ranged over the entire Mediterranean area: Grosseto, Pomigliano, Capodichino, Pratica, Pisa, Lagnasco, Foggia.

Like *I. Gruppe*, following its transfer to the Mediterranean *II. Gruppe* had to expect casualties. After isolated attacks on transport flights, on 13 April Castelvetrano was bombed. The following Me 323s were destroyed or damaged: WNr. 1116 (60%), WNr. 1221

(100%), WNr. 1232 (40%), WNr. 1233 (60%), WNr. 1235 (40%). Of the fourteen *Giganten* which were shot down off Cape Bon, eight were from *II. Gruppe*, including the aircraft of the *Gruppenkommandeur*, *Oberstleutnant* Werner Stephan, who was killed (see chapter titled "Cape Bon").

On 23 April 1943 Hptm. Hans Fischer was placed in command of *II. Gruppe* and promoted to *Major*.

When German troops retreated from Tunis on 7 May 1943, WNr. 1260 C8+FN "*Mücke*" was incapable of taking off and was blown up.

In May 1943 the *Gruppe* was renamed *II./TG 5*. on 6 June 1943 the *Gruppe*, or what was left of it, moved from Pomigliano to Risstissen near Ulm, where it was disbanded on 22 June. At the same time *III./TG 5* (with almost no aircraft) was renamed *II./TG 5* and received sufficient new Me 323s to bring it up to authorized strength. In the weeks that followed, there were several minor moves for the *Gruppe*, which was virtually a new formation. It went to Istres for a time in order to support *I./TG 5* from there. The airfields were bombed almost daily, resulting in losses.

On 10 July 1943 Allied forces landed on Sicily and following the removal and arrest of Mussolini on 25 July Italy could no longer be regarded as an ally. *TG 5* withdrew to Pistoia in northern Italy. On 17 August the Allies carried out a devastating bombing raid against the huge airfield at Istres. Aircraft of the air landing, paratrooper, glider and transport units were lined up as if on parade, and more than 180 of them were destroyed or damaged. The number of dead was 40 to 50. *II./TG 5* lost two *Giganten* destroyed and another damaged. In northern Italy, too, the aircraft of *TG 5* were subjected to increasingly frequent attacks by enemy aircraft.

On 25 August 1943 the new *Kommandeur* of *II. Gruppe*, *Major* Fritz Barthel, reported for duty to the *Geschwaderkommodore*. The evacuation of Corsica began on 30 September 1943. Me 323s WNr. 1216 and 1285 of *II./TG 5* were shot down by fighters near Borgo while en route from Corsica to Elba. WNr. 1112 RD+QL of *II./TG 5* had to be left behind at Poretto, Corsica. German soldiers blew up the aircraft. On 10 October 1943 the *Gruppe* moved from Lagnasco to Goslar. The focus of operations now shifted to the Eastern Front.

III. Gruppe

In contrast to *I.* and *II. Gruppe* the *III. Gruppe* existed for only a short time. It was formed from the *K.Gr.z.b.V. 900*, which on 3 February 1943 had returned from operations on the Eastern Front, flying its Ju 52s to Münster-Handorf. The *Gruppe* was renamed *III./KG.z.b.V. 323* and by 20 March had reequipped on the Me 323. The *Gruppe* subsequently moved from Münster to Leipheim, from where it flew sorties to Istres and the Balkans. The unit's first *Gruppenkommandeur*, *Oberst* Alfred Wübben, was probably relieved by *Major* Markus Zeidler on 3 June 1943. On 22 May 1943 the *Gruppe* was renamed *III./TG 5* and then on 22 June became *II./TG 5*. If the *III. Gruppe* retained its previous organization of four *Staffeln* (plus *Stabsstaffel*), with twelve Me 323s and one Ju 52 on strength, in March 1943 it had just three *Giganten* per *Staffel*. In April 1943 the entire *Gruppe* consisted of just one Me 323 and one Ju 52! All of the other *Giganten* had gone "to other units." As *I. Gruppe* received twelve *Giganten* "from other units" at about the same time, it may be assumed that they all came from *III. Gruppe*. No new aircraft were received prior to 22 June 1943, when *III./TG 5* and the remnants of *II./TG 5* were combined to form a new *II. Gruppe*.

Other Units which Used the Me 323

On 27 May 1942 the *Lehr- und Ausb.Kdo. 323* (instruction and training detachment) was formed in Dornstadt near Ulm for the purpose of training pilots on the Me 323. The unit, which initially was supposed to exist for six months, was later transferred to Stendal and Munich-Oberwiesenfeld under the command of Hptm. Mehring. On 30 August 1943 the *Lehr- und Ausb.Kdo. 323* was disbanded and *Fl.Techn.Schule 3* (aviation ground school) in Munich formed a *Lehrgruppe Verlastung* (loading training group). The school had already given courses for "loaders for high-capacity aircraft." On 20 March 1943 the *Erg.St.z.b.V. 323* (replacement training *Staffel*) was created from *5./K.Gr.z.b.V. 300* in Leipheim and in June it was equipped with five new Me 323s. *Staffelkapitän* was Hptm. Oswald Brien. In September 1943 the unit was renamed *5./Erg.Transportfliegergruppe*. On 13 October 1943 the *Staffel* moved from Leipheim to Liegnitz, then to Schroda and finally, on 15 June 1944, to Tonndorf (Posen). By the end of June it gave up its aircraft (corps reserve, conversion to weapons carrier?) and on 21 July 1944 was disbanded, one month before TG 5.

Gigant operations by GS 1 and 2 in the east ended in November. At Leipheim they awaited other assignments. (Nowarra)

End of October 1942: the first Me 323s ready to move to the Mediterranean area. (Peter)

The engines were checked over thoroughly. (Radinger)

Right: Major Günther Mauß was involved from the beginning. Here he is seen wearing the German Cross in Gold while Kommandeur of I./TG 5. (Petrick)

Going-away party for I./K.Gr.z.b.V. 323 in Leipheim before its transfer to Italy. From left to right: unidentified, unidentified, Major Oskar Unruh, Oblt. Waldemar Kost, unidentified, unidentified, Major Günther Mauß and his wife, Oblt. Josef "Sepp" Stangl, Oblt. Ernst Peter. (Peter)

Final preparations, the takeoff-assist rockets are mounted beneath the wings. (Hellwig)

Waiting to take off on the flight to Eleusis. (Peter)

The crew of DT+IA has one more look around the aircraft. (Peter)

Takeoff. With rockets burning, the first Giganten lift off for the Mediterranean. (Peter)

Supply goods of all kinds are loaded aboard the Giganten. (Hellwig)

The aircraft via Vienna, Belgrade and Sofia to their initial destination, Eleusis, Greece. From there they flew supplies to Crete. (Radinger)

Below: This Gigant of I./K.Gr.z.b.V. 323 has just landed at Lecce, Italy. (Petrick)

The aircraft were serviced at Pomigliano, like the Me 323 sitting in the background. Major Unruh and a crew from the Stabsstaffel pose for the photographer. On his left is Fw. Kochale. (Hellwig)

The Alfa Romeo company airfield at Pomigliano d'Arco near Naples. (Storm)

The Giganten of I. Gruppe land at Pomigliano. (Ott)

Pomigliano was K.Gr.z.b.V. 323's base of operations until the end of supply flights to the Afrika-Korps. (Quest)

The Giganten wait for their next mission. (Hellwig)

The Me 323s often flew to Africa as part of mixed formations. Here they are accompanied by Ju 90 J4+KH, WNr. 0009, of Lufttransportstaffel 290. (Radinger)

When everything went well the Giganten returned to Pomigliano. (Ott)

Fl.Hpt.Ing. Kurt Müller (center) of the E-Stelle Rechlin, the author of the "Me 323 front-Line Experience Report." Here he is seen relaxing at the Café Nied in Leipheim with other members of the E-Stelle and Ing. Bernhard Schwarting (left of Müller), who was responsible for power plant installation. (Vogel)

When Müller was assigned to the K.G.z.b.V., only 40 to 60% of the unit's Me 323s were serviceable. Undercarriage changes as seen here were quite rare, on account of the amount of labor required. (Hellwig)

The engines were very maintenance-intensive. The technicians of the Stabsstaffel soon converted this Opel-Blitz into a mobile crane, which simplified the job of changing engines at Pomigliano. (Hellwig)

Fl.Hpt.Ing. Müller found that loading and unloading was conducted "with commendable speed." This was of particular importance in Tunis, where the threat of air attack was always present. (Peter)

Even on Sardinia, the crew endeavored to get the gun out of the aircraft and into safety as quickly as possible. (Ott)

The loadmasters faced a variety of challenges: bulky equipment ... (Griehl)

Höherer Kommandeur
der fliegertechnischen Schulen.

Befähigungsnachweis

Nach Teilnahme an einem Lehrgang
vom 3. 4. 1943 bis 1. 6. 1943
bei der Flg. Techn. Schule 3

und auf Grund des Prüfungsergebnisses
vom 1. 6. 1943 wird dem
Uffz. Hermann Schladerbusch
bestätigt, daß er die Prüfung zum

Verlaster
für Großraumflugzeuge

bestanden hat.

München, den 1. 6. 1943

für die Prüfungskommission

i. A. *Fritz*
Flg. Stabsingenieur

i. V. *Kulen*
Oberstleutnant

In his report, Fl.Hpt.Ing. Müller proposed that ground personnel receive a thorough briefing on loading. In fact, for the most part it was the flight engineers who were trained as loadmasters for large-capacity aircraft. (Schladerbusch)

... heavy equipment ... (Ott)

... mixed loads ... (Nowarra)

... optimal utilization ... (Griehl)

... and, unfortunately, wounded. Though the Me 323 was often used to transport wounded, there is no evidence that it was ever marked as an ambulance aircraft. (Schladerbusch)

In Tunisia local youths were always on hand to assist in rapid loading or unloading. (Peter)

Fl.Hpt.Ing. Müller also found that refueling consumed too much time. (Griehl)

Flight engineer Korzenewski with two Tunisian helpers. In the background is Oblt. Ernst Peter's aircraft DT+IG "Peterle." (Peter)

At low level over the Mediterranean. According to Fl.Hpt.Ing. Müller, the type's inadequate aileron effectiveness made flying into the slipstream of a preceding aircraft an "extremely unpleasant" experience. (Peter)

A deceptive picture: the aircraft's fuel capacity was considered inadequate for supply missions to Africa. (Storm)

In the tent camp at Pomigliano: belting ammunition and cleaning the weapons for the Giganten. Müller was especially critical of the Me 323's armament, calling it "practically unusable." (Hellwig)

In fact, the Me 323's weak defensive armament led the crews to install a dorsal turret from the He 111 P above the cockpit. (Handbook)

Later versions of the Me 323 were equipped with more effective defensive weapons on the production line, however they still remained vulnerable. (Nowarra)

In his report Fl.Hpt.Ing. Müller also mentioned the casualties suffered by the unit to date. On 10 November 1942, Me 323 RD+QG burnt out on the Tunis-El Aouina airfield following a strafing attack by Allied aircraft. After the surrender of Army Group Africa the victorious Allies counted eleven more or less destroyed Giganten at El Aouina. The wreck depicted here may have been the first Me 323 lost in Africa. (Nowarra)

A Gigant flying to Africa alone and at low level. An Me 323 flying in this manner was doomed if Allied fighters found it. At first the Allied pilots thought the unidentified type was an Italian flying boat. (Nowarra)

In spite of intense gunnery training, the Gigant gunners had little chance of fighting off an attacking fighter. (Rößmann)

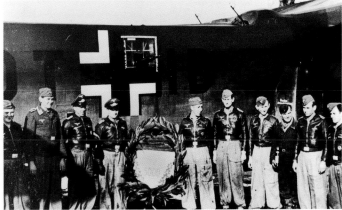

On 17 February 1943 I./KG.z.b.V. 323 celebrated the transport of 5 000 metric tons of supplies. The milestone was reached by Obfw. Eitel and the crew of DT+IB. The side-mounted MG FF cannon was installed with materials on hand. A standard MG 131 installation was later introduced as standard. (Peter)

Something else to celebrate. The side-mounted defensive armament is once again a retro-fit. A wrecked Gigant is visible in the background. (Roba)

Deadly threats were omnipresent: a Gigant has been hit in an air raid on Pomigliano airfield and caught fire. (Hellwig)

There is nothing the firefighting truck can do, the Gigant burns out. (Hellwig)

The result of a bombing raid on the Tunis-El Aouina airfield. (Roba)

Right: The fuel goes up with a tremendous explosion. (Hellwig)

This Me 323 D-2 escaped damage in an air raid on Lecce. (Petrick)

Giganten in a hail of bombs falling on Castelvetrano airfield (Sicily) on 13 April 1943. (Aders)

The crew sits beneath their wrecked Gigant, one of a total of eleven which was later counted there. (Roba)

Me 323 C8+AA of the Stabsstaffel I./KG.z.b.V. 323 was forced to make an emergency landing after it was fired on. (Peter)

After the heavy losses suffered by the Ju 52 units, on 19 April 1943 the order was issued: from now on formation flights to Tunis by Me 323s only! (Hellwig)

Damage caused by mechanical failure: this Me 323 rolled between parked aircraft after its brakes failed. (Hellwig)

Undercarriage damage after a hard landing. Repairing the damage was hard work. (Peter)

This Gigant wears the palm tree emblem of the Africa Corps in addition to the simplified emblem of the Stabsstaffel I./KG.z.b.V. 323. (peter)

Oblt. Peter's DT+IG at Trapani with gunner Obfw. Schröder and his tiny mascot. (Peter)

Before the return flight from Tunisia to Italy. All had not gone smoothly, as the man with the bandaged head would suggest. In the middle a Tunisian helper. (Hellwig)

An Me 323 at Castelvetrano in spring 1943. Note the circular window in the nose door. The purpose of the window is not known. (Petrick)

In January 1943, after 250 flying hours, DT+IG became due for an inspection in Leipheim. Here Major Mauß is involved in a lively discussion shortly before departure from Pomigliano. (Peter)

Group photo prior to departure for Germany. From left to right: Major Mauß, Oblt. Kost, Ing. Henckel of Messerschmitt, Oblt. Peter, Oblt. Schalkhauser, Waffeninspektor Kollmann.

Gigant designer Fröhlich and his deputy Petri also visited Pomigliano to examine the situation on the spot. Behind them, partly concealed, is pilot Starbati. (Vogel)

The crew of the Me 323 D-2 in front of the aircraft in which the milestone mission was flown. (Hellwig)

In June 1943 I./TG 5 celebrated its 1,000th transport mission at Pomigliano airfield. (Ott)

The occasion was also used to present decorations to several soldiers. In the background, ten kilometers away, Mount Vesuvius. (Hellwig)

At about the same time, on 11 June 1943 the Italian island fortress of Pantelleria was taken by the Allies without a fight after a bombardment lasting several days. The ring was closing around the German forces in Italy. (USAF)

Right: A departure: shortly before the unit's transfer back to the Reich, the Major Oskar Unruh, commander of the Stabsstaffel I./TG 5, retired. (Hellwig)

Below: Major Unruh's official departure: the men have fallen in to hear his farewell speech. (Hoffmann)

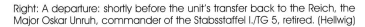

Gruppenkommandeur Major Mauß in informal summer uniform, Major Unruh in dress uniform. (Hellwig)

Then began the pleasant part. On the wall the emblem of I./TG 5. Beneath the picture of Göring is Major Mauß, to his right Major Unruh, beside him Hptm. Stangl, who took over the Stabsstaffel. Next to Stangl is the Gruppe medical officer, Dr. Opitz, while beneath the picture of Hitler is signals officer Oblt. Templ. (Hellwig)

Group photo standing ... (Hoffmann)

... and sitting. (Hellwig)

This going-away party put a permanent end to the period in which there were two Majors in I. Gruppe. (Hellwig)

On 18 July 1943 I./TG 5 moved from Pomigliano to Pistoia near Florence and on 6 August from Pistoia to Leipheim. The "Foot People" (ground personnel) of course went by train. (Hellwig)

On 11 October 1943 Generalleutnant Ulrich Buchholz, the Transportfliegerführer Mittelmeer, released all of TG 5 from his area of command.

The clover leaf was actually the emblem of FFS B 8 in Wiener Neustadt, however K.Gr.z.b.V. 104 was probably formed using personnel from the training school. The unit flew the Ju 52 until March 1942. (Roba)

In March 1942 K.Gr.z.b.V. 104 was equipped with the Go 244. This motorized version of the Go 242 did not prove a success on operations in the east. In October 1942 the Gruppe returned to Leipheim where it relinquished its Go 244s. In January 1943 K.Gr.z.b.V. 104 became II./KG.z.b.V. 323. (Roba)

K.Gr.z.b.V. 104's equipment arrived in Leipheim by train in December 1942. (Roba)

Generalfeldmarschall Erhard Milch planned to use the Giganten of the recently-formed II./KG.z.b.V. 323 in his airlift in support of the 6th Army encircled at Stalingrad, even though these aircraft were urgently needed to supply Army Group Africa. (Roosenboom)

Landing at Pomigliano. Pilots of II. Gruppe ferried several Me 323s from Leipheim for the I. Gruppe and then returned by train. (Hellwig)

The Luftwaffe's largest transport aircraft and its most widely used. While the Me 323 did not see action at Stalingrad, 133 Ju 52s were lost and another 84 damaged while participating in the airlift. (Griehl)

The Luftwaffe's largest transport glider and its most widely used. Neither the Me 321 nor the much more numerous Go 242 saw action in the Stalingrad airlift, as the situation had rendered this impossible. (Nowarra)

The impressive sight of an Me 323 approaching to land often resulted in a quick photo – even if a windshield wiper was in the way. (Petrick)

Raising a large cloud of dust, an Me 323 taxis to takeoff position. Other aircraft visible on this Italian airfield include a Ju 88, a Bf 110 and a DFS 230 glider. (Quest)

Munich-Riem on 23 June 1943: the crew waits to take off, its mission to deliver the Gigant to Grosseto. On takeoff the Gigant lost both folding plexiglas panels from the two flight engineer positions. (Storm)

In the course of transfer and ferry flights the crews were often required to cross the Alps. (Roosenboom)

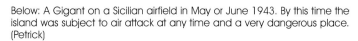

An advance detachment from 6./TG 5 had already arrived in Istres and on 13 July 1943 began erecting a tent camp in the so-called "Oasis." The actual transfer of II. Gruppe from Mengen to Istres began on 30 August. (Schladerbusch)

Below: A Gigant on a Sicilian airfield in May or June 1943. By this time the island was subject to air attack at any time and a very dangerous place. (Petrick)

Short break before the next mission. Until the very end a few examples of the D-2 with fixed-pitch two-blade wooden propellers remained on strength with the Staffeln. (Roba)

Last missions to Sicily. Allied forces landed on the island on 10 July 1943. (Petrick)

The American 5th Army lands at Salerno on 9 September 1943. Less than one month later, on 1 October, German troops abandoned Naples. I./TG 5 moved from Pomigliano to Pistoia on 18 July. (USAF)

The evacuation of Corsica began on 30 September 1943. Prior to this, flights into the area by the Giganten had become extremely dangerous due to the constant presence of Beaufighters, Marauders, Mitchells and other heavily armed Allied aircraft in the area. Here an Me 323 is being attacked by a Martin Marauder near Cape Corse. (Nowarra)

A Gigant goes down west of Cape Corse after being attacked by a Martin Marauder in September 1943. (Griehl)

On 30 July 1943 Obfw. Honig took off from Istres in VM+IW to fly to Rome, however he was attacked near Cape Corse and forced to crash-land on the island of Corsica. (Roba)

Below: This Gigant was also attacked by a Marauder near Cape Corse. It is most likely the aircraft of Obfw. Walter Honig. (Griehl)

The Gigant was wrecked in the hard landing. (Roba)

All of the thirteen persons on board (crew of 9 and 4 drivers) were injured to some degree. (Roba)

No one was killed, however. Obfw. Honig (with bandaged knee) displayed great skill, but was also very lucky. (Roba)

The Giganten were no longer safe on any Italian airfield either. In the final weeks before the retreat from the Mediterranean area more than one Gigant crew left its aircraft … (Hellwig)

… only to return and find it like C8+ , seen here in Pisa. It had been totally destroyed in a bombing raid during the night of 23 September 1943. At that time Uffz. Rößmann and his crew were billeted in a hotel in the city. (Rößmann)

Everything that could still be used was salvaged from the Gigant. (Roba)

Wie ein urweltliches Ungeheuer zieht das sechsmotorige Großtransportflugzeug „Gigant" vom Baumuster Me 323 mit der riesigen Spannweite von 55 m seine Bahn. Deutlich ist das Fahrwerk zu erkennen, das aus 10 Rädern besteht und so angelegt ist, daß es, ähnlich einem Raupenrollwerk, Bodenhindernisse überwinden kann. Eine besonders starke Bewaffnung sichert den Großtransporter vor überraschenden Feindangriffen. Trotz ihrer Größe kommt die Me 323 mit einer Besatzung von nur 5 Mann aus

DER «GIGANT»

Me 323, das größte Landflugzeug der Welt

Als erste Zeitschrift veröffentlicht der ADLER Aufnahmen von dem seit einiger Zeit bei der deutschen Luftwaffe eingesetzten Großraumflugzeug Me 323, das wegen seiner riesigen Ausmaße den Beinamen „Gigant" erhalten hat. Deutsche Konstrukteure haben mit diesem sechsmotorigen Flugzeug der Messerschmitt-Werke, dem größten Landflugzeug der Welt, einen Transporter geschaffen, der sich bei den militärischen Operationen der jüngsten Vergangenheit über weite Strecken außerordentlich bewährt hat

Fast unerschöpflich ist der Bauch des „Gigant" mit seinem Laderaum von 100 cbm. Munition, Verpflegung, Mannschaften mit voller Ausrüstung bis zu 130 Köpfen, ja sogar Geschütze, Panzer und vollbeladene Lastkraftwagen nimmt der Rumpf auf

Startklar! Die sechs Motoren sind dröhnend anlaufen, gleich wird der „Gigant" über die Startbahn rollen und sich trotz seiner großen Belastung leicht in die Lüfte erheben

PK-Aufnahmen
Kriegsberichter Seeger (Atl)

echts: Behutsam werden ie Verwundeten vom Sanitspersoal aus der Me 323 erausgetragen. Ihre weit ber dem Durchschnitt egenden Ausmaße lassen ach Transporte bis zu Verwundete in Betten ohne Schwierigkeiten zu

The Gigant was revealed to the German public for the first time in Issue 23 of the magazine "Adler" published on 9 November 1943. The photographs in the magazine were seven months old and had been taken at the time of the costly Mediterranean operations.

The Lehr- und Ausb.Kdo. 323 was also equipped with the Me 323. (Petrick)

A newcomer is familiarized with the huge aircraft. (Ott)

For most pilots, converting to such a large aircraft also required a change of attitude, which was accomplished more easily with a little humor. (Ott)

Loading practice was carried out in Leipheim or, more often, in Dornstadt. Calculating the center of gravity and properly securing the load were vital to safe operation of the aircraft, and specialized courses were given on both subjects. Here a company of trainees has fallen in in front of an Me 323. (Kuettner)

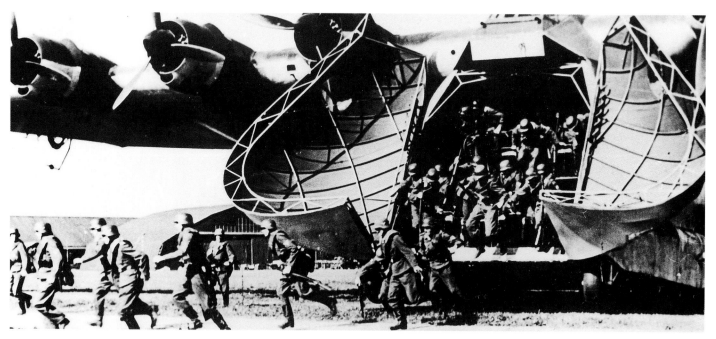

Focal point of the exercise: quick entry and even quicker exit plus maximum discipline on board. To the pilots the soldiers were an "amorphous mass", unpredictable in critical situations. (Peter)

The soldiers are marched off after the exercise. (Radinger)

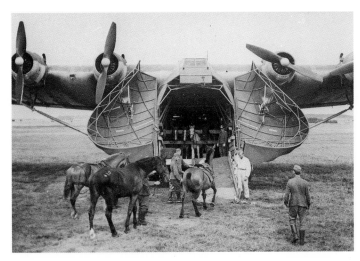

Since horses were important elements of the supply system, especially in the east, care had to be taken in transporting them. (Radinger)

The horses have been safely put aboard and the doors can be closed. The animals still had to be watched during the flight. (Radinger)

Here a crew practices loading an 88-mm anti-aircraft gun. There was always the danger that the long barrel of the gun might damage the control cables, therefore the loading ramp was moved forward and lengthened. (Thiele)

The Gigant was also capable of accommodating the Model 18 Heavy Field Howitzer (150 mm) and its Sd.Kfz. 7 tractor (8 tonnes). This, too, required practice. (Radinger)

Gun and tractor were loaded in such a way that they were able to exit the aircraft without difficulty. (Radinger)

9

The Drama off Cape Bon - 22 April 1943

Holy Thursday, just before Easter 1943, was the blackest day of all for the Me 323s and their crews. The following account of the incident is based on war diary entries, teletype messages of the *Luftwaffe* operations staff and statements by men who were there.

Ten Ju 52s of *Kampfgruppe z.b.V. 106* took off from Pomigliano at 0640 hours bound for Tunis. The formation was led by *Staffelkapitän* Oblt. Biedermann. The Junkers were supposed to fly to Tunis with a group of fourteen Me 323s which took off from Pomigliano at 0710 hours and the maximum available fighter escort. Each *Gigant* was carrying about 12 metric tons of fuel or ammunition destined for Army Group Tunis, the embattled remnant of the former *Afrika-Korps* commanded by Rommel's successor, *Generaloberst* von Arnim. Sixteen Me 323s were originally supposed to take part in the mission, which was to be a repetition of a successful mission on 19 April when all aircraft returned safely. The sixteen aircraft were not the last still available to *KG.z.b.V. 323*, as has been claimed in various publications. According to *Geschwader* strength reports from April 1943, at the beginning of the month *I. Gruppe* had fifteen aircraft, while *II. Gruppe* had 23 Me 323s, although not all were serviceable.

One of the *Giganten* assigned to the mission on 22 April could not be made ready to fly and aircraft C8+BN of Obfw. Karl Kandzia went unserviceable as it was preparing to take off. Following engine run-up, two engines failed during the takeoff roll. In addition, one tire blew and the aircraft was unable to achieve flying speed. Kandzia's Me 323 rolled off the end of the runway past the DF shack and ended up in a field. It was later recovered.

The fighter escort of 39 Bf 109s assembled over Trapani at 0830 hours. Another 65 fighters were supposed to fly out from Tunis to meet the formation. At 0835 hours the formation overflew the island of Marettimo west of Sicily and descended to a height of 20 to 50 meters above the sea. The specified route of flight <u>was not</u> over Cape Bon, a fact which had been stressed at the flight briefing the previous day, but over Cape Farina, which lay approximately 75 kilometers farther west. The area around Cape Bon was considered especially dangerous. The Ju 52 group was flying on the right, the Me 323s on the left. Approximately halfway between Sicily and Tunisia the Me 323s separated from the Ju 52 formation and, contrary to orders, set course for Cape Bon. Why the *Gruppenkommandeur* of *II./KG.z.b.V. 323*, who was flying in *Gigant* C8+AR, ordered this course change will never be known. Most of the escort fighters which had taken off from Sicily stayed with the Ju 52s and did not go after the Me 323s until the fighters from Tunis had reached the Junkers. This splitting of the fighter escort meant that the *Giganten* had only 36 escorts instead of the planned 104.

Oblt. Biedermann saw the attack on the Me 323s beginning in the distance, however he and his formation of Ju 52s reached Cape Farina unmolested at about 0935 hours. Biedermann was supposed to take his aircraft into the holding area near Cape el Fortass. Instead, however, he led his formation to a German fighter base at Andeless and circled there until he received clearance to land at Tunis.

At 0925 two large groups of enemy fighters began attacking the Me 323s between Cape Bon and the island of Zembra. Conditions were hazy. The first group of enemy fighters engaged the Bf 109s of *II./JG 27*, which were flying at an altitude of about 2 400 meters, and forced them away from the transports. This allowed the second formation, which was larger and made up mainly of P-40 Kittyhawks of the South African Air Force, to attack the *Giganten*. The arrival of the fighters was no accident. First, Tunis and the surrounding airfields were the transports' only possible destination and they could only arrive within certain hours. Second, a secret transmitter, which was discovered that same day, had been sending information to the Allies on all German flight movements from Trapani. The radio was hidden in a confessional in a church on Monte Giovanni above Trapani. Under these circumstances it was no problem for the enemy fighters to intercept and destroy the transport units, especially since shortages of personnel and aircraft meant that they were usually weakly escorted.

The enemy fighters estimated the size of the Me 323 formation at 20 aircraft instead of the actual 14. Once attacked, the Me 323s took evasive action and the wedge-shaped formation disintegrated. The huge, cumbersome transports had little chance of even reaching the African coast. Usually able to sustain a great deal of battle damage, on this day the *Giganten* were carrying volatile cargoes and most caught fire or exploded after a few hits. Though they put up stiff resistance, shooting down five to seven enemy fighters, the Me 323s were shot down one after another until the last *Gigant* crashed into the sea in flames. The escort fighters from Tunisia were still with the Ju 52s and were too far away to intervene. In any event, it is likely that they could have done little to alter the outcome of this uneven battle.

Flight-Lieutenant Edwards of No. 260 Squadron arrived on the scene toward the end of the massacre and discovered the last surviving Me 323, which had so far escaped attack. He and two other pilots gave chase. They opened fire on the *Gigant*, which caught fire and crashed into the sea.

Only after he had arrived in Tunis did Oblt. Biedermann contact the adjutant of the *Fliegerführer* by telephone and inform him of the air battle. On reading Oblt. Biedermann's written report, the *Geschwaderkommodore* of *KG.z.b.V. 323, Oberstleutnant* Gustav Damm became furious and demanded to know why the air-sea rescue service had not been alerted by radio. The belated (beginning at about 1200 hours) rescue – Fieseler Storks dropping one-man life rafts, most of which missed their targets – was hampered by heavy seas and rain. Some men were picked up by motor torpedo boats, with the Storks circling overhead to guide the boats to the men in the water. The last survivors were picked up at about 1800 hours, after 8 1/2 hours in the water.

Aircraft losses: 14 Me 323s with 700 drums of fuel. Personnel losses: the initial tally was 2 killed, 113 missing (including 6 officers), 4 badly injured and 14 with less serious injuries. In the end, however, it was found that only 19 of the 138 men involved had survived this tragedy. *Oberstleutnant* Werner Stephan was among the dead and he was officially honored by *Generalfeldmarschall* Albert Kesselring for his "heroic actions." In transport officer circles, however, it was believed that Stephan had arbitrarily changed course to reach Tunis more quickly and thus led the *Giganten* to their destruction. Had he lived, he would probably have been required to answer for his actions before a court-martial.

Me 323 Losses (parent *Gruppe* in brackets)

C8+ER, WNr. 1114 (II.), pilot Fw. Wagner, 4 killed, 5 injured.

C8+AR, WNr. 1115 (II.), pilot Lt. Wiedemann, 6 killed, 4 injured (on board this aircraft was the *Kommandeur* of *II./KG.z.b.V. 323, Oberstleutnant* Stephan).

RD+QZ, WNr. 1126 (I.), pilot Oblt. Drewes, 9 killed.

RF+XH, WNr. 1134 (I.), pilot Oblt. Meyer, 15 killed.

RF+XI, WNr. 1135 (I.), 7 killed, 2 injured.

C8+EP, WNr. 1124 (II.), pilot Obfw. Sczotka, 9 killed.

C8+CP, WNr. 1225 (II.), pilot Obfw. Oerlich, 9 killed.

C8+DP, WNr. 1226 (II.), pilot Hptm. Kube (*Staffel* leader), 9 killed, 1 injured.

C8+AC, WNr. 1239 (II.), pilot Hptm. Ruge (*Staffel* leader), 10 killed (aircraft was a D-2 with fixed-pitch two-blade wooden propellers).

SG+RP, WNr. 1242 (I.), pilot Oblt. Müller, 8 killed, 1 injured.

C8+DN, WNr. 1245 (II.), pilot Oblt. Keil, 9 killed.

SG+RV, WNr. 1248 (I.), pilot Obfw. Löneke, 8 killed, 1 injured (D-2).

VM+IA, WNr. 1253 (I.), pilot Lt. Knecht, 6 killed, 3 injured.

C8+CC, WNr. 1254 (II.), pilot Oblt. von Kalinowski (killed, further casualties not known).

The following confirmed kills were awarded to Allied fighter pilots who took part in the attack on the Me 323s:

No. 4 Squadron SAAF
Lt. Marshall (2), Lt. Green (2 1/2), Lt. Brunton (1), Lt. Crosley (1), Lt. de Kock (1), Lt. M. Dougall (1), total of 9.

No. 5 Squadron SAAF
Maj. Parsonson (2 1/2), Lt. Weingartz (2), Maj. Human (1), Lt. Sansom (1), Lt. Coad (1 1/2), Lt. Britten (1), Lt. Pollock (1), Lt. Clarke (1), Lt. Block (1), Lt. Humphrey (1), Lt. van Niekirk (1/2), total of 13.

No 260 Squadron RAF
Flt.Lt. Edwards (1)

According to Me 323 pilot Oblt. Ernst Peter, from the end of November 1942 to 22 April 1943 *KG.z.b.V. 323* had transported 15,000 metric tons of equipment to Tunis and Bizerta in approximately 1,200 sorties. Among the items delivered: 309 trucks, 51 medium prime movers up to 12 tonnes, 209 guns up to 150-mm caliber, 324 light guns, 83 anti-tank and anti-aircraft guns, 42 anti-aircraft radars including "Würzburg Riese" and 96 armored troop carriers and self-propelled guns. In April 1943 alone, the *Geschwader* lost 21 Me 323s to enemy action and 7 from other causes. The unit's actual strength on 30 April 1943, including new arrivals, was thirty-five Me 323s.

The transport of supplies by sea and air was vitally important to the troops on the ground in Africa. The Allies knew this, and they attacked the Axis supply lines wherever they could. Here a formation of B-25 Mitchells has come upon a group of Ju 52 transports. The Mitchell carried as many as thirteen 12.7-mm machine-guns. (USAF)

The outnumbered Axis fighters often had to fly close-support missions and fly escort for transport flights on the same day. Constantly outnumbered, the fighter units lost irreplaceable men and equipment. This photo shows the burnt-out remains of a German fighter in the desert sands of Tunisia. (US Army)

The Me 323 could absorb a considerable amount of punishment and keep flying, however when loaded with 12 metric tons of fuel, or as in this case ammunition, it became a flying powder keg. (Obermaier)

Equipment from the Giganten was serviced in the tent camp on the perimeter of Pomigliano airfield. The inflatable dinghies proved of little use in the disaster off Cape Bon. (Hellwig)

Below: Giganten on the Pomigliano airfield, from where supply missions were flown to Tunis. The light-colored strip is the concrete runway. (Peter)

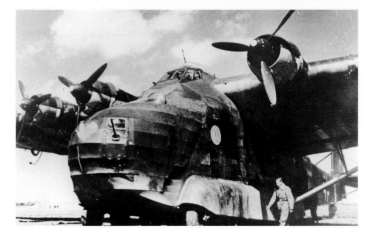

When the standard defensive armament was found wanting, many Me 323s were fitted with additional guns at the unit level. This additional armament was not enough to save any of the Me 323s attacked off Cape Bon, however. (Koos)

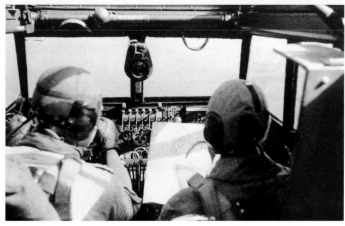

Pilots Obfw. Kandzia and Fw. Binder in their Me 323. Kandzia's Gigant escaped destruction off Cape Bon as it was grounded with engine and tire problems. (Ott)

The jettisonable cockpit cover enabled a few Me 323 pilots to escape the aircraft at the last second. (Roba)

The chief figures in the aerial supply effort to Army Group Africa (from left to right): Major Hornung (commander K.Gr.z.b.V. Frankfurt), Oberstleutnant Stephan (commander II./KG.z.b.V. 323), Oberst Damm (commander KG.z.b.V. "N"), Major Mauß (commander I./KG.z.b.V. 323), and Major Hagenah (commander III./KG.z.b.V. 1). They were photographed at Pomigliano on 14 April 1943 while awaiting the arrival of Generalmajor Buchholz, the Air Transport Commander Mediterranean. (Bundesarchiv RL 10/239).

The Me 323 was a huge target for enemy fighters and with its explosive cargoes stood little chance if attacked. (Nowarra)

A seldom-illustrated scene: 14 Me 323s and two other aircraft en route to Africa. This may have been the fateful flight of 22 April 1943. (Bundesarchiv 421/2073/9)

The Kittyhawk proved deadly to the Me 323s off Cape Bon. Most of the attacking fighters that day were of that type. (Air Ministry)

Fighter pilots of No. 5 Squadron SAAF after returning from the attack on the Gigant formation off Cape Bon (from left to right): Major Human, Major Parsonson, Lt. Humphrey, Lt. Weingartz. (IWM)

The Fi 156 Storks began their search and rescue effort much too late, and when they did get airborne they were hampered by bad weather. (Griehl)

Right: In expressing his regrets over those killed in the slaughter of the Giganten off Cape Bon, Generalfeldmarschall Kesselring made no mention of the course change initiated by Oberstleutnant Stephan, who was killed after "an heroic struggle." (Mayburg)

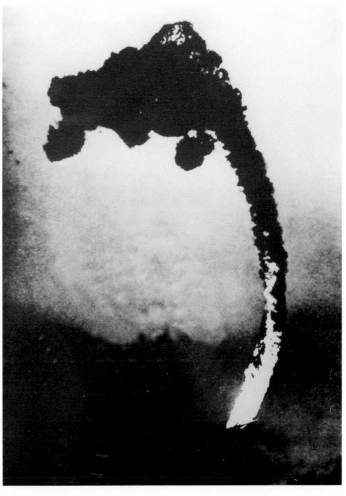

Shot down over the Mediterranean. Whether or not the aircraft is an Me 323 is uncertain, however this is what a fuel-laden Gigant looked like in the last few seconds before it crashed. There are no known photos of the engagement on 22 April 1943, as it appears that none of the fighters was equipped with a gun camera. (Nowarra)

10

Me 323 Operations in the East
until the Disbandment of TG 5

Following their transfer from Pistoia, Italy, on 6 August 1943 the *Giganten* of I./TG 5 found themselves in Leipheim. II./TG 5 moved to Goslar on 10 October 1943. All surviving *Giganten* had thus been withdrawn from the Mediterranean area and transferred to the Reich. For the rest of their service lives the Me 323s see action mainly on the Eastern Front.

On 4 November 1943 *II. Gruppe* transferred from Goslar to Biala-Podlaska in Poland, near the Russian border. On 28 November *General* Fritz Morzik, the *Transportfliegerführer*, arrived there to find a suitable location for the Stab (headquarters) of TG 5. *II. Gruppe* flew missions to Lvov, Kalinovka, Bobruisk, Baranovice, Breslau, Dresden, Schroda, Wiener-Neustadt, Belgrade-Semlin, Bacau, Bucharest, Vienna-Aspern, Kecskemet, Kraiova, Mamaia, Zilistea and Prague, among others. On 12 November *I. Gruppe* also moved to Poland, to the Warsaw-Okecie airfield. From there it flew missions to Kovno, Riga, Plesta, Bobruisk, Zhitomir, Kiev, Proskurov, Nikolayev and other destinations.

On 28 February 1944 Me 323 C8+DF, WNr. 1295 of *2. Staffel, I./TG 5* was obliged to make a forced landing near Kunki, 14 km west of Tomaszow. On 31 March the aircraft was stripped and probably blown up. Lt. von Rettberg wrote a brief report dated 2 March 1944 describing the circumstances of the forced landing and the difficulties which ensued, typical of that period:

"At 1205 hours on 28 February 1944 I took off from Proskurov for Warsaw in Me 323 C8+DF. After takeoff I shut down engine number two after the oil pressure fell to 1 atm. The pitch control motors for engines four and six also developed problems. As the aircraft was relatively lightly loaded (21 passengers) it was still able to make 175 km/h and I proceeded on course. From Lvov I picked up the rail line which proceeded from there to Rava Ruska and Zamosc and followed it at an altitude of 200 meters above ground. Abeam Narol I came under rifle and machine-gun fire from bandits in a wood between Narol and Plazow. Observers on the ground saw only rifles firing at me initially, later six to eight machine-guns. The aircraft took a number of hits in the engines, fuselage and wings. Engine number one stopped. The starboard flight engineer Uffz.

Schweer received minor wounds. Losing height, I turned east so as to reach large wooded area near Tomaszow as quickly as I could and, if possible, head from there to Mokre airfield. With the two port outboard engines gone and engines four and six producing less than full power, I lost height steadily and made preparations to land on the next open field. The forced landing occurred at 1425 hours without damage to personnel or materiel.

There was enough room to take off again, however this was ruled out for the time being as the ground was very soft. The right side of the undercarriage was almost axle-deep in the mud. The approach roads were in fair condition and to the north had been mined in places by bandits. The rail line had been blown by bandits near Susiec.

After landing I posted sentries to guard the aircraft and had the crew remove all weapons and valuable items of equipment. Meanwhile two gunners organized several sleighs and teams of horses. The locals said that there was a strong bandit group in the area and my first concern was to get everyone to safety. I made the village elder of Grabowice responsible for the safety of the aircraft and told him that the entire village would be destroyed if anything should happen to it. Our sleigh column reached Tomaszow. I went to the police and tried to obtain guards and ascertain the bandit situation. Officer Langenkemper told me about a bandit group about 1,500 men strong which was holding the village of Susiec. It was believed that the group was armed with machine-guns, mortars and anti-tank guns. It was therefore necessary to post a strong guard around the machine. I requested assistance from every available agency, but without success. *Oberstleutnant* Schäfer of *General* Grünwaldt's staff refused to give me any support, stating that guarding the aircraft was purely a matter for the *Luftwaffe*. Police *Hauptmann* Streitmann, who happened to be in Tomaszow with two platoons, was prepared to help but was forbidden to do so by *SS-Oberführer* Schermann in Narol. The Zamosc-Mokre airbase finally provided the guard, 26 men, none with any infantry experience.

On 29 February the area around the aircraft was fortified and with the help of Polish workers foxholes were dug. The weapons which had been removed were reinstalled as was the battery needed to operate the MG 131s. The guard could only be supplied every three days and hot food was impossible. On 1 March, as per orders, the crew left Tomaszow, leaving behind two gunners to operate the MG 131s."

Author's note: Partisans were generally referred to as "bandits" in the official parlance of the *Wehrmacht*, police and the SS.

A brief entry concerning these events appears in the unit war diary on 29 February 1944: "Me 323, WNr. 1295, C8+DF, tactical code X1M, of *I./TG 5* fired on by bandits near Grabowice (about 70 km from Lvov) and force-landed. One man slightly injured."

A recovery effort was initiated and then called off, and ultimately the machine was stripped and abandoned. It is noteworthy that the tactical code X1M still forms part of the identification, even though by that time it had become largely irrelevant.

Whereas the *Giganten* of *TG 5* had been decimated mainly by Allied fighters and bombers in the Mediterranean area, in the east attrition was mainly due to the difficult operating conditions: non-stop operations with little maintenance of troublesome engines and propellers, makeshift repairs, softened ground, partisan activities and the threat of ground fire and Soviet aircraft as the Red Army steadily advanced. All of this is reflected in the unit war diary. Some typical entries:

08/03/44: Uman and Przekumir airfields abandon due to proximity of the enemy. Me 323 C8+GS of *II./TG 5* unable to take-off because of badly softened ground. This machine was blown up, together with C8+GP and C8+EP.

13/03/44: Me 323 C8+BB of *I./TG 5* cannibalized and blown up at Vinnitsa due to proximity of enemy.

17/03/44: Me 323 X1H of *I./TG 5* made forced landing 40 km southeast of Stanislau after developing engine trouble.

18/03/44: Me 323 X1V of *I./TG 5* crashed after taking off from Odessa 3 with 70 troops on board and was completely destroyed in the crash and ensuing fire. Cause: sabotage. One crew and 63 passengers killed, the rest injured. (Fw. Blanke, who was flying troops to the Crimea returning from leave, circled the airfield in his *Gigant* together with other transport aircraft, waiting for the promised fighter cover. "We had been in the air for about 20 minutes when we saw a *Gigant* taking off. After lifting off, the machine climbed about 70 to 100 meters into the air. It seemed to stop in midair and then rolled over to the right. I saw it crash. Several people ran out the rear door.")

20/03/44: Me 323 X1J, C8+EE, WNr. 330001 of *I./TG 5* force-landed near Ottynie (Poland) due to bad weather, 85% damage. The aircraft, which was no longer usable anyway, was blown up on 31 March with the approach of enemy troops.

22/03/44: Me 323, WNr. 1222, C8+BF of *I./TG 5* crashed on takeoff after engine failure and burned out. Three killed, two seriously injured, two with minor injuries. The aircraft's cargo (tank spare parts) was completely destroyed.

24/03/44: Me 323 C8+AP, WNr. 330009 of *II./TG 5* obliged to make a forced landing 5 km south of Stanislau because of engine trouble. The aircraft was blown up on 29/03/44.

The situation on 25 March 1944: eight Me 323s stranded after forced landings in the countryside or on other airfields caused by engine failure or other problems. On 27 March eleven *Giganten* were unserviceable on other airfields and four in poor terrain (which probably meant that the machines had to be abandoned). On 26 March 1944 the *Kommodore* issued an order that no more Me 323s were to be sent to Odessa or Tiraspol because of the proximity of the enemy and bad visibility (in the area of the Carpathians). Aircraft were only sent to Lvov. These and many similar reports were everyday occurrences for the *Gigant* units in the east. The aircraft were flown until they fell apart, became stuck in the mud, were shot up or could not obtain any more fuel. Each day the *Gigant* crews faced the dangerous, difficult task of supplying the front and evacuating men and materiel before the Red Army inevitably launched its next offensive.

There was a change in the command of TG 5 at this time. On 14 March 1944 *Oberstleutnant* Guido Neundlinger, previously *Kommandeur* of *II./TG 1*, was named to succeed *Geschwaderkommodore Oberstleutnant* Gustav Damm, who had fallen ill and was in hospital. On 1 April 1944 Neundlinger was promoted to *Oberst*. Previously, the *Kommandeur* of *I./TG 5*, *Major* Günther Mauß, had served as acting *Kommodore* from 22 January to 14 March 1944.

On 28 March 1944 *I./TG 5* began transferring to Focsani, Romania, escorted by two Me 323 *Waffenträger*. *II./TG 5* was supposed to go to Schroda in Posen, however this was delayed because the necessary rail transport was not available due to acts of sabotage by partisans. As soon as *II./TG 5* arrived in Schroda it would have to carry out a "*Führer*" Order" direct from Hitler: transport anti-tank guns with a total weight of 145 metric tons to Zilistea. The transfer was completed on 1 April 1944 and twelve *Giganten* took off for Vienna-Aspern to carry out the "*Führer*" Order", but as soon as they arrived in Vienna, the transports were grounded by bad weather. Six Me 323s of *I./TG 5*, which were still en route to Focsani, were also grounded in Vienna.

One day later two more *Giganten* arrived from Schroda to take part in the Zilistea mission. One Me 323 flew to Minsk-Krossonow with air-drop cargo containers on an unspecified "important mission." On 3 April 1944 some of the aircraft of *II. Gruppe* were en route from Vienna to Belgrade and some from Belgrade to Zilistea. Because of the loss of a radio station reports from Belgrade to Zilistea were sparse, but it was reported that the first Me 323 had already returned to Schroda.

On 6 April 1944, Zilistea, to where the *Geschwaderstab* and *II. Gruppe* were also supposed to transfer, reported that eight Me 323s of *I. Gruppe* had arrived there and that thirteen Me 323s had fulfilled the "*Führer*" Order." On 3 April aircraft C8+FR flown by Uffz. Rößmann developed engine trouble and had to make a forced landing near Péterréve, Hungary and thus could not complete its mission. The guns the aircraft was carrying were unloaded by soldiers of the Hungarian Army and taken away. This seems to have been the only casualty of the entire operation. *I. Gruppe* now had some of its *Giganten* in Zilistea and no longer had to fly the dangerous route along the Carpathians. It could again fly to Odessa and Tiraspol and evacuate wounded from there together with aircraft of *II. Gruppe*.

For many other missions the growing shortages of pilots and aircraft was already becoming an increasing problem. The missions piled up, however the available resources were far short of what was required.

On 12 April 1944 Headquarters, XIV Air Corps telephoned with orders for the *Geschwaderstab*, *II./TG 5* and *7./ETG* (Ar 232) to move to Zilistea. Outstanding transport missions were set aside. Me 323 C8+GP (WNr. 130031) of *II./TG 5* was destroyed in a bombing raid on Wiener Neustadt. The aircraft was loaded with 10 metric tons of ammunition. The same day the Red Army launched its offensive against the German 17th Army, which withdrew to Sevastopol. Hitler refused to evacuate the Crimea and instead ordered that reinforcements be sent to the army. The operations staff arrived in Zilistea on 13 April. Attached to *TG 5* were: *I./TG 5*, *II./TG 5*, *7./ETG*, *Tr.Fl.St. 5*, *T.Gr. 30*, *Schleppgruppe 2* and *I.* and *II./TG 1*. Towed missions to the Crimea with the Go 242 were no longer possible because of Russian fighters, and the He 111 towplanes were employed as transports. The aircraft of these units flew day and night, delivering troops to Sevastopol and flying out wounded. These missions were not without incident. As well, on 16 April the Belgrade-Semlin airport was bombed. At the same time the airfields around Sevastopol were also bombed. The *Transportfliegerführer 2* subsequently banned further Me 323 missions to the Crimea. Losses rose to the point where daylight missions were suspended. All available means were used to evacuate wounded from Romania. On 17 April 1944 *II./TG 5*'s had not yet completed its transfer; furthermore, Belgrade-Semlin, which was used as an en route stop, had been bombed again. A total of six Me 323s of *I.* and *II./TG 5* was damaged there on those two days.

In Sevastopol the situation was becoming ever more critical. On 19 April 1944 one Ju 90, One Pi 108, one Ar 232 (Kommodore on board) and twelve He 111s (ten of the He 111s flew two sorties) landed there. One day later all night-capable aircraft were ordered to fly two sorties per day to the Crimea. Daylight missions to the mainland and night missions to the Crimea continued until 5 May 1944. Operations were hampered by the growing fuel shortage. On 9 May Russian artillery destroyed the Khersonyes and Sevastopol airfields. Eighteen He 111s of *T.Gr. 30* and *Schleppgruppe 2* flew to Sevastopol on the night of 9-10 May. With nowhere to land, the aircraft were forced to turn back.. A few Ju 52s managed to land on makeshift strips that night and the following night and fly out wounded.

On 10 May 1944 Hptm. Sepp Stangl and his co-pilot *Oberfähnrich* Schäferlein flew their Me 323 to Ploesti and evacuated 140 female signals auxiliaries to Kecskemét, Hungary. This was followed by a relatively quiet period for the personnel of *TG 5*.

The inevitable evacuation of Sevastopol ended on 12 May 1944 and many of TG 5's aircraft were lost. Lack of fuel limited the number of missions flown until 12 May, and no missions at all were flown to the Crimea after the loss of Sevastopol.

In addition to losses at the hands of enemy aircraft and anti-aircraft fire, accidents continued to take a toll of personnel and equipment. On 15 May 1944, while taking off from Kecskemét for Sofia, Me 323 L5+GN of *5./ETG* struck the chimney of a house. The aircraft crashed and burned out, resulting in six dead and three injured.

The *Geschwader* itself remained on the move: on 9 May 1944 *Stab TG 5* moved to Kecskemét, *II./TG 5* to Tonndorf, Posen, while *I./TG 5* remained in Kecskemét. On 21 May the *Stab* moved on to Nagy-Korös, approximately 12 km north of Kecskemét, and from there on 27 May to Posen airbase. By 15 June 1944 *5./ETG*'s days were numbered. The training *Staffel* was transferred from Schroda to Tonndorf and was attached to *TG 5* for operational purposes. As of 30 June 1944 the strength returns no longer showed any training units with Me 323s (although *5./ETG* had eleven Me 323s on strength until 30 May 1944).

There was little for the *Geschwader* to do and thus *Major* Mauß, the *Gruppenkommandeur* of *I./TG 5*, found time to write a letter to Willy Messerschmitt:

"Dear Professor,
The *Gruppe* is sending you a commemorative print on the occasion of its 2,000th sortie on the Me 323.

While the first 1,000 sorties were flown in the south, the second 1,000 were completed in the difficult conditions of the Russian winter. We approached this new mission with the same enthusiasm as when we began operations and with the same belief in the practicality and necessity of large-capacity transport aircraft and mastered it. The success of this mission, which was ordered by the *Führer*, was greatly influenced bringing the *Gruppe* up to strength with E-series Me 323s. With the exception of the uncorrectable shortcomings which are known to both you and us, we are very satisfied with the E-series. Unfortunately the engines are becoming even worse and the situation has caused us serious concerns such as never existed before with the Messerschmitt. We therefore hope to see a German engine in this airframe. Coincident with the 2,000th sortie, the first Me 323 airframe reached 500 flying hours.

The decision not to continue building the *Gigant* has hit us hard, because we have become so used to the aircraft. (Author's note: the last three machines were delivered in April 1944, ending production.) Nevertheless, we continue to hope that, following a decisive turn in the war which is expected soon, the *Gigant* will be developed and built on a much larger scale than was previously the case. For us there is no fonder wish than to be a part of this. As creator of the *Giganten*, you, Herr Professor, will surely be allowed to realize your ideas in the area of large-capacity transports, for this type of aircraft will also be part of the future after the war.

With best wishes for you personally and for your work, which is decisive to Germany's life and death struggle, I respectfully salute you with *Heil Hitler*,

Mauß "

The letter was accompanied by an artfully-done commemorative print recalling *I. Gruppe*'s missions from the beginning of operations to Kecskemét. Did the *Gruppenkommandeur* perhaps have an inkling that *TG 5* would cease to exist in a few weeks?

TG 5 flew no missions in the period to 20 July 1944. *Gruppe* personnel were kept busy making and keeping the aircraft serviceable. "Headquarters, XIV Air Corps and attached units are subordinated to Air Fleet 15 formed on 1 July 1944." (Author's note: This is obviously a printing error; the intended unit was surely Air Fleet 10.) On the Eastern Front the Soviets had launched a summer offensive on 23 June 1944. Army Group Center was shattered. The Red Army took Minsk on 3 July. The military situation went from threatening to almost hopeless. Unlike their opposite numbers in the Ju 52 units, the Me 323 crews were almost incapable of flying transport sorties. There were shortages of everything and the enemy's air superiority was becoming more marked. Reacting the situation at the front and in the Reich, on 20 July 1944 *Oberst* Claus Count von Stauffenberg made an unsuccessful attempt to assassinate Adolf Hitler. A few days later Joseph Goebbels was named "General Authorized for Total War."

In the period from 21 to 31 July 1944 TG 5 was ordered to halt all operational flying. On 1 August II./TG 5 received a verbal order from XIV. Fliegerkorps to move to Chrudim south of Pardubitz (Protectorate) in order to free Tonndorf for bomber units from the east. During the course of this transfer, on 3 August *Waffenträger* W.Nr. 330004, C8+GC, was lost in a crash (see chapter "Waffenträger"). The *Stab* of TG 5 now received orders to find a new command post in the Chrudim area. The move was completed by 10 August, and no further missions were flown during this period. One day later Stab TG 5's transfer was stopped again. According to entries in the war diary, consideration was being given to disbandment on account of the adoption of the total war strategy and the inactivity of the Geschwader. Then, on 12 August 1944, the order was issued: *Stab, I.* and *II./TG 5* were to make preparations to disband. Each *Gruppe* was to be reduced to a single *Staffel*. The end of the Geschwader was at hand, however even at that late date further missions were flown: beginning on 13 August at least six of II./TG 5's Me 232s flew the Insterburg-Riga-Insterburg route.

These flights resulted in further losses. On 15 August Me 323 C8+EC, W.Nr. 130023, was shot down by four Russian fighters while flying the route. The aircraft's pilot, Obfw. Pötschke, wrote the following (slightly abridged) combat report:

"While on the return flight from Riga to Insterburg, which was being made on five engines as one engine had lost a cylinder (with three female passengers), the aircraft was attacked by four Russian fighters and set on fire while flying its desig-

nated course. The bullet strikes immediately set a fuel tank in the right wing and the right side of the fuselage on fire. I prepared to land on a meadow into the wind. At a height of 5 to 10 meters I felt the control column jerk, after which elevator control could be moved back and forth with no resistance. I therefore completed the landing using trim. The landing was completely normal. On the roll-out the right side of the machine sank into the softened ground (the tires on the right side must have been shot through). The aircraft came to a stop with a heavy jolt, swinging sixty degrees to the right and tearing the nose doors off in the process. The crew and passengers left the aircraft, which burned out completely apart from the outer wingtips and parts of the engines.

When the fighters attacked from behind, taking us completely by surprise, the gunner in the right cannon turret (Uffz. Butz) immediately opened fire, however after firing just a few shots he and his gun were put out of action. Four members of the crew (Fw. Seifert, Uffz. Butz, Gefr. Ellerbrock and Gefr. Eckert) and one of the female passengers sustained minor burns or bullet/fragment wounds.

Three hours after the incident a Latvian doctor provided first aid and arranged for my four crewmen to be transported to the *Luftwaffe* hospital in Liebeau. I left the German-Latvian police to watch over the remains of the aircraft. The usable ammunition and machine-guns (which I had removed from the aircraft) were placed in a truck. I subsequently made my way to Hasenpoth and turned them over to the local police."

Then came the end of the *Geschwader*. TG 5 was disbanded during the period 23 to 30 August 1944. *Stab, I. Gruppe* (Kecskemét) and *II. Gruppe* (Chrudim) were instructed to form two *Staffeln* of 12 Me 323s, which were to be transferred to IV./TG 4.

Assembly points were Skutsch and Chrudim. The following entry appears in the war diary under 23 August 1944: "In accordance with Headquarters, XIV Air Corps Abt. Ia Br.B.Nr. 792/44 G.Kdos dated 13/08/44, two *Staffeln* of twelve Me 323s each are to be formed from *Stab TG 5, I./TG 5* and *II./TG 5* and incorporated into IV./TG 4. The remaining elements of the *Geschwader* are to be disbanded. *Stab/TG 5* is responsible for formation of the two *Staffeln* and the disbandment of the two *Gruppen*."

At that time a major Russian offensive was under way against Army Group South Ukraine. The Romanian government under Senatescu had declared war on Germany. The Romanian armies, formerly allied to Germany, ceased fighting against the Russians and abandoned their sectors of the front. In the subsequent battles against the *Wehrmacht* the Romanians lost another 169,000 killed and wounded by the end of the war. Germany thus faced another enemy and an increased need for evacuation transport, in which the Me 323s took part.

I./TG 5's orders: proceed to Romania with all available aircraft. One Me 323 landed near the city of Alba-Julia in northern Romania and its crew of three was taken prisoner. Another crew (type of aircraft not known) tried to prevent their capture. The aircraft crashed while attempting to land, killing all on board. In the evening a Me 323 landed at the Bucharest-Otopeni airport, which was still in German hands. The aircraft probably came from Albania and had a special detachment on board.

On 26 August 1944 two Me 323s were shot down by Bf 109 Gs of the Romanian *Grupu 7 vânatoare*. The first Me 323 went down at 1400 hours. Twenty of those on board were captured, however four died as a result of their injuries. The second Me 323 was shot down at 1615 hours and 77 men were taken prisoner. On the same day two Me 323s were shot down near Ploesti and another damaged by Romanian mortar fire on the Târgsor airfield. One day later three more Me 323s were attacked by Bf 109 Gs of fired on by Romanian anti-aircraft fire, making landings in Bucharest impossible. The first Me 323 was obliged to make a forced landing at 0800 hours, and 66 men were taken prisoner. Eighty-one soldiers on board the second Me 323 were captured, while the third was found empty and burnt out. In the area of the Protectorate two Me 323s were strafed and destroyed on Prossnitz airfield near Olmütz by Mustangs of the 15th Air Force. The American fighters were returning from a bomber escort missions (against the oil refineries in Blechhammer).

On 29 August 1944 five *Giganten* landed in the area around Bucharest at various times. 158 soldiers were taken prisoner. The only Me 323 not captured landed near Dobra with 31 soldiers on board. On that same day the Allies laid the groundwork for the destruction of most of the remaining Me 323s. Aircraft of the American 4th Fighter Squadron (52nd Fighter Group, 15th Air Force) based at Madna airfield in Italy spotted what they described as "about 100" Me 323s on a Bohemian airfield, probably Skutsch. As was often the case, the Allied pilots greatly overestimated the number of enemy aircraft, for according to German sources, there were only 56 Me 323s on strength with the *Transportgeschwader* at that time. Two days later P-51s of the 4th Fighter Squadron attacked these aircraft, destroying about twenty. Aerial reconnaissance later determined that the wrecks had been bulldozed to the side of the airfield.

The slaughter of the *Giganten* went on. On 31 August P-51 Mustangs of the American 15th Fighter Group strafed German aircraft which had assembled on the Szászrégen airfield in eastern Hungary during the German retreat from Romania. Among the more than 100 aircraft which were destroyed were several *Giganten*. Romanian reconnaissance discovered aircraft identified as Me 323s on airfields at Marosvásárhely and Debrecen in eastern Hungary.

In spite of the dramatic developments in Romania, the *Gruppen* continued preparations for the disbandment of the *Geschwaderstab TG 5*. As per orders, the Me 323 pilots handed over their aircraft at Skutsch and Chrudim, after which they were transferred to other units. Those who had previously flown Bf 110s stood a good chance of transferring to night fighters, however many were sent to the infantry. *Major* Mauß, who had commanded *I. Gruppe* from beginning to end, took command of the "*Teilgruppe Ju 52*", later renamed the *Großraum-Transportstaffel* (large capacity transport squadron). The commander of his *Stabsstaffel*, Hptm. Stangl, was assigned to Mühldorf in Bavaria, where he began training on helicopters with the newly-formed *Tr.Gr. 40*.

By the end of August 1944 *TG 4* had taken over the remaining Me 323s. The unit submitted the following strength report on 31 August 1944:

12. Staffel:
28 acquisitions, 21 losses through enemy action (some on missions in Romania), 1 loss for reasons other than enemy action, leaving six Me 323s on strength.

13. Staffel:
28 acquisitions, 16 transferred "to other units", leaving 12 Me 323s on strength.

Total of 18 Me 323s on strength.

TG 4 had thus received 55 Me 323s from *TG 5*. This was all the aircraft available to the *Geschwader* (one other was undergoing repairs). But the Me 323s with 12. and 13. *Staffel* of TG 4 were not listed as belonging to those units. Also not known is the number of aircraft unserviceable at various locations: grounded for lack of spare parts, lack of fuel, lack of personnel, or stranded and abandoned in difficult terrain. For certain not all of these *Giganten* were destroyed, however they did not see action again.

On 25 September 1944 Hitler issued a decree calling for the formation of the *Volkssturm*. The Red Army was drawing ever nearer and one German city after another was pulverized by Allied bombs. The fighter arm had been given absolute priority, consideration was only given to other branches of the air force in conditions of grave emergency. This of course affected the *Giganten* too. TG 4's final strength reports: on 30 September 1944 18 Me 323s on strength with *IV./TG 4*, 2 acquisitions, 6 transferred to other (unidentified) units, for a total of 14 Me 323s on strength. No indication was given as to which *Staffel* they were assigned to.

On 31 October 1944: 14 Me 323s on strength, now assigned to *16. Staffel*. Two gone (1 lost through enemy action, 1 sent for overhaul), leaving 12 Me 323s on strength. No change on 30 November 1944. On 31 December 1944 the unit still had 12 Me 323s on strength. One acquisition, one departure, leaving 12 Me 323s. None of the subsequent strength returns appear to have survived. According to Czech historian Jiri Rajlich, on 28 December 1944 six Me 323s of *IV./TG 4* were strafed and destroyed on Chrudim airfield by Mustangs of the 15th Air Force. The fighters, which were from the 325th Fighter Group, were returning from a bomber escort mission to Pardubitz and the Kolin oil refineries.

It is not known whether the Me 323s of TG 4 saw any further use. It seems very likely that they did not. In 1945 the remaining flyable Me 323s were still idle at Skrudim and Skutsch. For the most part they were stuck in the softened earth. The Red Army did not occupy the two airfields until the period 9 to 11 May 1945. This can be documented with certainty, for the fanatical *Generalfeldmarschall* Schörner did not surrender his remaining forces of Army Group Center in Bohemia until 11 May, after the official German surrender. When the fighting ceased the remaining *Giganten* were probably cannibalized by the local population.

An Me 323 D-1 during II./TG 5's stay in Goslar from 7 October to 9 November 1943. (Giesecke)

The main entrance to Warsaw-Okecie airport. (Hellwig)

Hangar 9 at Okecie airport. Visible on the left of the photo is the starboard wing of an Me 323 E-2. (Hellwig)

Left: Generalmajor Fritz Morzik, air transport commander. (Nowarra)

A collection of aircraft on the Okecie airport, seen from the radio operator's position of an Me 323. (Hellwig)

This assembly of transport aircraft was also photographed at Okecie. From left to right: Ju 52, Ar 232, Me 323, Go 242. (Hellwig)

Returning to base at dusk. (Hellwig)

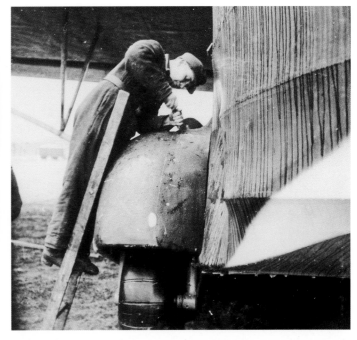

After the tire had been changed the undercarriage fairing was replaced. (Hellwig)

From 12 November 1943 I./TG 5 was based at Okecie, where its aircraft were also serviced and repaired. Operations in the east were conducted under the harshest conditions, which is reflected in the condition of the aircraft. Here repairs are made to an aircraft's undercarriage. (Hellwig)

New engines have arrived. (Hellwig)

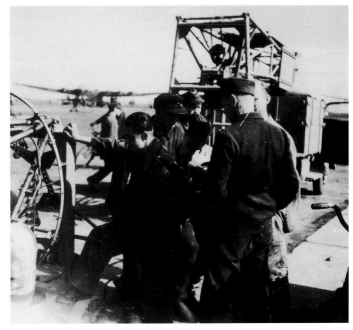

The job done, the crew takes a brief rest. (Hellwig)

Right: The mobile cranes approaches in preparation for an engine change. (Hellwig)

Waiting for the signal from the mechanics on the wing that all is ready to proceed. (Hellwig)

This photo was taken some months later, but it also depicts an engine change at Warsaw-Okecie airport. (Hellwig)

More than a few soldiers had more faith in the "Wellblechtante" (Corrugated Auntie) Ju 52 than the "Leukoplastbomber" (Band-Aid Bomber) Me 323. (Petrick)

Ju 52s and Me 323s stand ready to transport troops to the front. (Nowarra)

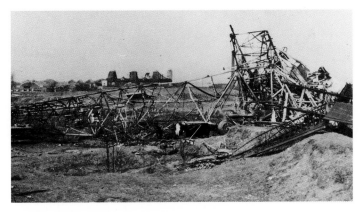

In fact the Giganten were involved in many dangerous situations. How this Me 323 was destroyed is not known. (Hellwig)

It may have ground-looped on takeoff or been wrecked in a landing crash. (Hellwig)

On the other hand the aircraft may have been destroyed in an enemy attack. The Me 323's immense size made it an easy target and attacking pilots could scarcely miss seeing it. (Hellwig)

Damaged undercarriage? Damage which was not outwardly visible could prove disastrous on the next takeoff. (Roba)

A damaged tire needs replacing, which means that a pit has to be dug beneath the affected wheel. (Storm)

This aircraft crash-landed at Schroda airfield in March 1944. The Me 323's entire undercarriage was ripped off in the accident. (Storm)

Flight engineer Gerhard Storm stands in front of the crash-landed Gigant. (Storm)

The Gigant, which appears to have recently undergone repairs, was written off. (Petrick)

Forced landing by C8+CE, tactical code X1F, at Wohyn (40 km southeast of Biala-Podlaska. (Ott)

The aircraft was forced down in partisan country in December 1943 after it lost two engines and a propeller. The propeller smashed through the fuse-lage door. (Ott)

The Me 323 was obviously repaired, for it was destroyed by Allied aircraft at Kecskemét on 14 April 1944. (Ott)

Also photographed at Odessa 3 airfield on 18 March 1944: Me 323 C8+GE crashed and exploded as a result of sabotage. Sixty-three passengers died in the crash, a few survived with serious injuries. (Ott)

Uffz. Rößmann and his crew with their Gigant C8+ER on 18 March 1944 before taking off from Odessa 3. The flight was completed without incident. (Rößmann)

Inspecting the remains of the Gigant. (Ott)

It is difficult to believe that a few soldiers were pulled from the wreckage alive. (Ott)

This Me 323 E-2, still wearing its tactical code X1U, was totally destroyed in a crash-landing. (Hellwig)

Inspecting the wreckage. (Hellwig)

At least the airplane did not catch fire. (Hellwig)

In this case the Gigant exploded after a bombing raid ... (Hellwig)

... and was destroyed by fire. (Hellwig)

This Gigant was abandoned somewhere on the Eastern Front and was probably set on fire by German troops. (Petrick)

The winter of 1942-43 saw only a few Giganten flying on the Eastern Front. The winter of 1943-44 was undoubtedly the busiest for the Me 323s, for only a few missions were flown in 1944-45. This amount of snow must have presented flight control with some interesting problems. (Roba)

In spite of all the difficulties presented by the weather, the aircraft kept flying and a mission was only aborted when conditions were extremely poor. (Roba)

Left: Snowed in. This Gigant would soon be ready to fly again. (Schladerbusch)

Right: Snow was shoveled off the wings ... (Roba)

Below: ... and the wings were de-iced ... (Storm)
Bottom: ... a job which took several hours. (Storm)

Repair work also had to be done in the harsh cold. (Petrick)

Somehow the work is completed and the Gigant is ready to fly again. (Nowarra)

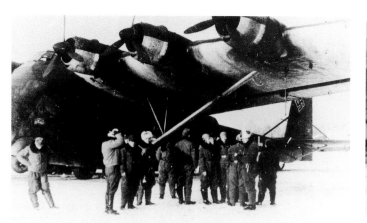

Shivering from the cold, the soldiers wait for departure. (Auer)

Acquaintances and even friendships were made. A souvenir photo before taking off. (Roba)

Waiting for departure, this time in Golta in the Ukraine, 13 January 1944. (Storm)

"Thawing out" the engines with a torch. (Griehl)

DT+IC at Stuhlweissenburg in the winter of 1943. Whether the pack animal was one of the passengers is not known. (Roba)

Successful takeoff, smooth flight, no engine trouble: C8+EP lands in Biala-Podlaska. (Schladerbusch)

On 14 March 1944 Oberstleutnant Guido Neundlinger replaced Oberstleutnant Gustav Damm as Geschwaderkommodore of TG 5. On 1 April Neundlinger was promoted to Oberst. Here he (left) is seen sitting at a table with Oblt. Wasserkampf, Staffelkapitän of Transportfliegerstaffel 5, in Mühldorf, Bavaria. (Kössler)

As soon as II./TG 5 completed its transfer to Schroda it had to carry out a "Führer Order" issued by Hitler personally: transport anti-tank guns with a total weight of 145 tonnes to Zilistea in Romania. (Radinger)

The Kommandeur of I./TG 5, Major Günther Mauß, assumed temporary command of the Geschwader from 22 January to 14 March 1944. (Peter)

Below: Most of the Giganten were grounded by weather in Vienna-Aspern until 3 April, but then the mission was completed quickly. (Bernád)

These large weapons were no problem for the Me 323. The guns were loaded in Ohlau and the first Gigant took off for Zilistea via Vienna and Belgrade on 1 April 1944. (Petrick)

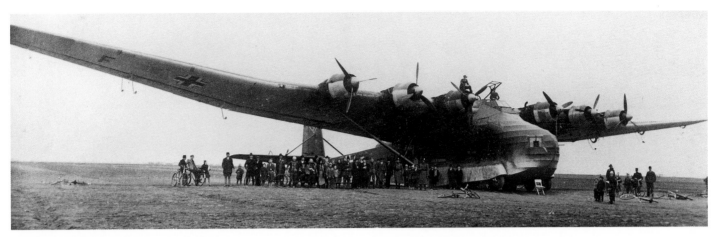

Uffz. Rößmann's C8+FR had bad luck while carrying out the "Führer Order." After problems with engines 2, 4 and 6, on 3 April 1944 the pilot was obliged to make a forced landing near Péterréve. (Rößmann)

The guns were unloaded by Hungarian soldiers and two tanks prepared to tow the Me 323 to more solid ground. (Rößmann)

On 13 April 1944 7./ETG was attached to TG 5 for operational purposes and examples of the Ar 232 flew with the Gruppe's Me 323s. (Hellwig)

Until then the Me 323 was guarded by the Hungarians. Here a Csendör (gendarme) stands in front of the aircraft. (Bernád)

The attempt failed, and the Me 323 was not able to take off until a few days later after three new engines had been installed. (Rößmann)

German aerial photograph of Sevastopol. The Wehrmacht occupied the Crimea by 16 November 1941, however Sevastopol did not fall until 1 July 1942. The Red Army recaptured Sevastopol on 9 May 1944 and those German troops not killed or captured withdrew by 12 May. (Dabrowski)

Entertainment for the troops on the Eastern Front: Major Mauß (left) bids farewell to the Leo Kraus orchestra. (Hellwig)

In mid April 1944 the Giganten were banned from flying further missions to the Crimea. (Bernád)

This apparently unarmed Me 323 E-1 flew the artists and their equipment back to Germany. (Hellwig)

A Gigant meets its end in Kecskemét. Obfw. Karl Blanke recalled that the Me 323, which was flown by a "generally unpopular flight instructor", crashed into the DF shack for reasons unknown and burnt out. (Hellwig)

After the evacuation of the Crimea and the completion of its transfer, for TG 5 there began a period of relative quiet with few missions. (Hellwig)

The aircraft underwent necessary maintenance and were cleaned ... (Griehl)

... refueled and readied for the next flight. (Griehl)

In May 1944 I./TG 5 recorded its 2,000th transport sortie, which of course received official recognition. (Petrick)

This was followed by the issuing of "morale ammunition." (Hellwig)

Thus equipped, the "pleasant part" could begin. The E-2 in the background wears an as yet unidentified tactical emblem on its tail. (Hellwig)

This commemorative print was sent by the Gruppe to the creator of the Gigant, Professor Messerschmitt. (Peter)

Left: There was also the "Gigantenlied" (Giant Song): bitter verses with no confidence in victory. It is unlikely that this page was also sent to Professor Messerschmitt. (Peter)

Obfw. Blanke flew to Bobruisk in his C8+BS one more time before the city fell to the Red Army on 27 June 1944. 70,000 German soldiers surrendered there on 29 June. (Giesecke)

This unfortunately rather blurry photo depicts Giganten in Romania at the time of that country's declaration of war on Germany. For the German forces in the country this marked the start of a dangerous retreat. (Bernád)

A rectangular cutout may be seen in the nose doors. This may have been an additional gun position, as the threat of fighter attack had increased dramatically. (Giesecke)

Right: This was Skutsch airfield: a few huts and a runway. Because of the unevenness of the terrain, pilots could not see the end of the runway from the takeoff point. The photo was taken in 1943. (Haferland)

It looks as if the fuselage of C8+BS had recently been repaired. (Giesecke)

Giganten parked on the Chrudim airfield near Pardubitz in autumn 1944. (Zazvonil)

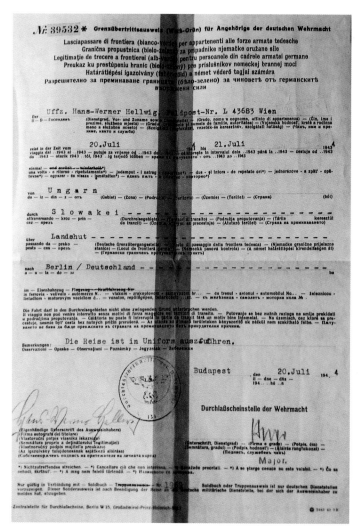

Many members of TG 5 were assigned to the infantry. (Hellwig)

An Me 323 parked on the Skutsch airfield, photographed in spring 1945. (Petrick)

Some of TG 5's personnel were reassigned shortly before the unit handed its Me 323s over to TG 4. A form like this was important in getting past the numerous checkpoints on such a long trip. (Hellwig)

Right: At Skutsch the aircraft were marked as aircraft of IV./TG 4. This Me 323 received the code G6+NQ. The tactical emblem of I./TG 5 was overpainted. (Rajlich)

The fuselage code G6+LQ identifies this aircraft as also belonging to IV/TG 4. Photographed on Skutsch airfield in January 1945, it is unlikely that this Gigant saw any further action. (Rajlich)

Of course the collection of Giganten in Skutsch and Chrudim did not escape the attention of the Allied photo reconnaissance aircraft. Positions were built ... (Roba)

... and anti-aircraft guns, such as this cannon apparently removed from a Gigant, were emplaced, however this did nothing to deter the Allied bombers. (Roba)

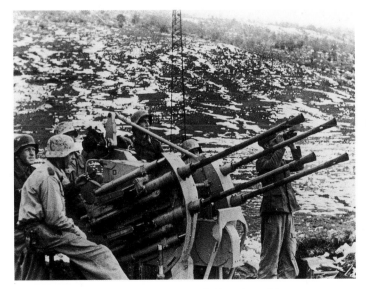

Four-barreled anti-aircraft guns (Vierlingsflak) such as this one were very scarce, and the few that were available inflicted little damage on the attacking aircraft. (Nowarra)

Right: Chrudim in the winter of 1944-45: delivering ammunition for the EDL 151/20 turrets of an Me 323 E-2, G6+FQ. The start trolley suggests that a mission was planned. (Roba)

Attack on the Giganten in Chrudim. (Roba)

Another Gigant hit at Chrudim. (Roba)

The last Giganten in Skutsch and Chrudim (seen here), met their end in May 1945. They were either destroyed or used as a welcome source of raw materials by the Czechs.

Giganten could be found on airfields everywhere in the former theaters of war. Either they were totally destroyed ... (Hellwig)

American soldiers wonder at and photograph the still impressive remains of a Gigant. (Ostrowski)

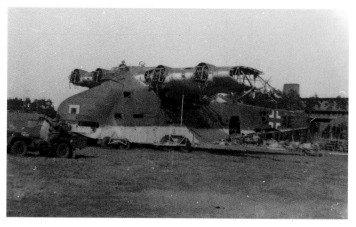

... or cannibalized, as here in Gardelegen where Me 323s were repaired. Those illustrated here probably served as sources of spare parts. (Ostrowski)

This may be the last surviving remnant of a Gigant: a main spar at Leipheim airfield. After the war it was used for many years as a bridge over a small stream in Bavaria. (Schlaug)

Above: These are some of the people who were involved in the Gigant program at Leipheim in 1942:

1. Engineer Kurt Brandt (supervision of drawings, Fröhlich's deputy); 2. Wachinger (technical draftsman); 3. Engineer Oskar Fischer (empennage construction); 4. Achinger; 5. Engineer Meyer (blueprint office); 6 . Engineer Wilhelm Steinhauser; 7. Engineer Molt (fuselage and wing construction); 8. Engineer Bernhard Schwarting (engine installation); 9. Pfaffeneder; 10. Dipl.-Ing. Lechner (bench test); 11. Frl. Erna Nied (Fröhlich's secretary); 12. Engineer Petri (Fröhlich's deputy); 13. Senior Engineer Josef Fröhlich (design head Me 321 / Me 323); 14. Engineer Förster (electrics); 15. Drescher (draftsman, electrics); 16. Gerda Lippert (typist clerk); 17. Ost (typist clerk); 18. Emmi Schlumberger (technical draftsman); 19. Elfriede Goldschmid (typist clerk); 20. Engineer Stehle (operational matters); 21. Engineer Holzmeier (electrics); 22. Erdle (office worker); 23. Lindenmeyer (technical draftsman); 24. Heinz Sorge.

Also present were persons from the following companies: Blohm & Voss, Roßmeyer & Thanner, Wiener Neustädter Fluzeugbau. (Vogel)

The last reunion of the "Old Giant Builders" in the Café Nied in Leipheim on 7 June 1975. Edmund Eisele sent the invitations, which read: "We would like to get together in Leipheim one more time, before one after another of us goes to his final reward." From left to right, back row: Edmund Eisele, Kurt Brandt, Bernhard Schwarting, Josef Fröhlich, Hilmar Stumm, Wolfgang Degel, Josef Bitz. Front row: Molt, Emmi Schlumberger, Frau Fröhlich, Erna Vogel (nee Nied), Maier. (Vogel)

11

Attack on Kecskemét

On 14 June 1944 thirty-nine Lockheed P-38 Lightning long-range fighters carried out a low-level attack against Kecskemét airfield and the surrounding area.

Approximately fourteen days earlier the Allies had conducted high-altitude reconnaissance of the area. Evaluation of the photographs revealed that in addition to Hungarian aircraft, a number of German large-capacity transports, "probably Giants", were present on Kecskemét airfield. It was decided that aircraft based in Italy would attack the airfield on 3 June 1944, however deteriorating weather made it necessary to abort the mission when the aircraft were over Yugoslavia.

Eleven days later, at 0850 hours on 14 June, forty-two Lightnings took off from airfields in central Italy and set course for Hungary. The force consisted of 14 aircraft from the 95th Fighter Squadron, 18 from the 96th Fighter Squadron and 10 from the 97th Fighter Squadron. Three aircraft turned back due to mechanical problems. The rest, some carrying bombs, arrived over Kecskemét at 1050 hours.

Major Phillips, leader of the 95th F.S., spotted the first Me 323 in front of a hangar and subsequently strafed it and set it on fire. Lt. Holloway destroyed a "Giant" and a Fi 156 *Storch* utility aircraft. The 95th Squadron was followed in by the bomb-carrying P-38s of the 96th Squadron. The 97th Fighter Squadron had other targets: it bombed runways, hangars, airfield buildings and a nearby railway station.

There was no organized defense at Kecskemét. The only return fire came from a few machine-guns and defensive weapons mounted in the *Giganten*. None of the attackers was shot down. On the way back to Italy the Lightnings attacked other targets: the railway stations at Kiskunhalas and Baja, shipping on the Danube near Mohács and Apati and an oil refinery near Osijek in Serbia. Two aircraft sustained minor flak damage, however all 39 Lightnings landed safely at their bases in Italy at 1300 hours.

The pilots claimed to have destroyed six *Giganten*. In five cases their locations were given: two were parked in front of hangars, one was on the north side of Kecskemét airfield and one on the west side. Also claimed destroyed were the Storch and one other unidentified aircraft, possibly a Bf 109. (Author's note: both of these aircraft probably belonged to the Hungarian Air Force. The Hungarian report lists the following damage at Kecskemét: two hangars collapsed, four German transport aircraft destroyed, 23 tank cars set on fire at the railway station.

The following entry appears in *Transportgeschwader 5*'s war diary under 14 June 1944: I./5 Kecskemét reported: 1045 hours concentrated attack, approximately 30 American fighters. Casualties: 1 killed, 3 injured, 5 Me 323s (four of them from I./5):

WNr. 1209	C8+AF	100%
WNr. 130016	C8+EG	100%
WNr. 130041	C8+HE	100%
WNr. 130055	C8+DE	100%
WNr. 130037	C8+CE	100%

plus one Ju 52

WNr. 640191	C8+DB	90%

The Ju 52 was used by *I. Gruppe* as a supply and personnel transport and was attached to the *Stabsstaffel*. *Gigant* WNr. 130037 belonged to the air corps reserve and was therefore not on the strength of *TG 5*.

These young Hungarian soldiers pose proudly for a photograph in front of a Gigant in Kecskemét. (Hellwig)

The low-level attack began at 1045 hours. The Lightnings met negligible resistance. (Hellwig)

On 14 June 1944 a group of 39 Lightnings appeared over Kecskemét and turned the airfield into an inferno.

Uffz. Hellwig, a member of the ground personnel. The EDL 151/20 turret's plexiglas cupola is absent. The turret was apparently removed from a damaged Me 323 and converted into a defensive fixture on the airfield. (Hellwig)

All quiet and peaceful on the airfield. (Ott)

From a safe distance, this group of soldiers watches the Lightnings attack. (Roba)

The dispersed Giganten escaped, however the soldiers could only watch helplessly as the others were destroyed. (Roba)

Five Giganten and one Ju 52 were destroyed on the airfield, along with hangars and vehicles. (Roba)

This was I./TG 5's only Ju 52. The aircraft (WNr. 640191) belonged to the Stabsstaffel. Coded C8+DB, it was flown by Obfw. Lohmann until destroyed at Kecskemét. (Hellwig)

Burning aircraft and a fuel train at the railway station in Kecskemét produced huge columns of smoke which were visible for kilometers. (Roba)

All that was left of the Giganten was smoldering steel skeletons. (Ott)

When the attack was over the damage and casualties were added up. (Ott)

These engines belonged to Ju 52 C8+DB. Damage was assessed at 90%, a virtual write-off. (Roba)

12

The *Waffenträger* (Weapons Carrier)

For many years it was believed that just one example of the *Waffenträger* (WT) variant of the Me 323 was built and aviation literature portrayed it as an unsuccessful design. It is now known with certainty, however, that a number of these *Waffenträger* were constructed or converted from standard Me 323 transports. A heavily-armed version of the Me 323 E-2 with a crew of twenty, the *Waffenträger* was designed solely for the escort role. The type was so rare that only a few members of the *Luftwaffe* were even aware of its existence. Unfortunately, much still remains unknown concerning the production and operational use of the *Waffenträger*.

At the beginning of summer 1943 at Leipheim, the Me 323 V15 (VM+IT, WNr. 1272) was fitted with two HDL 151 turrets each mounting one 20-mm MG 151 cannon in addition to its standard defensive armament. The two armored turrets were mounted semi-submerged in the upper surface of the wings between the outer and center engines. Because of their high drag they were soon replaced by more streamlined EDL 151 turrets. After the conclusion of weapons trials at Tarnewitz/Ostsee and the completion of several modifications by the Luftschiffbau Zeppelin in Friedrichshafen, in September 1943 the cannon turrets were adopted as part of the standard armament of the Me 323 E-2. Subsequently the number of turret-mounted MG 151/20 cannon carried by the V15 was raised to five. Two additional EDL 151 turrets were installed in the wings, near the fuselage, and an HDL 151 turret was fitted in the nose doors, which were permanently closed. Six more MG 151/20 cannon were installed in armored weapons positions in the fuselage plus four MG 131 heavy machine-guns. The fuselage positions were protected by 20-mm armor plate and 90-mm armor glass. Flight testing of the prototype *Waffenträger* was conducted by Luftschiffbau Zeppelin.

So equipped, in November 1943 the V15 returned to the *E-Stelle Tarnewitz*, which was responsible for armaments. Initial ground firing trials began in December 1943. Unfavorable weather and an engine fire delayed the commencement of air firing trials until 31 December 1943. These continued until 25 February 1944 with von Günther as pilot. Seven flights were made to determine the accuracy of the weapons and their possible effects on the air-craft when fired simultaneously, such as changes in controllability, vibration or possible damage to aircraft components. The test flights were flown parallel to the Baltic coast. Air firing trials were photographed and the ballistic paths of the projectiles measured.

On 4 March 1944 the aircraft took off for Leipheim. Conditions were critical, There was a land breeze and almost no wind. The pilot, Oblt. Hermann Gatzemeier, positioned the aircraft at the very end of the north runway, which only recently had been extended by 200 meters, increasing its total available length to 1 200 meters. The V15 needed every meter, and Oblt. Gatzemeier got the machine off the ground just before a tall wire fence. The flight to Leipheim was made by way of Gardelegen.

Why had the *Waffenträger*, also called the "Flak Cruiser", been built? The idea probably originated at the time of the costly supply flights to North Africa. Testing of the heavily-armed Me 323 did not begin until September 1943, however, almost six months after the *Afrika-Korps* had surrendered and the cessation of massed flights.

The first mission recorded in TG 5's war diary occurred on 27-28 March 1944, when two *Waffenträger*, also called "Flak Carriers" in the east, were ordered to escort *I./TG 5* during its transfer flight from Warsaw-Okecie to Focsani. On 29 March 1944 one *Waffenträger* with the code RL+UE was in Rechlin for testing. While there it was flown by Fl.St.Ing. Böttcher. The same *Waffenträger* was later at Warsaw-Okecie (date not known). A similar aircraft was sighted at the south end of Finsterwalde airbase. Its armament was used to bolster the anti-aircraft defenses of the base, from which KG 200 operated captured enemy aircraft.

Leipheim was bombed on 24 April 1944 and several Me 323s in the process of being converted into *Waffenträger* were destroyed. On 3 August 1944 *Waffenträger* WNr. 330004, C8+GC of *II./TG 5* crashed while en route from Tonndorf to Chrudim. After takeoff the pilot of the *Waffenträger* put the aircraft into a steep turn. The machine subsequently disintegrated in flight and crashed. Sixteen crewmembers were killed, three were injure3d and one escaped uninjured.

The fates of at least two other *Waffenträger* are not known. One other is known to have been completed; the last two letters of its fuselage code were HT. It appears that there was again a requirement for the aircraft in the summer of 1944, when the disbandment of TG 5 was imminent. A Major from the RLM appeared in the office of the head of the LZ's aircraft development department, Walter Stender, and demanded that he "immediately" have a Me 323 converted into a *Waffenträger*. It is likely that the aircraft was intended for use in connection with the transfer of the remaining *Giganten* to TG 4 to Skutsch and Chrudim. The *Major* told Stender that 150 flak soldiers would assist in the work. Production of the *Gigant* had ceased in April 1944 and Zeppelin's only responsibility was further development (see chapter titled "Further Developments"). Stender tried to explain to the *Major* that the *Waffenträger* conversion could not be done "immediately." The latter then threatened to have Stender shot, whereupon he replied dryly, "Then it will take even longer." Work on the *Waffenträger* conversion never began.

Me 323 E-1 RF+XM over Lake Constance. In addition to a strengthened airframe, the E-series had a stronger defensive armament with an additional four MG 131 machine-guns. (Petrick)

The port outer EDL 151/20 turret in the wing of a Waffenträger. (Nowarra)

Production Me 323 E-2s were also fitted with two additional MG 151/20 cannon in wing-mounted turrets. (Nowarra)

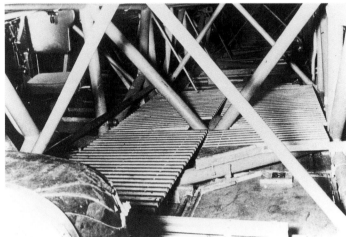

Walkway to the outer turret in the wing of an E-2. (Griehl)

The radio operator's position in Waffenträger RL+UE. (Hellwig)

In addition to the outer wing turrets, the Waffenträger was equipped with two inner wing turrets, as seen here on RL+UE. The rectangular window was in the radio operator's position. (Hellwig)

The Waffenträger mounted a fifth MG 151/20 cannon, which was located in an hydraulically-operated rotating turret in the nose of the aircraft. (Hellwig)

Below: For a long time these were the only two known photographs of a Waffenträger, which led to the conclusion that very few of these aircraft were built. (Nowarra)

Interior view of the nose turret. (Nowarra)

The four MG 151/20 cannon in the wing-mounted turrets are clearly visible here. This Waffenträger was very probably aircraft SL+HT. (Deutsche Aerospace)

Repair work on Waffenträger RL+UE at the Warsaw-Okecie airport in spring 1944. (Hellwig)

The four men in front of the Waffenträger may have been members of the aircraft's crew. The names of two of them are known: on the far left is Obfw. Schoene, on the far right Schirrmeister. The emblem of the aviation-technical service is visible on the cuffs of the two men on the left. The emblem was also worn by some aircrew-weapons personnel. (Hellwig)

Then the other engines were started one after another. (Hellwig)

Following repairs, one of the Waffenträger's engines is given a test run. Seen from this angle, it is easy to understand why the Waffenträger was given the nickname "Nashorn" (Rhinoceros). (Hellwig)

Below: Waffenträger RL+UE just before takeoff at Warsaw-Okecie. (Hellwig)

Though of poor quality, this is the only known photo of Waffenträger C8+GC, which crashed on 3 August 1944. (Nowarra)

At least three Waffenträger were completed, but how many were destroyed before delivery? Most of the Waffenträger under construction or being converted from standard transports were destroyed in the devastating air raid on Leipheim on 24 April 1944. This one is only identifiable by the mount for the turret in the nose. (Petrick)

Another Waffenträger destroyed prior to completion. (Schmoll)

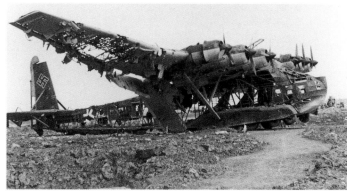

This Waffenträger was also reduced to scrap. (Thiele)

The only indication that this pile of wreckage was a Waffenträger is the armored gun position in the side of the nose. (Schmoll)

Below: Another view of the same Waffenträger. (Schmoll)

This Waffenträger was literally thrown into the air by the force of the exploding bombs. (Thiele)

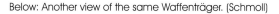

13

The Me 323 Flying Workshop

One Me 323 was fitted out as a "Flying Workshop." Contained within the fuselage were all the tools and equipment required to repair aircraft, vehicles and other technical devices, from lathe to welding torch. The crew of this Me 323 were able to assist wherever something was in urgent need of repair and could be reached by a field workshop.

The "Workshop Messerschmitt" was originally conceived as a flying spare parts repository with which to restore unserviceable *Giganten* to flying condition. Wheels, engines, propellers, etc were always carried and the necessary repair gear was stored in a truck which was also aboard the aircraft. Later, in practice, the "Workshop Messerschmitt" usually carried just the replacement parts needed to complete the repair in question and the truck. Repairs were not limited to *Giganten*. The original cargo compartment was outfitted with everything a mechanic, welder, electrician, precision mechanic or carpenter might need. In addition to the crew, there was always on board a 12- to 15-man technical team plus one mad to take care of the inevitable paperwork.

Obergefreiter Richard Hoffmann, who for six months served as pilot of the "Workshop Messerschmitt", still remembers the aircraft and its crew very well. He even remembers the names of the crew:

Pilot Fw. Rudolf Köhler
Co-pilot Obgefr. Richard Hoffmann
Radio operator Uffz. Bernhard Wolter
Flight engineers Fw. Möbius and Fw. Hild
Head of the technical team Fw. Luftmann, replaced by Technical Inspector Bruno Wesse in summer 1944
Electrician Uffz. Axmann
Mechanics and drivers of the workshop truck Uffz. Naumann and Uffz. Remer
Precision mechanic Gefr. Lampe
Mechanic and gunner Gefr. Ludwig Jendroska
Welder Gefr. Herzlieb
Mechanic Gefr. Bäsler
Carpenter Gefr. Haase

Sailmaker Gefr. Finke (repairs to fabric covering)
Uffz. Rudolf Schulze ran the "office."
In addition, there were two or three men on board whose names and functions Hoffmann can no longer remember.

In January 1944 Obgefr. Hoffmann was sent to Biala-Podlaska in Poland, where II./TG 5 had been based since 4 November 1943. In February Hoffmann was transferred to Lvov in the Ukraine, where he was familiarized with the special aircraft based there (RD+QU, WNr. 1112). It was a Me 323 D-1 with Gnôme-Rhône engines in Bloch cowlings and belonged to the *Stabsstaffel* of *I. Gruppe*. All of the *Geschwader*'s mechanics were members of this *Staffel*. The *Staffelkapitän* was Hptm. Peter "Sepp" Stangl, who had replaced *Major* Oskar Unruh as technical officer.

From Lvov repair missions were flown to Radom, Warsaw, Cracow and Proskurov. On 6 March 1944 the aircraft flew a repair mission from Lvov to Proskurov. The Me 323 was supposed to return to Lvov on 9 March, however its wheels became stuck in the mud. The crew of a heavy tank, probably a "King Tiger", which was on its way to the front some seven kilometers away, noticed the difficulties in which the "Workshop-Me" found itself and offered to help. With the Tiger's 700 H.P engine and the six engines of the *Gigant* at full power, the aircraft was extracted and returned to takeoff position. To avoid a repetition of the first attempt, weight had to be removed from the aircraft. The truck came off, and the technicians drove it back to base. Thus lightened, the *Gigant* successfully took off early on 10 March 1944 when the ground was frozen.

In the spring I./TG 5 moved from Warsaw-Okecie to Focsani, Romania and then to Kecskemét, Hungary, while in April 1944 II./TG 5 transferred from Biala-Podlaska to Schroda and in May moved to nearby Tonndorf. The "Workshop Messerschmitt" remained at Warsaw until 17 March 1944 (a planned flight to the Crimea did not take place), then it went to Radom and at the beginning of April via Cracow to Vienna-Aspern. RD+QU, which still belonged to the Stabsstaffel I./TG 5, had by then become an "independent unit" with its own office and even its own administrative authority. Each member of the crew had his own sleeping bag and necessary accessories such as mosquito netting, emergency rations and flashlight. A few tents were also kept on hand and there was also the truck.

On 15 April 1944 the aircraft flew from Vienna to Belgrade-Semlin, where the next day Allied bombing damaged five *Giganten*. RD+QU sustained only minor splinter damage. Following repairs, on 2 May the aircraft was flown to I./TG 5 in Kecskemét. From there it flew a number of missions, first back to Belgrade-Semlin, then one each to Deva and Zilistea. While the technicians were busy carrying out repairs, the crew were kept on standby and were used for other purposes, often making transport flights in other *Giganten*. When RD+QU was in Zilistea, the crew were used to ferry a *Waffenträger* from there to Belgrade. The heavily-armed aircraft was not a factory conversion, lacking the nose-mounted HDL 151 turret. On board the aircraft was a detachment of ten to twelve men commanded by a Leutnant. During the flight, roughly abeam the Iron Gate, the Leutnant had his men conduct firing practice while in cloud. Unfamiliar with the handling characteristics of this special variant of the *Gigant*, the ferry crew made a rather rough landing in Semlin.

The "Workshop Messerschmitt" escaped the attack on Kecskemét on 14 June 1944 as it was still in Zilistea. In the days that followed, the technicians were kept busy near Deva and especially in Zilistea. On 18 July RD+QU departed for Kecskemét, however during the flight the plexiglass panel over the radio operator's compartment flew off with a bang, taking approximately three square meters of fabric covering with it. The aircraft began to vibrate and lost altitude, and the *Gigant* was obliged to make a forced landing on a makeshift fighter field near Alba-Julia in northern Romania. The latter was little more than a large meadow on which about fifteen cows were grazing. A Leutnant was in command there. All the airfield had to show for itself was a few fuel drums plus tents for the handful of men stationed there. The landing was uneventful as the sound of the engines had scared the cows away.

Days passed as the men waited for replacement parts to arrive. They were given a warm reception by the local population. Then, on 25 August, came news that the Senatescu government had declared war on Germany. Things had to move quickly. Romanian guards had arrived, making it impossible to blow up the aircraft. The technical personnel had already made the necessary repairs, only the plexiglass panel was missing. The engine mechanics made the basically flyable aircraft ready for takeoff. Those in the vicinity of the *Gigant* (most were quartered away from the airfield) climbed aboard the workshop truck and tried to reach the Hungarian part of Transylvania in the two days the Romanian government had given the Germans to leave the country. The Romanians subsequently cancelled this grace period (allegedly because the Germans continued to fight in their country) and the men in the truck were captured. Pilots Fw. Rudolf Köhler and Obgefr. Richard Hoffmann, radio operator Uffz. Bernhard Wolter and gunner Gefr. Ludwig Jendroska managed to escape. After three days on foot they crossed the Hungarian border and from Klausenberg they returned to Kecskemét. Arriving there on 1 September 1944, they learned of TG 5's disbandment. Like most other members of the *Geschwader*, Richard Hoffmann was assigned to other duties. He went to the Field Maintenance Battalion in Eschwege, where he served as a "Special Courier" until December. Then in January 1945 he went to the combat pilot assembly point in Quedlinburg. Hoffmann was supposed to join the day fighters, however this never took place. His war ended on 18 April 1945 in Nuremberg after four days of house FG.

Note: According to Hungarian sources, at 0900 hours on 5 September 1944 seven German aircraft attacked the Drâmbari airfield near Alba Julia. One of the attackers was shot down by flak. The others destroyed four aircraft on the ground, among them a seemingly flyable Me 323 which had been captured by the Romanians. This could have been the "Workshop Messerschmitt", which from a distance appeared to be undamaged.

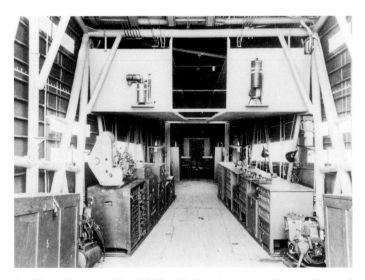

The "Flying Workshop" Me 323 RD+QU. This photo shows the machine as it emerged from the factory. (DaimlerChrysler Aerospace)

This is how the "Flying Workshop" looked in service. (Hoffmann)

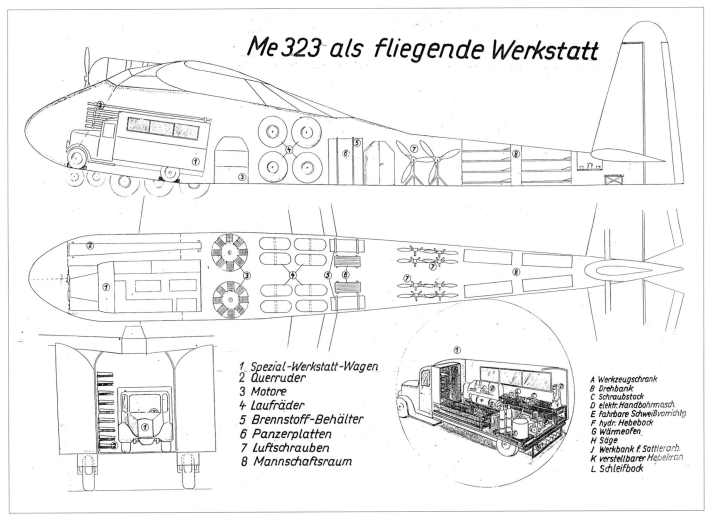

Me 323 als fliegende Werkstatt

1 Spezial-Werkstatt-Wagen
2 Querruder
3 Motore
4 Laufräder
5 Brennstoff-Behälter
6 Panzerplatten
7 Luftschrauben
8 Mannschaftsraum

A Werkzeugschrank
B Drehbank
C Schraubstock
D elektr. Handbohrmasch.
E fahrbare Schweißvorrichtg.
F hydr. Hebebock
G Wärmeofen
H Säge
J Werkbank f. Sattlerarb.
K verstellbarer Hebekran
L Schleifbock

General arrangement drawing of the "Workshop-Me" as it was originally supposed to be equipped. (Radinger)

Vital engine maintenance. (Koos)

The "Workshop-Me" was summoned whenever engine changes or repairs (as seen here in Warsaw) were impossible as a result of an unplanned landing away from base. (Hellwig)

The co-pilot, Obgefr. Richard Hoffmann (right), here with his brother Ernst. (Hoffmann)

Left: The pilot of RD+QU, Fw. Rudolf Köhler. (Hoffmann)

Radio operator Uffz. Bernhard Wolter at his position in RD+QU. (Hoffmann)

Left: On the left flight engineer Fw. Möbius, right Fw. Luftmann, head of the technical personnel assigned to the "Workshop-Me." (Hoffmann)

On the left Uffz. Remer, mechanic and driver of the on-board truck, in the middle pilot Fw. Köhler, right Uffz. Schulze, who managed RD+QU's "office." (Hoffmann)

Electrician Uffz. Axmann in front of the "Workshop-Me" at Lvov in February 1944. (Hoffmann)

The "Workshop-Me" and its on-board truck at Lvov, February 1944. (Hoffmann)

14

Braking Parachute Tests and the Heuberg Accident

The Me 323 completed a number of flights in which aircraft fuselages or test projectiles were dropped from high altitude. The purpose of these flights was to test braking parachutes designed to rescue pilot and airframe in the event of an emergency at near sonic speeds. The test projectiles had to be very heavy in order to reach the desired speed and the Me 323 was the only aircraft capable of carrying them. In mid-1943 the *E-Stelle Rechlin* had conducted test drops over Müritz Lake with 1:5 scale models of the Me 262 in order to test the aircraft's general configuration. Two "live" research flights were made with an Me 262 fuselage suspended beneath the starboard wing of the Me 323. The test fuselages, which were painted bright red, were hung inverted, probably to prevent the tail from damaging the Me 323's wing when dropped. The first flight of this type took place on 11 February 1943, the second on 23 October, prior to the start of series production of the jet fighter. In order to enable the Me 323 to safely reach the desired drop altitude of 7 200 meters, it was also towed by an He 111 Z, which had been specially designed to tow the Me 321 glider. The He 111 Z was capable of reaching an altitude of 8,000 meters. The tests took place over Lake Constance. The first test flight saw the parachute open as planned. The second ended in the loss of the Me 262 fuselage when the parachute failed to deploy.

A braking parachute was also requested for the Do 335, which had to be capable of decelerating from 1 050 to 500 km/h in ten seconds while in a dive. (The Do 335 V1, CP+UA, was first flown by *Flugkapitän* Hans Dieterle on 26 October 1943 in Mengen.) Six drops were carried out at the *E-Stelle Rechlin* with bomb-shaped projectiles weighing 6.5 metric tons. For the purpose of these trials a hatch was installed in the floor of the Me 323 V18, WNr. 130027, BM+GM. Also installed in the aircraft was a Lotfe 7 C bombsight. Thus modified, the aircraft was capable of dropping the projectiles, each of which was assembled from ten separate cast-iron discs, from altitudes of 4,000, 5 500 or 6,000 meters at an airspeed of approximately 180 km/h. The aircraft's crew consisted of: pilot and co-pilot, two flight engineers plus a third acting as coordinator between fuselage and wing, a radio operator, an observer manning the bombsight and two men responsible for dropping the test ob-

ject. There were thus nine men on board, plus representatives of the firms involved or other observers. Pilots Hirschberg and Eisermann took part in the test flights conducted from Rechlin and Lärz. Because of the extensive preparations involved, the initial process of rotating crew members was dropped in favor of a fixed crew roster.

On 27 April 1944 a test flight had to be aborted when an engine caught fire at an altitude of 4,000 meters. The fire was extinguished and the aircraft landed safely.

Companies which took part in the experiments were Dornier (test body), Kosteletzky (braking parachutes) and the Graf Zeppelin Research Institute (FGZ).

On 21 May 1944 the Me 323 V18 was destroyed in a bombing raid on Rechlin/Lärz, furthermore there were insufficient cast iron discs to assemble a complete (test body). Dornier was ready to begin high-speed trials with the Do 335 and pressed to have the experiments continue. At this point the Luftschiffbau Zeppelin took over the program from the *E-Stelle Rechlin*. In autumn 1944 the Me 323 V16 (DU+QZ, WNr. 130010), the prototype for the planned F-series with redesigned tail surfaces and six Jumo 211 F engines (1,340 H.P.) was modified to transport and drop the Dornier test body. It is worth noting that production of the Me 323 in Leipheim and Obertraubling had ceased almost six months earlier and that no production of the Me 323 F was contemplated.

This time the test body would be carried inside the fuselage instead of beneath the wings. The test vehicle would be slid nose first through a large opening in the floor of the *Gigant* and achieve the desired speed in free fall, after which the braking parachute would deploy.

The modified and reinforced Me 323 F conducted test drops with concrete blocks prior to the start of actual test flights. These were conducted under conditions of great secrecy at the Heuberg troop training grounds, which was also used as a second-line airfield.

By 30 September 1944 all was ready. Early that morning the *Gigant* took off from Heuberg under its own power (no He 111 Z was used) with the test vehicle on board and climbed to the assigned drop altitude of 7,000 meters. The crew consisted of pilot

Walter Starbati (chief pilot with Zeppelin), co-pilot Dr. Joachim Kuettner (Zeppelin's director of flight testing), radio operator Hans Boje and flight engineers Georg Schmitt and Otto Schlicht, who were at their stations in the wing between the engines. Also on board the aircraft were Fl.Ing. Herbert Popin (test observer from the *E-Stelle Rechlin*), Test Engineer Hans Scherer (Dornier test director), flight engineer Josef Haag (Dornier test mechanic) and *Oberfeldwebel* Wagner of *KG 2 "Holzhammer"*, who operated the Lotfe 7 C bombsight and was responsible for dropping the test vehicle. *KG 2* was disbanded in September 1944. Its *III. Gruppe* was supposed to be equipped with the Do 335, however this never happened.

During the climb the aircraft developed engine trouble and it took the better part of an hour to reach the assigned altitude of 7,000 meters and speed of 270 km/h. The test vehicle slid through the opening in the fuselage floor. At that point the *Gigant* still weighed 37.5 metric tons and vibrations during the release were acceptable. Sitting on the left, pilot Starbati was supposed to watch to see that the parachute opened properly, and co-pilot Dr. Kuettner on the right took over the controls. He put the Me 323 into a left turn to give Starbati a better view. Suddenly things went wrong. The controls had become ineffective. What had happened to the new tail surfaces? Later investigations revealed that the top of the rudder had broken off. The upper end of the control surface was not mass-balanced (the Wolf Hirth Company, which had built the tail surfaces, had made the fateful decision not to install one even though it knew that the rudder's torsional stiffness was marginal). The top of the rudder, which had only two attachment points, broke off and both halves of the elevator. The entire tail section broke off and the *Gigant* went down. Starbati and Dr. Kuettner jettisoned the canopy roof but had difficulty getting out of the machine, which was in a spiral dive. The outer wings broke off. Starbati made it out of the aircraft. Dr. Kuettner struggled to free himself from cables and hoses, and after dropping another 1,000 meters he got clear of the aircraft at a height of approximately 6,000 meters. The cables and hoses in which he was tangled prevented his parachute from deploying, however. The *Gigant* continued to disintegrate and beneath him the fuselage fell to earth. None of the unfortunates inside was able to get out. Some may not have been wearing their parachutes, contrary to

orders, and were unable to reach them in the spinning aircraft. It is known for certain that radio operator Boje, Dr. Kuettner's best friend, was not wearing his.

What was left of the fuselage crashed tail-first into the town of Oberglashütte, only a few kilometers from Heuberg. Miraculously, the only casualty on the ground was a woman who suffered a leg injury. Part of a wing with a still-running engine whizzed over the town and landed in an open field.

At the same time, Dr. Kuettner's situation appeared increasingly hopeless as the earth rushed toward him. Blocked by the jumble of cables, the parachute could not deploy. Then at 200 meters he succeeded in freeing the worst tangles and pulled the release handle. It worked! Kuettner's luck held: he was swinging badly during the last few meters, and when he struck the ground he was at the extreme point of a swing and thus his vertical speed was almost zero. He was unhurt, but being rather dazed, he walked about aimlessly for a few minutes until he came upon some people.

Test Engineer Scherer and Oberfeldwebel Wagner jumped through the opening in the floor with their parachutes. Another, Popin or Haag, jumped without his parachute. Sitting between the engines, flight engineers Schlicht and Schmitt had no chance. Radio operator Boje was pulled from the wreckage of the *Gigant* with a fractured skull and was at first mistaken for one of the pilots.

The crash mobilized the entire area. Everyone who could walk or pedal a bicycle headed for the crash site near the houses at the outskirts of town until soldiers cordoned off the area and forced the people back.

Other pieces of wreckage were scattered all around the town. Walter Stender, Zeppelin's head of development, immediately flew to the area and searched the crash site for pieces of wreckage, especially from the tail section, of which he had been critical from the beginning. He found the remains in a wood and his suspicions that the crash had been caused by a design or construction error were confirmed.

This may have been the last research flight by a *Gigant*. The Me 323 V18 had been destroyed in an air attack and the V17 was obviously not completed. *TG 5* had been disbanded at the end of August 1944 and *TG 4*, which had fourteen Me 323s on strength in September, was not used for that purpose.

Me 323s were present at Rechlin on several occasions, whether for testing or as test-beds for other equipment. This photo was taken at Rechlin on 3 September 1943; from left to right: Oberst Edgar Petersen (commander of all test stations), Albert Speer (Minister of Armaments and War Production), unidentified, Major Edmund Daser (commander of E-Stelle Rechlin). (F. Selinger)

Extensive trials were conducted in 1943 to investigate the Me 323's flutter characteristics prior to the commencement of drop tests with experimental bodies. For this purpose a camera was mounted on a rigid mast beneath the wing, pointing toward the fuselage. (Kuettner)

A white field with red (?) horizontal lines was painted on the fuselage. The behavior of the mast made it possible to determine torsion and bending. The houses on the bottom left of the photo suggest that the aircraft was in a steep turn when this photo was taken. (Kuettner)

Dr. Kuettner (left) and radio operator Boje (right) in front of an Me 323 D-1. It was probably the aircraft which carried the Me 262 fuselage aloft. (Kuettner)

The bright red Me 262 fuselage beneath the wing of the Gigant. (Kuettner)

Right: The He 111 Z towplane ready to go. (Kuettner)

The two aircraft slowly gain altitude. (Petrick)

The Me 262 test fuselage about to be dropped. The second Me 323 probably carried representatives of companies and institutions involved in the experiments. (Kuettner)

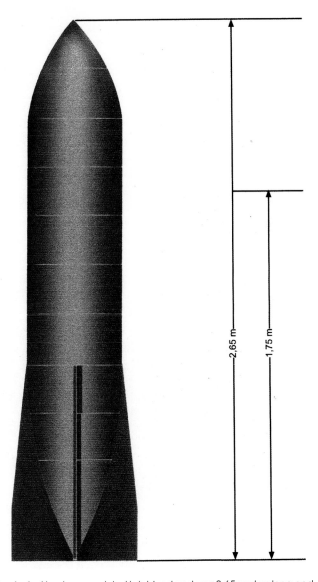

The Dornier test body was painted bright red and was 2.65 meters long and had a diameter of 0.50 meters. By way of comparison, the average human body has a diameter of about 1.75 meters. (Dabrowski)

Dr. Joachim P. Kuettner was director of flight testing at Luftschiffbau Zeppelin, Aircraft Department. This photo was taken in the 1970s. (Kuettner)

Radio operator Hans Boje was Dr. Kuettner's best friend. He died in the crash of the Me 323 V16 on the Heuberg. (Kuettner)

Walter Starbati was Luftschiffbau Zeppelin's chief pilot. He was later killed while testing the Fieseler Fi 103 Reichenberg manned flying bomb over Müggel Lake. (Kuettner)

The Do 335 heavy fighter was one of the fastest propeller-driven aircraft of its day, and the use of a braking parachute was planned. The Me 323 took part in braking parachute trials with an air-dropped weighted body. (Nowarra)

Tail section for the proposed Me 323 F. The Me 323 V16 was fitted with a similar tail prior to its crash on the Heuberg. (P.F. Selinger)

All control inputs to the new tail section were by way of control rods instead of cables as before. (P.F. Selinger)

Emergency escape procedure: the canopy roof could be jettisoned to allow the cockpit crew to bail out, however this was not always possible in a spinning Me 323. (Ott)

The cockpit glazing of an Me 323. (Griehl)

In an emergency the flight engineers could exit the machine through this jettisonable hatch. Because of their cramped cabins, they did not always wear their parachutes, and putting them on was not always possible in a sudden emergency. (Roba)

Observers had the presence of mind to photograph the Me 323 V16 as it crashed. By the time this photo was taken the tail section and outer wings had broken off. Those still in the machine had no chance of escape. (Kuettner)

A few seconds before impact: several soldiers on the Heuberg troop training grounds watch in horror as the Me 323 V16 crashes. (Kuettner)

The Gigant crashed inverted on the outskirts of Oberglashütte. Miraculously none of the townspeople were killed. (Kuettner)

Both photos show how close the houses were to the crash site. (Kuettner)

Right: A member of the crew killed in the crash. (Kuettner)

15

Further Developments

Operational experience with the *Giganten* resulted in improved armament and, beginning with the E-series, more powerful Gnôme-Rhône 14 R engines producing 1,180 H.P. for takeoff. Equipped weight rose to 29 metric tons compared to the 27.9 metric tons of the Me 323 D-1, while payload dropped to 9 metric tons. The E-2, deliveries of which began in 1944, carried the following armament: two MG 131s in a dorsal turret, one MG 131 in a nose turret, two MG 151/20s in wing turrets, two MG 131s in the sides of the forward fuselage and two MG 131s in the "bay window" positions in the aft fuselage. If required, up to six additional machine-guns could be installed in window positions in the fuselage sides. The added armament raised the size of the crew to eleven. Design improvements could have raised the aircraft's payload by 50%, however these proved impossible. Improved performance would also have required a redesign of the aircraft.

With Messerschmitt occupied with other projects, in the autumn of 1942 responsibility for development of the Me 323 was transferred to the Luftschiffbau Zeppelin's aircraft department. When the war began, Zeppelin had been forced to abandon its airship development program. As the war progressed, the greater became the danger that the company's experienced design team would be irretrievably scattered. The directors of the Luftschiffbau Zeppelin therefore decided to form an aircraft department in order to keep its workers active and possibly continue the Zeppelin tradition by producing competitive commercial aircraft. This department was established in the autumn of 1942, a time when Germany suffered several serious defeats which marked a turning of the tide in the war.

The Luftschiffbau Zeppelin regarded the further development and ultimate completion of the Me 323 program as a first step in a program of its own. The company's aircraft department began work in the spring of 1943. The leader of the design team which had created the Me 321 and Me 323, *Oberingenieur* Josef Fröhlich, moved with his people from Leipheim to Friedrichshafen on Lake Constance, while the head of the Leipheim operation, Ing. Hans Spieß, remained in charge of series production of the Me 323. At the time the program was transferred a new version of the *Gigant*,

the Me 323 V14, was under test. The type was powered by four Jumo 211 F engines and was not intended for series production. The Me 323 V15, prototype for the E-2 series with two HDL 151 cannon turrets (later EDL 151) on the wing upper surfaces, appeared in 1943. It is also interesting that several Me 323 E-2s were converted to flak cruiser standard at Leipheim and were used by the units as "escort aircraft" (see chapter titled *Waffenträger*). Design of the Z Me 323 F was begun by Messerschmitt and continued by Zeppelin. This work had a significant influence on the company's design for its own large-capacity transport.

In charge of the project was Ing. Walter Stender, for years head of research at Blohm & Voss and close advisor to Dr. Vogt. Since 1936 Ing. Stender had played an increasingly important part in design work on the Bv 222 and Bv 238 flying boats, which weighed 45 and 85 metric tons respectively. Their outstanding performance and ease of handling were in large part his accomplishments. Among the outstanding engineers working in the Luftschiffbau Zeppelin's aircraft design department was Arthur Förster, who since the 1920s had been head statistician and chief designer of the airship framework construction department. His skill in designing incredibly light yet strong airship frameworks is well documented.

The Z Me 323 F, which was essentially a Messerschmitt project similar to the Me 323 E-2 in design and equipment, was to be fitted with six Jumo 211 F engines with annular radiators and Junkers variable-pitch propellers. It was planned to increase payload to 18.2 metric tons. Strengthening of the airframe resulted in an increase in equipped weight to 33.2 metric tons and takeoff weight to 56 metric tons. Defensive armament was the same as that carried by the Me 323 E-2. Flight testing of the Z Me 323 F began at the end of 1943 with the Me 323 V16. The type did not enter production, as work shifted to a completely redesigned variant designated the Z Me 323 G. This aircraft's fuselage was completely redesigned. It was to be powered by six Gnôme-Rhône 14 R-4-5 engines each producing 1,600 H.P. for takeoff. In the spring of 1944 the Luftschiffbau Zeppelin halted work on the Z Me 323 G project, which was in the mock-up construction stage. Zeppelin's aircraft department was largely destroyed in two heavy air raids on

Friedrichshafen on 15 and 18 March 1944 and the design bureau moved to Weissenau near Ravensburg. Soon afterwards Oberingenieur Fröhlich was called away to Frankfurt/Oder to join the Fighter Staff, remaining there for a few months. From summer 1944 he was active with the Oberammergau Research Institute in Upper Bavaria. Among the projects he worked on there was a single-engine jet fighter of simple modular design for rapid production.

While development of the Z Me 323 G and project work on the Z Me 423 were under way in August Zeppelin aircraft department began designing an even larger six-engined transport. Dr. Eckener's good reputation as a pioneer of civilian aviation may have helped secure the assistance of a French company, which otherwise would not likely have entered into such a collaboration. It was the *Societe Nationale des Constructions Aeronautiques du Sud-Ouest*, or SNCASO, which at that time had the largest design bureau in France. A working agreement was reached with SNCASO aimed at creating the new aircraft and also securing a true business partner at a later date. Both parties hoped that the agreement would lead to a closer relationship after the war. The type designation ZSO was derived from the names of the companies, to which was added the RLM number 523. Work began on the six-engined Zeppelin-SNCASO ZSO 523 transport.

With Ing. Walter Stender as coordinator, project development by the two companies proceeded quickly. SNCASO was responsible for the bulk of the design work. The ZSO 523 retained most of the general design principles of the Me 323, such as steel-tube construction, mainwheels arranged in rows on the fuselage and the loading through clamshell doors at the front of the fuselage. A new undercarriage was designed which could be lowered hydraulically to ease loading. In addition to the clamshell doors and side doors, the aircraft was to have an opening in the rear floor. Two 22-meter-long traveling crane extended the length of the cargo compartment. A significantly lighter rhombus form was developed for the fuselage framework. The wing skinning of pressure-formed plywood panels was incorporated into the torsion system and all skinning was weatherproof. The wing of the braced shoulder-wing monoplane was built in three sections, like that of the Me 323. The broad center-section was braced against the fuselage by an I-strut on each side. The wing, which spanned 70 meters with an area of 455 square meters, had eight-part landing flaps in the center-section and three-part ailerons with trim tabs in the outer sections. Like the Me 323, the wing construction consisted of a steel tube framework with pres-sure-formed plywood skinning. Crawlways extended to the wingtips, allowing the engines, firewalls, fuel tanks and ailerons to be checked. Likewise, the fuselage was accessible to the extreme tip of the tail, allowing examination of the entire elevator mechanism and most of the rudder systems. All of the controls could be operated without power assistance, this achievement being based on Ing. Stender's work with Blohm & Voss which he continued at the Luftschiffbau Zeppelin. The horizontal stabilizer was of vee configuration with twin fins and rudders. The four-part elevator was equipped with trim tabs and the rudder was in two parts. The cockpit featured extensive glazing and sat on the fuselage nose. The cargo compartment of the 40.25-meter fuselage measured 280 cubic meters with a loading surface of 67 square meters. The intended power plants were six Gnôme-Rhône 18 R radial engines producing a combined 12,600 H.P. for takeoff.. Other data: height 11 m, equipped weight 48.2 metric tons, takeoff weight 85 metric tons, useful load 36.8 metric tons (overload takeoff weight 95 metric tons), wing loading 186 kg/m2, power loading 67.5 kg/H.P., maximum speed at 4,000 meters 345 km/h, cruising speed at 3,000 meters 300 km/h and range at 3,000 meters at 300 km/h 2 300 km (85 metric tons).

Work on the project was forced to end with the Allied occupation of France. At almost the same time the original Me 323 construction program ended for good.

By the time production ceased in April 1944 (three Me 323s were delivered that month, the Messerschmitt factories built a total of 201 aircraft of this type. Production breakdown by year: 1942: 27, 1943: 140, 1944: 34. The *Luftwaffe* took delivery of 26 aircraft in 1942, 121 in 1943 and 34 in 1944. It is not completely certain whether or not the figure of 201 includes converted Me 321s.

The six-engined Me 323 *Gigant* was the largest land-based aircraft of World War Two. Showing clear signs of improvisation, the Me 323 required relatively few man-hours to build and used cheap non-strategic materials in its construction. Nevertheless, the *Gigant* introduced several innovations to military air transport. For the first time ever, complete vehicles and guns, bulky goods or a complete company of infantry with equipment could be transported by air to combat zones several hundred kilometers by air, relatively economically and quickly. The type did not even require paved runways.

The *Gigant* was the first of the battle zone transports, which are even larger today and capable of carrying much greater payloads. Without these giants worldwide logistics would be impossible.

The last production variant, the Me 323 E-2 had more powerful engines and was more heavily armed than the D. (MBB)

On the other hand, its payload was drastically reduced. (MBB)

Transfer of the Me 323 from Messerschmitt to the Luftschiffbau Zeppelin at Leipheim in the autumn of 1942. Second from the left is Dr. Ludwig Dürr, in the middle wearing the dark coat is Knut Eckener, to his right Obering. Fröhlich, next to him Dipl.-Ing. Degel. (Radinger)

They make their way to the site of the handover to Luftschiffbau Zeppelin. Second from the left is Obering. Josef Fröhlich, with arms crossed is Zeppelin director Dr. Hugo Eckener, and on the right of him is Bley then Knut Eckener. (Radinger)

The moment of the former transfer of the Gigant program to Luftschiffbau Zeppelin. Dr. Eckener assumes responsibility for further development from Messerschmitt operations manager Theo Croneiß (died 07/11/42). In the background is the Me 323 V14 DT+IW equipped with four Jumo 211 engines. (Radinger)

Dipl.-Ing. Walter Stender, acknowledged expert in the design of large aircraft. (Reinhardt)

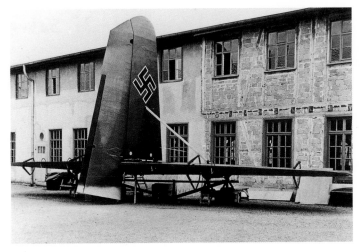

Prototype tail section built by Schempp-Hirth. This tail unit was intended for variants designed by the Luftschiffbau Zeppelin, beginning with the Me 323 F. (P.F. Selinger)

Right: A drawing of Dipl.-Ing. Walter Stender's ZSO 523 from the project description. (Dabrowski)

The city of Friedrichshafen on Lake Constance was struck by heavy air raids on 15 and 18 March, 29 April, and 15 and 20 July 1944. Friedrichshafen-Löwenthal airport, which was used by Luftschiffbau Zeppelin, was also hit. This Me 323 was riddled by splinters while parked there. (Kuettner)

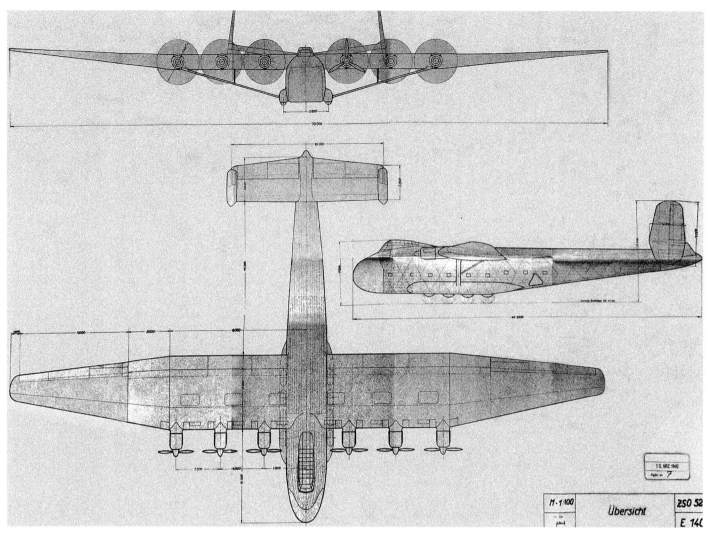

General arrangement drawing of the ZSO 523 dated 15 March 1945. The ZSO 523 was a heavy transport aircraft proposed by Zeppelin. (Dabrowski)

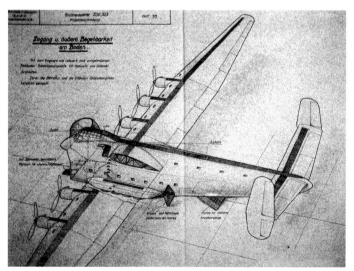

Drawing showing ground access to the ZSO 523. (Kössler)

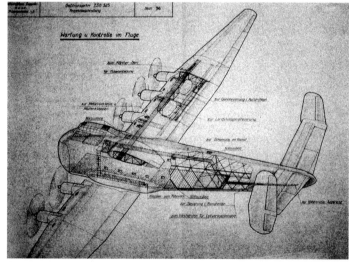

Depiction of servicing and checks in flight. (Kössler)

16

Misc. Gallery

C8+HE in a front-line repair facility. The tactical code X2D was previously unknown. (Petrick)

On the perimeter of Warsaw-Okecie airport. (Hellwig)

Takeoff preparations. (Rößmann)

Transfer to the east. (Giesecke)

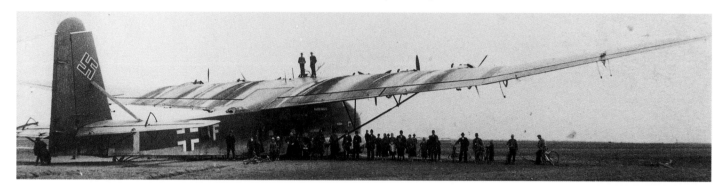

Forced landing in Hungary, 1944. (Rößmann)

Breslau-Schöngarten airport: in the foreground an Me 323 D-6, left an Me 323 D-2; in the center a Ju 52, right an Hs 129. (Hellwig)

On a forward airfield. (Nowarra)

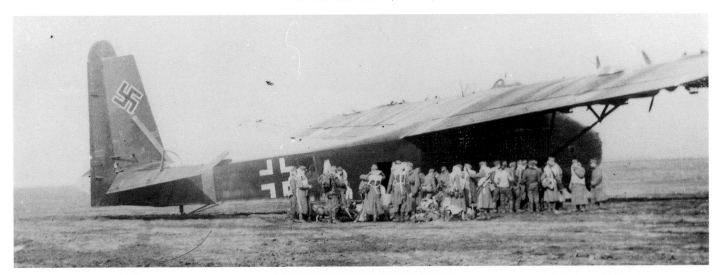

An Me 323 E-2 and its passengers. (Petrick)

An Me 323 D-2 during refueling on a forward airfield. (Petrick)

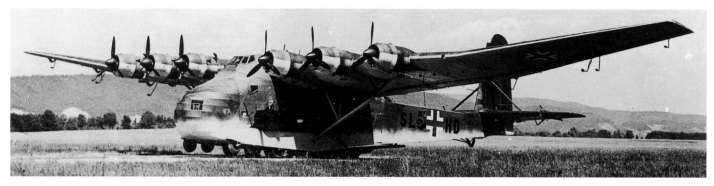

Official postcard motif. (Postcard)

Me 323 on approach to land. (Roosenboom)

About to touch down. (Nowarra)

A truly "gigantic" sight. (Griehl)

RF+XH over Lake Constance. (Radinger)

Me 323 E-1 as postcard motif. (Postcard)

This Me 323 of 7./TG 5 flown by Lt. Seewald ended up in a vineyard after suffering brake failure. With a total of three landing accidents, he was given the unflattering title of "Crash Pilot." (Storm)

Lt. Seewald's crew. The "Crash Pilot" is second from the left. (Storm)

W9+SA, converted from an Me 321, during flight trials. (Radinger)

Interior view of a Gigant with nose doors open. (Hellwig)

Interior view of a Gigant with nose doors closed. (Hellwig)

Defensive position in the nose doors during flight. (Storm)

The sheep do not seem overly impressed by the Gigant. (Griehl)

Landing among the sheep on an Hungarian airfield. (Schladerbusch)

Gigant C8+BR made a forced landing near Handscha, Hungary as a result of engine trouble and remained there from 9 to 19 May 1943. To pass the time the crew tried their hand at milking sheep, with mixed success. (Rößmann)

A Gigant photographed in autumn 1944 on a makeshift airfield in Szászrégen (German: Sächsisch Regen). The people in front of the aircraft are Székely from the eastern part of Transylvania. (Schladerbusch)

One can only speculate as to the reason why this aircraft was given the name "Pechvogel" (bad luck bird). (Petrick)

Photo with dedication for the head of the design team. The text reads: To Dipl.-Ing. Fröhlich with grateful appreciation for his extraordinary accomplishment in creating this aircraft. Messerschmitt 6/8/42. (Vogel)

Me 323 D-1 and Me 321, probably at Leipheim. (Griehl)

Me 323 V2, W9+SA in Leipheim. (Nowarra)

SL+HN in Dessau. (Petrick)

Vehicles for the Africa Corps. (Peter)

„Siehste, das haste von deinem saudummen Looping. Die ganze Ladung ist nach hinten gerutscht, und ich möchte sehen, wie wir wieder herumkommen!"

Gigant humor in the magazine "Der Adler." (Hellwig)

„Na bitte, die Spitfires drehen ab. Sie haben Respekt vor unserem Giganten — wahrscheinlich halten sie das Langrohrgeschütz für eine neue Bewaffnung!"

Gigant humor in the magazine "Der Adler." (Hellwig)

The pilots often flew visually, following rail lines or rivers. (Griehl)

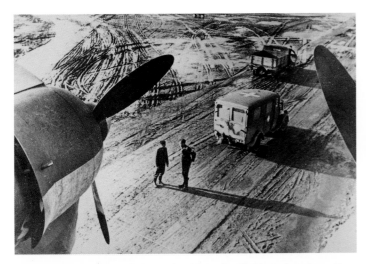

Transporting wounded, photographed from the flight engineer's position. (Schladerbusch)

The doors in the sides of the Gigant's fuselage were also used to load the aircraft. (Hellwig)

Flight engineer Uffz. Bolze of 6./TG 5 sits in a lofty height on one of the engines of DU+PK. (Schladerbusch)

A captured Russian SIS-5 truck moves into position to take on cargo. (Nowarra)

An Me 323 is towed to takeoff position. (Griehl)

The runway seems to extend to infinity, however for a fully-laden Gigant it often seemed all too short. (Griehl)

I./KG.z.b.V. 323 Christmas party in December 1942. In the background may be seen Major Mauß and Major Unruh. (Hellwig)

The huge tail was often used as a photographic background. (Schladerbusch)

Refueling an Me 323 E-2. (Griehl)

Unloading shells. (Schladerbusch)

Unloading shells. (Aders)

Me 323 E-2, RL+UJ in winter. (Roba)

Warming up the engines during winter operations. (Hellwig)

Group photo on the tail of X1C. (Roosenboom)

Below: Me 323 SG+RA. (Radinger)

Me 323 DT+IT on the Eastern Front. (Petrick)

On the Eastern Front: in the foreground the wing of an Hungarian Fi 156, in the background a Ju 52 in winter camouflage finish, an Me 323 and a Junkers W 34. (Bernád)

Giganten in the snow. (Roba)

Giganten in the snow. (MBB)

Giganten in the snow. (MBB)

Giganten in the snow. (Petrick)

Raw conditions for man, animal and aircraft – winter 1943-44. (Roba)

Gigant repair work at Gardelegen airfield, 1944. (Petrick)

Engine change after a forced landing. (Rößmann)

Changing the Bloch power plant of an Me 323 D-1. (Petrick)

Changing the Bloch power plant of an Me 323 D-1. (Petrick)

Loading a vehicle of unidentified origin. (Ott)

Loading heavy bombs in Warsaw. (Hellwig)

Loading an aircraft engine. (F. Selinger)

Common cargo: large crates. (Obermaier)

Loading an Sd.Kfz. 7 (8 tonne) with 150-mm heavy field gun. (Nowarra)

Loading an Sd.Kfz.222 eight-wheel heavy armored car from an Me 323 D-2 at Castelvetrano, spring 1943. (Petrick)

Loading a 105-mm light field gun and an Opel Blitz truck (3 tonne). (Hellwig)

Loading an Sd.Kfz. 250/1 medium armored troop carrier. (Hellwig)

Generalfeldmarschall Albert Kesselring talks to a soldier as a French Citroën car is loaded. (Nowarra)

Loading a Marder II tank-destroyer. (Hellwig)

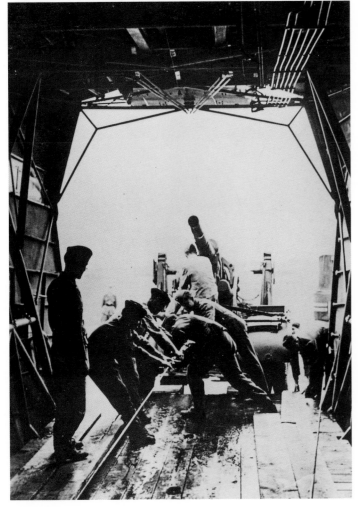

Loading an anti-aircraft gun with the help of a winch. (Schladerbusch)

Right: Loading an ambulance. (Griehl)

A light armored car rolls into the Gigant's cargo compartment. (Nowarra)

This Gigant was to transport Ju 52 spares to the front. (Koos)

This photo was taken at the beginning of 1944 and shows clearly just how young these non-commissioned officers were. (Hellwig)

A crew of Stabsstaffel I./KG.z.b.V. 323 in Italy in front of their Me 323 D-1. (Hellwig)

Right: The crew of C8+BP in front of their aircraft. (Roba)

Above: Army soldiers, probably a guard platoon, have positioned themselves in front of an Me 323. (Roosenboom)

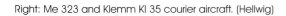

Right: Me 323 and Klemm Kl 35 courier aircraft. (Hellwig)

Below: Two Messerschmitt products: Me 323 D-6 and Bf 108 Taifun. The Kapitän of Stabsstaffel I./TG 5, Hptm. Stangl, enjoyed flying the Taifun. (Petrick)

Above: Such a meeting was only possible in Göttingen: Me 323, tactical code X1F, and a Horten H II flying wing. (Griehl)

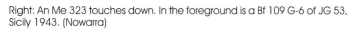

Right: An Me 323 touches down. In the foreground is a Bf 109 G-6 of JG 53, Sicily 1943. (Nowarra)

Below: Two more by Messerschmitt: in the air a Bf 110, which often flew escort for the Me 323 over the Mediterranean. (Petrick)

17

Color Gallery

The Luftwaffe's first and most used transport glider was the DFS 230. Seen here is an aircraft of LLG 1 on a Greek airfield in May, 1941. Following its successful use in the attack on the Belgian fortress of Eben Emael in 1940, the DFS 230 became the Luftwaffe's standard transport glider. The aircraft was capable of carrying a pilot and nine troops, or an equivalent weight of cargo. It was designed by Dipl.-Ing. Hans Jacobs in 1936-37. Wingspan 21.98m, length 11.24m, takeoff weight 2,100kg., total built, probably 1,591. (Kuntz)

Another widely used transport glider was the Go 242. Shown here are two aircraft of the Verbindungskommando (S) 4 on an airfield in southern Russia, in autumn 1942. The Go 242 was designed by Dipl.-Ing. Albert Kalkert and production began in 1941. The aircraft had a crew of two and was capable of transporting twenty-one soldiers or an equivalent weight of cargo. Wingspan 24.5m, length 15.8m, equipped weight 3,226kg. A total of 1,528 were built, plus 324 examples of the relatively unsuccessful Go 244, which were later converted back to Go 242 standards. (Petrick)

In service the Me 323 retained its factory-applied camouflage finish, namely RLM Green 70 and 71 on the upper surfaces and sides in a splinter pattern and Pale Blue 65 on undersurfaces. In contrast to the Me 321, there are no known cases of Me 323s being repainted to match operating conditions, for example white winter camouflage or sand-yellow desert camouflage. Although Giganten were often used to transport wounded, none are known to have been marked as medical evacuation aircraft. (Petrick)

In some cases the tips of the spinners were painted in the Staffel color and the undersides of the wingtips were painted yellow (same color as fuselage band, indication use on the Eastern Front) (Petrick)

Me 323 DT+IT "Himmelslaus" during repairs in Lvov on 15 February 1943. (Schmeelke)

The Gigant sustained 15% damage in a hard landing there. (Schmeelke)

Die Kennzeichnung der Flugzeuge beim K.G.z.b.V.323 und beim T.G.5

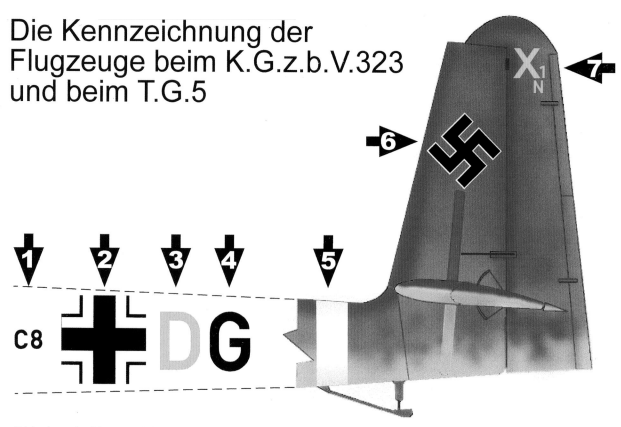

❶Verbands-Kennzeichen in gleicher Größe wie die Staffelkennzeichen oder, wie bei diesem Beispiel, in verkleinerter Form.
❷Balkenkreuz auch ohne schwarze Winkel oder nur aus weißen Winkeln bestehend.
❸Buchstabe in der jeweiligen Staffelfarbe (hier: 3. Staffel) kennzeichnet das Flugzeug in der Staffel.
❹Staffel-Buchstabe (hier: 3. Staffel).
❺Rumpfband weiß (Einsatzgebiet Mittelmeerraum) oder gelb (Einsatzgebiet Ostfront Südabschnitt), Position zwischen Rumpfkennzeichen und Leitwerk sowie die Breite des Bandes uneinheitlich.
❻Hakenkreuz mit oder ohne schwarzer Füllung.
❼Taktisches Kennzeichen: I. Gruppe X 1 A bis X 1 Z, danach X 2 A bis mindestens X 2 D.
II. Gruppe Y 1 A bis mindestens Y 1 O. Durch Abgabe von Flugzeugen an die I. Gruppe Y-Kennzeichen auch dort möglich.

Die Gruppen und Staffeln des K.G.z.b.V.323 und des T.G.5
Der farbige Buchstabe kennzeichnet das Flugzeug innerhalb der Staffel, der schwarze Buchstabe kennzeichnet die Staffel selbst.

I. GRUPPE lange mit Stammkennz.

A B Stabsstaffel
B E 1. Staffel
C F 2. Staffel
D G 3. Staffel
4. Staffel existierte nicht

II. GRUPPE

A C Stabsstaffel
B N 5. Staffel
C P 6. Staffel
D R 7. Staffel
E S 8. Staffel

III. GRUPPE wahrscheinl. nur Stammkennz.

A D Stabsstaffel
B T 9. Staffel
C U 10. Staffel
D V 11. Staffel
E W 12. Staffel

Opposite
Me 323 Markings:

1. The unit code was the same size as the Staffel code or was much reduced in size.

2. The Balkenkreuz was applied following official guidelines, although it was sometimes seen without the black outline or in white outline form.

3. The first letter to the right of the Balkenkreuz was always applied in the Staffel color and numbered the aircraft within the Staffel (for example, D = the fourth aircraft).

4. The actual Staffel letter identified the Staffel to which the aircraft belonged, following a fixed sequence of letters.

5. The fuselage band (white for the Mediterranean theater, yellow for the southern section of the Eastern Front) was located between the fuselage code and the tail. The exact position of the band and its dimensions varied.

6. The Swastika appeared with solid black interior and outline only versions.

7. Before the Me 323 carried the unit code C8, it was flown on operations wearing its Stammkennzeichen, a four-letter code assigned during production (for example, DT+IG, RD+QL, SG+RD, RF+XA). The KG.z.b.V. adopted so-called "Tactical Codes" to instill some sense of order in their units, which were assembled from widely differing sub-units. Those used by the Me 323 units were: I. Gruppe = X1A to X1Z, then X2A to at least X2D, II. Gruppe = Y1A to at least Y1O. The transfer of aircraft from II. Gruppe to I. Gruppe may have resulted in Y-codes there as well. No tactical codes are known to have been used by III. Gruppe. Tactical codes were still seen after the reorganization of the transport units in May 1943, although they were no longer of any significance.

The fuselage codes of the Me 321 were unusual. The Stammkennzeichen was generally retained in service and was an alpha-numeric sequence: the code W1 to W9 appeared in front of the Balkenkreuz and the letters SA to SZ behind it. This was probably done to clearly distinguish the aircraft from powered machines produced by Messerschmitt. There was some crossover when the first Me 321s were converted into Me 323s, which initially retained the glider codes. Whereas 200 Me 321s were completed at most (probably less), and the complete code sequence provided for 234 codes (9 x 26), there must have been gaps in the production blocks. (Dabrowski)

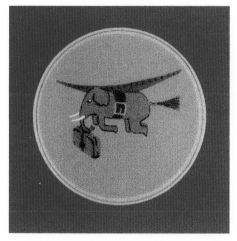

I./K.G.z.b.V.323   Stabsstaffel I./K.G.z.b.V.323   II./K.G.z.b.V.323

. Gruppe's emblem was a flying elephant carrying a suitcase. II. Gruppe's emblem consisted of the Baron Münchhausen figure riding on a cannonball pulled by six ducks. No III. Gruppe emblem is known. The only known Staffel emblem belonged to the Stabsstaffel of I. Gruppe: a 6 with propeller and two oak leaves.

It was an impressive sight to see an eleven-tonne Marder self-propelled gun drive out of an Me 323. Medium or heavy tanks were beyond the aircraft's ability, however. (Petrick)

This Me 323 D-1 has been retrofitted with guns in the nose doors. (Nowarra)

Below: A "Marder" self-propelled gun was successfully transported to Africa in a Me 323. (Petrick)

The drama off Cape Bon was the most costly off all the supply missions to Tunis. In spite of the valiant efforts of the transport crews, Army Group Africa could not be saved and on 13 May 1943 it surrendered.

This photo appears to depict Me 323 D-2 aircraft undergoing general overhaul in Leipheim. The machine in front has received new nose doors, the old ones lie on the ground. The undercarriage fairings have also been removed. (Petrick)

The loading of horses was also practiced in Dornstadt. (Petrick)

Right: Overflight by Me 323 RD+QQ. Low-flying Giganten were often subjected to ground fire from rifles and machine-guns. The armored cockpit protected the pilots, however the rest of the aircraft was vulnerable and engines were often hit. (Kuntz)

Generalfeldmarschall Erwin Rommel (seen here with the Fliegerführer Afrika, Generalmajor Stefan Fröhlich) achieved spectacular successes against the Allies in North Africa, however in the end even his great skill as a commander were no match for the enemy's vast materiel superiority.

The Ju 52 units bore the lion's share of the burden of supplying the Africa Corps. As Allied air superiority grew, the trimotors were intercepted more frequently before they could reach their destination airfields, and even there they faced the threat of air attack at any time. (Dabrowski)

Appendices

Persons Involved in the Design, Production and Testing of the Me 321 and Me 323
Messerschmitt AG and Messerschmitt GmbH
(list incomplete)

Concept .... Prof. Willy Messerschmitt
Operations Manager Messerschmitt .... Theodor Croneiß (until 1942, deceased)
Operations Manager Messerschmitt AG .... Rakan Peter Kokothaki (from 1942)
Operations Manager Messerschmitt GmbH .... Generaling. Roluf Lucht (from 1942)
Operations Management .... Ing. Wolfgang Degel
Works Management Obertraubling .... Karl Schmid
Works Management Leipheim .... Hans Spieß
Design Bureau Head .... Ing. Woldemar Voigt
Design Head .... Ing. Walter Rethel
Development Head .... Obering. Josef Fröhlich
Deputy .... Ing. Petri
Deputy, Blueprint Control .... Ing. Kurt Brandt
Secretary (Fröhlich) .... Erna Nied
Technical Draftsman .... Wachinger
Technical Draftsman .... Lindenmeyer
Technical Draftsman .... Emmi Schlumberger
Blueprint Office .... Ing. Meyer
Design
    Empennage .... Ing. Oskar Fischer
    Fuselage, Wing .... Ing. Molt
    Engine Installation .... Ing. Bernhard Schwarting
Systems .... Edmund Eisele
Systems .... Ing. Stehle
Andercarriage Systems .... Hilmar Stumm
Andercarriage Systems .... Horst Lattke
Electrics .... Ing. Förster
Electrics .... Ing. Holzmeier
Drawings, Electrical .... Drescher
Workshop Control and Test Flying .... Josef Bitz
Workshop Inspection .... Dipl.-Ing. Lechner
Company Photographer Messerschmitt AG .... Margarethe Thiel
Photographer Leipheim .... Egger
Typist .... Gerda Lippert
Typist .... Ost
Typist .... Elfriede Goldschmid
Office Worker .... Erdle
Prototype Testing .... Flugkpt. Karl Baur

Senior Command and Unit Officers

(associated with Me 323 operations) (List incomplete)

K.G.z.b.V. „N" - KG.z.b.V.323 - TG 5

Senior Commands

Transp.Fl.F. Mittelmeer	Generalmajor Ulrich Buchholz	?-11/10/43	
Transportfliegerführer 2	16/10/43-21/01/44		
	Gen.Kdo. XIV Fl.Korps (Tutow)	22/01/44-?	

Headquarters

Kommodores:	Oberstltn. Gustav Damm	18/12/42-24/01/44	(from K.Gr.z.b.V. Wittstock - Frontfl.-Sammelst. Quedlinburg)
	Oberstltn. Guido Neandlinger (promoted to Oberst 01/04/44)	14/03/44-?	
Adjutants:	Oblt. Walter Bühner (from K.Gr.z.b.V. Wittstock - II./TG 5)	21/04/43-03/03/44	
	Oblt. Alex Bielitzer	13/02/44-?	
Technical Officers:	Oblt. Hans-Joachim Griefahn (from E.TG. Schönwalde)	21/04/43-23/03/44	
	Lt. Hugo Trumpf	08/05/44-30/08/44	
Signals Officers:	Lt. Harald Wienbeck	?-?	
	Hptm. Hans Feldsien (from E.TG. Schönwalde)	08/09/43-21/05/44	
	Oblt. Templ	?-?	
	Oblt. Heinz Camen	03/08/44-23/08/44	
Operations Officers:	Hptm. Gerhard Dudek	24/04/43-?	
	Oblt. Hermann Hüter	29/05/43-30/08/44	
Paymaster:	Kurt Sülze	23/10/43-08/12/43	
Staff Major:	Hptm. August Schiffer	14/02/44-16/08/44	

I./323 – I./TG 5 (renamed 09/05/43)   ??/10/42-??/08/44

Gruppen-Kommandeur:	Major Günther Mauß	29/09/42-23/09/44
Adjutant:	Oblt. Waldemar Kost	?-?

Stabsstaffel C8 + .B

Staffelkapitän:	Major Oskar Unruh	?-?
	Hptm. Dr. Gerhard Opitz (Medical Officer)	?-?
	Oblt. Heinz Emil Müller	20/04/42-18/12/43
	Oblt. Ernst Peter	?-?

	Oblt. Josef Peter "Sepp" Stangl (T.O.)	?-?
	Oblt. Alfred Schumann	?-?
	Lt. Krüger	?-?
	Lt. Josef Huber	?-?

1. Staffel C8 + .E

Staffelkapitän:	Hptm. Josef Mies	25/04/42-01/09/44
	Oblt. Herbert Kaiser	?-?
	Oblt. Alfred Schumann	?-?
	Oblt. Wilhelm Seidel	from 04.42 (Formation)
	Lt. Werner Drewes (T.O.)	?-?
	Lt. Waldemar Balasus	?-?
	Lt. Johannes Meyer	?-?
	Lt. Konrad Grachernigg	?-?
	Lt. Josef Huber	?-?
	Lt. Paul Kruchen	?-?
	Lt. Krüger	?-?

2. Staffel C8 + .F

Staffelkapitäne:	Hptm. Edmand Auer	25/04/42-30/12/42
	Hptm. Joachim Bledow	01/01/43-14/05/43
	Hptm. Waldemar Kost	?-?
	Hptm. Heinz Jacob	?-?
	Oblt. Bernhard Hohenbruch	?-?
	Oblt. Schalkhauser	?-?
	Lt. Otmar Graf	?-?
	Lt. Rudolf Knecht	?-?
	Lt. Helmut Kranz	?-?
	Lt. Günther v. Rettberg	?-?
	Lt. Gerhard Schmitz	?-?

3. Staffel C8 + .G

Staffelkapitäne:	Hptm. Hans Fischer	15/02/43-22/04/43
	Hptm. Alfred Schumann	??/06/43-??/10/44
	Hptm. Heinz Jacob	?-?
	Oblt. Friedrich Bohl	?-?
	Lt. Paul Hartmann	?-?
	Lt. Gerhard Schmitz	?-?
Technical Officer:	Lt. Willy Söhnlein	01/04/44-21/09/44

4. Staffel   not formed

II./323 – II./TG 5   **??/11/42-??/08/44**

Gruppen-Kommandeure	Oberstltn. Werner Stephan	?-22/04/43
	Major Hans Fischer	23/04/43-27/05/43
	Major Fritz Barthel	25/08/43-31/08/43
	Major Paul Fischer (?)	?-?
	Lt. Bruno Heck	?-?

Stabsstaffel C8 + .C

Staffelkapitän:	Hptm. Schaffenberg	?-?
	Hptm. Rudolf Ruge	?-?
	Oblt. Gerhard v. Kalinowski	?-?

5. Staffel C8 + .N

Staffelkapitän:		
	Hptm. Joachim Zimmermann	07/04/43-14/06/43
	Hptm. Konrad Reithmüller	?-?
	Hptm. Walter Ehrlich	29/02/44-09/04/44
	Hptm. Josef Peter "Sepp" Stangl	13.06.44-14.04.44
	Hptm. Joachim Zimmermann	?-?
	Oblt. Walter Bühner	?-?
	Oblt. Jürgen Kell	?-?
	Oblt. Günther Seewald	??/06/43-??.??/44
	Lt. Lothar Krecker	?-?
	Lt. Heinz August Steinert	?-?

6. Staffel C8 + .P

Staffelkapitäne:		
	Hptm. Heinz Thöma	??.??.??-17/02/43
	Hptm. Ernst Kempen	15/05/43-14/06/43
	Hptm. Willy Schwarz	?-?
	Hptm. Joachim Zimmerreimer	02/04/44-01/08/44
	Hptm. Walter Ehrlich	?-?
	Hptm. Fritz Kube	?-?
	Lt. Heinz Gerdes-Röben	?-?

7. Staffel C8 + .R

Staffelkapitäne:		
	Hptm. Mölts	?-?
Deputy	Oblt. Ernst Bösmüller	15/03/44-05/10/44
	Hptm. Ernst Kempen	15/06/43-14/03/44
	Lt. Seewald	?-?
	Lt. Bruno Wiedemann	?-?

8. Staffel C8 + .S

Staffelkapitän:		
	Hptm. Hans Fischer	15/10/42-14/02/43
	Hptm. Joachim Zimmermann	?-?
	Hptm. Walter Ehrlich	10/04/44-14/10/44
	Hptm. Willy Schwarz	?-?

III./323 – III./TG 5   **??/03/43-??/06/43**

Gruppen-Kommandeure:		
	Oberst Alfred Wübben	15/05/43-02/06/43
	Major Markus Zeidler	?-?

9. Staffel C8 + .T

Staffelkapitän		
	Hptm. Konrad Reithmüller	?-??/04/43
	Oblt. Hans Werner Davignon	25/03/43-02/06/43
	Lt. Karl-Hans Schuster (T.O.)	?-?
	Lt. Heinrich Wettl	?-?
	Lt. Heinz August Steinert	?-?

5. Staffel/Erg.Tr.G. (former K.Gr.z.b.V.300)

Staffelkapitän		
	Hptm. Oswald Brien	??/03/43-?
	Lt. Gerhard Schmitz	

Erg.Staffel 323

Staffelkapitän		
	Hptm. Oswald Brien	??/03/43-??

Not Assigned

Hptm. Ernst Büsselmann (II./TG 5)	?/43-13/07/43
Oblt. Ernst Östmüller	?-?
Oblt. Gerhard Quietzsch	?-?
Oblt. Joachim Runze (I./323)	?-01/03/43 (†)
Oblt. Adolf Schleyer (I./323)	?-?/43
Lt. Karl-Heinz Vensky (I./TG 5)	?-?
Lt. Schalkl	?-?

16. Staffel IV./TG 4

Hptm. Walter Ehrlich	?-?

List of Me 321/Me 323 Prototypes and Variants

1940

On 04/10/40 Willy Messerschmitt proposed a "tank-carrying glider" to Ernst Udet. Soon afterwards the RLM issued specifications to Messerschmitt and Junkers.

	06/11/40 start of design work.
Me 261w	Design dated 01/11/40 (Fröhlich/Rethel).

1941

Me 263	so designated on a general-arrangement drawing dated 01/02/41.
Me 321 V1	First flight on 25/02/41.
Me 321 V2	First flight on 24/03/41.
Me 321 V3	First flight on 04/04/41.
Me 321 V4	First flight on 09/04/41.
Me 321 V5	First flight on 10/04/41.
Me 321 A	1 Pilot, possibility of second man behind him, maiden flight 07/05/41 in Obertraubling near Regensburg.
Me 321 B	2 Pilots, possibility of third man behind him, 15 examples converted to powered aircraft, initially designated Me 321 C and Me 321 D.
Me 321 C	4-engine, conversion planned from Me 321 B.
Me 321 D	6-engine, conversion planned from Me 321 B.
Me 323 A V1	4-engine, renamed Me 321C, maiden flight 21/04/41, possibly refitted with Heine two-blade propellers.
Me 323 B V1	6-engine, renamed Me 323 D, probably converted from the Me 323 A V1, Maiden flight ??/08/41.

1942

Me 323 C	4-engine, production planned, possibly converted from Me 321B, maiden flight 20/01/42, Obertraubling.
Me 323 D	Maiden flight?
Me 323 V2	
Me 323 V3	
Me 323 V4	
Me 323 V5	
Me 323 V6	
Me 323 V7	
Me 323 V8	
Me 323 V9	
Me 323 V10	
Me 323 V11	
Me 323 V12	100-hour test. All prototypes up to the V12 were test-flown by April 1942.
Me 323 D-1	Start of production July 1942, maiden flight August 1942, Bloch power plants, 3-blade Ratier variable-pitch propellers.

Me 323 D-2	LeO power plants, fixed-pitch Heine wooden propellers.
Me 323 D-3	6 Jumo 211 J engines, according to the delivery plan one example was to be delivered by February 1942, however it was probably not built.
Me 323 D-6	LeO power plants, Ratier variable-pitch propellers.

1943

Me 323 V13	Prototype E-1, increased fuel capacity, heavier armament.
Me 323 V14	Prototype with 4 Jumo 211 J engines.
Me 323 V15	Prototype E-2 with 2 HDL 151 turrets in the wings (production version with 2 EDL 151).
Me 323 E-1	Deliveries commenced September 1943.
Me 323 V16	Prototype Me 323 F with revised tail and Jumo 211 R engines. Crashed on the Heuberg 30/09/44.

1944

Me 323 V17	Planned prototype Me 323 G with 6 Gnôme-Rhône 14 R engines, mockup not completed.
Me 323 V18	Probably similar to the V16, made available for braking chute tests.
Me 323 E-2	Deliveries commenced 1944, last delivered April 1944.
Me 323 E-2/WT	Heavily-armed E-2 conversion, no cargo capability, only a few examples saw service.
Me 323 F	6 Jumo 211 F, drawings completed by 06/07/43, responsibility for development transferred to Luftschiffbau Zeppelin. Dropped from production schedule early 1944.
ZMe 323 G	Development by Luftschiffbau Zeppelin, computation dated 20/10/43, project abandoned.
ZMe 323 H	Project dated 18/05/44.
ZMe 423	Reference by Eckener to a telegram from the Special Committee in a letter dated 03/08/43. Not pursued further.
ZSO 523	Large transport design by Walter Stender, project description dated 30/09/44. Developed version of the Me 323, not realized.

Notes:

Me 321 = 166 examples delivered by November 1941. Probable production total: 175 to 200 examples.

Me 323 : 198 examples new production, 15 conversions (some as prototypes) from Me 321s = 213 examples altogether.

Approximately 180 examples delivered, rest lost in accidents and air raids.

Appendix 4

Formation and Movements of Me 321/Me 323 Units

Unit	Remarks
GS 1 Oblt. Meltzer	??/11/41 from the Eastern Front to Merseburg (disbanded)
GS 2 Oblt. Baumann	??/11/41 from the Eastern Front to Merseburg (disbanded)
GS 4 Oblt. Pohl	??/11/41 from the Eastern Front to Leipheim, renamed 4./KG.z.b.V.2 (1942 equipped with He 111 Z towplanes)
GS 22 Oblt. Schäfer	??/11/41 from the Eastern Front to Leipheim, renamed 3./KG.z.b.V.2 (1942 equipped with He 111 Z towplanes)
ex GS 2	31/12/41 from Merseburg to Leipheim
I./K.Gr.z.b.V.323	01/04/42 Order for formation of 1. and 2. Staffel
K.G.z.b.V.2	26/04/42 Stab from Berlin to Leipheim
I./K.Gr.z.b.V.323	26/04/42 formation
1. (GS)/z.b.V.2	01/05/42 renamed 1./K.Gr.z.b.V.323
3	(GS)/z.b.V.2 01/05/42 renamed 2./K.Gr.z.b.V.323
5	(GS)/z.b.V.2 31/08/42 1 He 111 Z, 1 Me 321
7	(GS)/z.b.V.2 31/08/42 1 He 111 Z, 11 Me 321
Ausb.Kdo.323	27/05/42 in Dornstadt near Ulm for 6 months, formed in chain of command, Kommandeur Hptm. Mehring. Later moved to Stendal.
1./K.Gr.z.b.V.323	01/11/42 Transfer order from Leipheim via Eleusis (Athens) to Lecce and Naples, Missions: Crete, Palermo, Bizerta, Tunis, Castelvetrano, Trapani, Marsala, Sidi Ahmed, Sardinia
K.Gr.z.b.V.104	15/12/42 with four Staffeln from ?????? to Leipheim
2./K.G.z.b.V.323	27/12/42 from Leipheim to Naples
K.Gr.z.b.V.104	13/01/43 four Staffeln renamed II./K.Gr.z.b.V.323, missions: Wiener Neustadt, Belgrad-Semlin, Saloniki, Athens-Eleusis, Grotaglio, Pomigliano
GS-Kdo. 2 (Me 321)	30/01/43 moved from ??? to Bagerovo
II./K.G.z.b.V.323	08/02/43 1. and 2. Staffel from Leipheim to Istres
II./K.G.z.b.V.323	12/02/43 3. and 4. Staffel from Leipheim to Istres, missions by all Staffeln: Grosseto, Pomigliano, Capodichino, Pratica, Pisa, Schifara, Avignon, Ferrara, Lagnasco, Foggia, Viterbo, München-Riem, Leipheim
1. Erg.St.z.b.V.323	?? /03/43 formation in Leipheim
5./ Erg.Tr.G.	20/03/43 formation in Leipheim (from K.Gr.z.b.V.300)
	Staffel was probably formed at beginning of March 1943 as 1. Erg.St./z.b.V. in Leipheim.
III./K.G.z.b.V.323	20/03/43 from Münster to Leipheim, missions: Istres, Balkans
K.G.z.b.V.323	01.05.43 renamed TG 5
III./K.G.z.b.V.323	22.05.43 renamed III./TG 5
GS-Kdo. 1 u. 2	End May 43 from Obertraubling to Reims and Istres
II./TG 5	06/06/43 from Pomigliano to Rißtissen (equipped with Me 323)

Erg.Staffel Me 323	22/06/43 renamed 5./Erg.Tr.G. in Leipheim.
	(authorized strength 5 Me 323, Staffelführer Hptm. Brien until disbanded on 21/07/44)
3.F.B.K./TG 5	22/06/43 from Warsaw to Leipheim
Lehr- und	
Ausb.Kdo.323	22/06/43 from Ulm-Dornstadt to München-Oberwiesenfeld
II./TG 5	22/06/43 disbanded in Rißtissen
III./TG 5 with 3.F.B.K.	22/06/43 renamed II./TG 5 with 2.F.B.K. (Leipheim)
III./TG 5 ceased to exist, II./TG 5 for all purposes newly formed	
1./TG 5	09/07/43 from Leipheim to Mengen
I./TG 5	18/07/43 from Pomigliano to Pistoia near Florence, missions: Corsica, Sardinia
II./TG 5	30/08/43 from Mengen to Istres (France)
3./TG 5	? ./09/43 from Leipheim to Kirovograd
5./TG 5	? ./09/43 from Leipheim to Sagan (Lower Silesia)
II./TG 5	02/09/43 from Istres to Airasca near Turin
Lehr- und Ausb.Kdo.323	08/09/43 disbanded in Munich-Oberwiesenfeld. Lehrgruppe Verlastung established.
II./TG 5	10/10/43 from Lagnasco to Goslar
5./Erg.Transp.Gr.	13/10/43 from Leipheim to Liegnitz
5./Erg.Transp.Gr.	20/10/43 renamed 5./E.TG.
II./TG 5	04/11/43 from Goslar to Biala-Podlaska, missions: Litzmannstadt, Warsaw, Lvov, Kalinovka, Bobruisk, Baranovice, Breslau, Dresden, Schroda, Wiener- Neustadt, Belgrade-Semlin, Bacau, Bucharest, Vienna-Aspern, Kecskemét, Kraiova, Bucharest-Baneasa, Mamaia, Zilistea, Brünn, Prague-Gbell, Schroda, Dresden-Schöngarten, Calerasi, Braila, Galatz
I./TG 5	12/11/43 from Leipheim to Warsaw-Okecie (Poland), missions: Kovno, Riga, Plesta, Bobruisk, Zhitomir, Kiev, Vinnitsa, Uman, Kirovograd, Proskurov, Nikolayev
GS-Kdo. 1 u. 2	??/12/43 disbanded, remaining Me 321s scrapped
II./TG 5	01/04/44 from Biala-Podlaska to Schroda
TG 5	12/04/44 order for Stab, II./TG 5 and 7.E.TG. from ??????? to Zilistea
I./TG 5	??/??/44 from Warsaw-Okecie to Focsani (Romania), missions: Tirana, Odessa, Sevastopol, Mamaia
I./TG 5	??/??/44 from Focsani to Kecskemét (Hungary), missions: Focsani, Bucharest, Ploesti
TG 5	19/05/44 Stab from Zilistea to Kecskemét (Hungary)
II./TG 5	19/05/44 from Schroda to Tonndorf (Posen)
TG 5	21/05/44 Stab from Kecskemét to Nagy-Korös(Hungary)
TG 5	19/05/44 Stab from Nagy-Korös to Posen airbase
5./E.TG.	15/06/44 from Schroda to Tonndorf (Posen)
5./E.TG.	??/06/44 disbanded
Erg.Staffel 323	21/07/44 disbanded in Leipheim (under command of Hptm. Brien for its entire existence in Leipheim)
TG 5	04/08/44 Stab supposed to locate new command post near Chrudim, stopped 11/08/44
II./TG 5	05/08/44 from Tonndorf (Posen) to Chrudim (Protectorate), ended 10/08/44
TG 5	30/08/44 Stab, I. and II. Gruppe disbanded, transferred Me 323s to IV./TG.4
	Spring 1945 last Me 323 in Skutsch and Chrudim .

Known Military Post Numbers

L 27545	1939 to spring 1944: 1.F.B.K. / TG 5
L 30467	1939 to end of 1943: 2.F.B.K. / TG 5
L 31751	1939 to beginning of 1944: 3.F.B.K. / TG 5
L 35369	???? to beginning of 1944 (disbanded): K.Gr.z.b.V.104 - II./K.G.z.b.V.323 - II./TG 5
L 43683	???? to ????: I./K.G.z.b.V.323 - I./TG 5 - 16./IV./TG.4
L 44132	???? to ????: Stab K.Gr.z.b.V.900 - III./K.G.z.b.V.323 - III./TG 5 - 16./TG.4

Appendix 5

Me 323 *Gigant* Construction List

The following list is based on the assumption, which has often been proved to be correct, that *Werknummer* (WNr.) and *Stammkennzeichen* (Stkz.) were allocated in blocks. Information in the list which has been confirmed by documents such as war diaries, logbooks and other official materials, which was obtained from reliable correspondence, or which was derived from photographs will appear in bold type. The remaining information is believed to be correct but lacks supporting documentation. This list cannot, therefore, be considered complete or 100% accurate. As well, there are many *Werknummer*, *Stammkennzeichen*, unit codes (Vkz.) and tactical codes (T.Kz.) which have not yet been assigned or identified. The possibility of typing errors (including in original documents) can also not be excluded.

Sequence of information: **Werknummer**, **Stammkennzeichen**, **unit code**, **tactical code**, **Gruppe** (if known). The remarks which begin in the second line appear in standard face even though in most cases the information is derived from documents.

456   **W1+SZ**
Me 323 A V1, four-engines, converted from an Me 321, probably the same aircraft later designated Me 323 BV1 with six engines.

—   **W9+SA**
V 2, six engines, converted from an Me 321

801?   **DT+DK**
Renamed Me 323 V2 W9+SA?

802   **with II. Gruppe**
Converted from an Me 321, crash landing at Leipheim on 26/01/43, 60% damage.

802?   **DT+DL**
Me 323 V3, training at Leipheim, mentioned 20/01/43 Obfw. Eckstein and escort.

803?   **DT+DM**
Me 323 V4, 08/08/42 Lechfeld, testing, Oblt. Seidel, Oblt. Mies.

804?   **DT+DN**
Me 323 V5

805?   **DT+DO**
Me 323 V6

806?   **DT+DP**
Me 323 V7

807?   **DT+DQ**
Me 323 V8

808?   **DT+DR**
Me 323 V9

809?   **DT+DS**
Me 323 V10

810?   **DT+DT**
Me 323 V11, 18/07/42 flown by Hptm. Braun, *E-Stelle Rechlin* (testing) 20/07/42 by Dipl.-Ing. Beauvais, also Rechlin (handling trials).

811   **DT+DU**
V12, undercarriage tests in Leipheim on 26/09/42.

812?   **DT+DV**
Me 323 V13

813?   **DT+DW**
Me 323 V14, 4 x Jumo 211

—   **DT+QB**
01/10/42 ferried from Obertraubling to Leipheim.

1101 – 1126: Me 323 D-1

1101   RD+QA

Crashed in Leipheim as a result of incorrectly attached ailerons.

1102   RD+QB

Takeoff with 8 takeoff-assist rockets after forced landing, mentioned 10/02/43, also 17/02/43, 21/02/43 Tunis—Naples, engine transport.

1103   RD+QC C8+DR II. Gruppe

24/0/43 explosion during flight to Warsaw-Okecie, 90% damage, 7 killed, 5 injured.

1104   RD+QD II. Gruppe

01/04/43 failed takeoff in Vicenza, 70% damage, 2 injured. RD+QD was the fourth production aircraft (Me 323 D), acceptance flight on 18/09/42.

1105   RD+QE C8+CR II. Gruppe

01/03/43 15% damage, destroyed in Konotop on 16/03/43, 5 killed, 1 injured.

1106   RD+QF II. Gruppe

02/01/43 15% damage in forced landing during flight from Tunis to Pomigliano, second crash near Tula (Sardinia) on 12/09/43, 1 killed, 2 injured.

1107   RD+QG I. Gruppe

10/11/42 destroyed in strafing attack by No. 272 Squadron on Tunis-Aouina airfield, first Me 323 lost in Africa.

1108   RD+QH I. Gruppe

19/12/42 written off after flying into hill near Rimini, 9 killed.

1109   RD+QI

Me 323 D-2

1110   RD+QJ I. Gruppe

23/11/42 80% damaged in bombing raid on Bizerta airfield.

1111   RD+QK I. Gruppe

11/01/43 shot down by fighters of the 14th F.G. off the coast of North Africa, crew of 9 and 16 passengers killed, pilot Lt. Krüger.

1112   RD+QL II. Gruppe

30/09/43 blown up by German troops near Poretto, Corsica.

1113   RD+QM

22/02/43 and 25/02/43 flights Tunis—Naples, engine transport.

1114   RD+QN C8+ER II. Gruppe

22/04/43 shot down by P-40 Kittyhawk of the SAAF near Cape Bon, 4 killed, 5 injured. Code C8+ER was subsequently reassigned.

1115   RD+QO C8+AR II. Gruppe

22/04/43 shot down by P-40 Kittyhawks of the SAAF near Cape Bon, 6 killed, 4 injured. Obstlt. Wilhelm Stephan, *Kommandeur* of II./KG.z.b.V. 323, was killed in this aircraft.

1116   RD+QP II. Gruppe

13/04/43 60% damage in bombing raid on Castelvetrano, Sicily.

1117   RD+QQ

24/03/43 ferried Leipheim—Brandis—Warsaw, pilot Obfw. Walter Lutz.

1118   RD+QR I. Gruppe

06/05/43 exploded in midair east of Ancona, 15 killed.

1119   RD+QS I. Gruppe

14/04/43 damaged 35% in fighter attack near Tunis, 1 killed, 2 injured.

1120   RD+QT

1121   RD+QU I. Gruppe

16/04/44 so-called "Workshop-Me' sustained 5% damage from bomb splinters in attack on Belgrade-Semlin, 18/07/44 forced landing near Alba Julia, Romania, abandoned by crew.

1122   RD+QV II. Gruppe

23/09/43 destroyed in bombing raid on Pisa.

1123   RD+QW II. Gruppe

mentioned on 16/01/43 as training aircraft at Leipheim, 50% damaged while landing at Tunis on 07/04/43.

1124   RD+QX

19/01/42 mentioned in training flight by Oblt. Seidel (instructor) / Eckstein (conversion trainee) in Leipheim.

1125   RD+QY C8+BC II. Gruppe

04/04/43 70% damage in heavy landing at Vicenza, 3 killed, 8 injured.

1126   RD+QZ I. Gruppe

22/04/43 shot down by P-40 Kittyhawks of the SAAF near Cape Bon, 9 killed.

1127 – 1152: Me 323 D-1 and D-6

1127   RF+XA C8+BF X1A I. Gruppe

26/10/43 Göttingen, pilot Ofw. Martin.

1128   RF+XB I. Gruppe

20/05/43 shot down by fighters of the 325th F.G. near Villacidro, Sardinia, 1 killed, 4 wounded.

1129   RF+XC C8+JE X1S I. Gruppe

16/07/43 35% damage in bombing raid on Pomigliano.

1130   RF+XD I. Gruppe

30/03/43 Me 323 D-6, crash-landing at Castelvetrano, 75% damage, 8 injured.

1131   RF+XE I. Gruppe

26/03/43 crashed on takeoff from Tunis-Aouina, 3 killed, 7 injured.

1132   RF+XF I. Gruppe

13/04/43 crashed in Tunis as a result of engine failure, 75% damage.

1133   RF+XG II. Gruppe

From 17/04/43 in Rechlin, pilot Müller. From 12/05/43 undercarriage tests by Fl.St.Ing. Hirschberg. On 31/07/43 crashed at Pontedera due to poor visibility, 30% damage.

1134   RF+XH I. Gruppe

22/04/43 shot down by P-40 Kittyhawks of the SAAF near Cape Bon, 15 killed.

1135   RF+XI I. Gruppe

Me 323 D-6, 22/04/43 shot down by P-40 Kittyhawks of the SAAF near Cape Bon, 7 killed, 2 injured.

1136   RF+XJ C8+NF I. Gruppe

Mentioned in Allied report.

1137   RF+XK I. Gruppe

30/05/43 destroyed in bombing raid on Pomigliano.

1138   RF+XL

Obertraubling

1139   RF+XM

Me 323 D-6, Obertraubling

1140   RF+XN II. Gruppe

17/08/43 70% damage in bombing raid on Istres.

1141   RF+XO

1142   RF+XP C8+AB X1C I. Gruppe

From 24/06/43 to 06/07/43 ferried from Leipheim to Pomigliano fir I./TG 5, pilot Fw. Karl Blanke. 21/07/43 50% damage in landing crash at Pistoia.

1143   RF+XQ II. Gruppe

17/08/43 destroyed in bombing raid on Istres.

1144   RF+XR II. Gruppe

29/07/43 40% damage in bombing raid on Pratica di Mare.

1145   RF+XS II. Gruppe

12/07/43 40% damage in crash-landing at Dijon, possibly Longvic, France.

1146   RF+XT

1147   RF+XU

10/09/43 flight from Airasca to Piacenza, pilot Obfw. Lutz.

1148   RF+XV II. Gruppe

24/12/43 to 04/01/44 Warsaw—Breslau—Dresden, pilot Fw. Blanke.

1149   RF+XW

03/09/43 in Rechlin, from 15/11/43 various trials, 16/02/44 Rechlin, pilot Fl.St.Ing. Böttcher.

1150   RF+XX Y1O II. Gruppe

Found by Allies in Venafiorita after cessation of hostilities, partly cannibalized.

WNr. 1151 to 1200 apparently not assigned.

(1201 – 1226: Me 323 D-1 and D-6)

1201   DT+IA I. Gruppe

Me 323 D-1, 09/09/42 from Obertraubling to Leipheim, 05/01/43 45% damage in collision at Trapani.

1202   DT+IB

28/10/42 ferried from Obertraubling to Leipheim.

1203   DT+IC I. Gruppe

02/10/42 from Obertraubling to Leipheim, on 22/11/42 60% damage in landing accident at Piacenza.

1204   DT+ID I. Gruppe

From 01/10/42 to 11/10/42 familiarization and conversion flights by Oblt. Edmund Auer and others at Leipheim. 20/11/42 ferried from Obertraubling to Leipheim. 02/12/42 crashed into Adriatic southwest of Termoli after engine failure, 3 killed.

1205   DT+IE I. Gruppe

Me 323 D-1, 10/03/43 destroyed in bombing raid on Tunis.

1206   DT+IF L5+BN 5. Staffel/E.T.G.

30/10/42 flown from Obertraubling to Leipheim with name "Hein". Mentioned in Pomigliano on 31/03/44, Obfw. Martin, Prüfmeister Ebner.

1207   DT+IG I. Gruppe

Me 323 of the Stabsstaffel with name "Peterle", pilot Oblt. Ernst Peter, 17/10/43 crashed near Radinow, 35% damage.

1208   DT+IH I. Gruppe
01/03/43 crashed near Trapani, 95% damage, 12 killed, 3 injured.

1209   DT+II C8+AF X1H I. Gruppe
14/06/44 destroyed in strafing attack by P-38 Lightnings of the 82nd F.G., Hungary. A C8+AF was also mentioned in the war diary on 17/03/44: developed engine trouble and made a forced landing 10 km south of Stryj (Ukraine) and on 28/03/44 was blown up "because of nearness of the enemy". Unless there was a typographical error, the unit code was reassigned after the loss of the first aircraft.

1210   DT+IJ C8+GR II. Gruppe
17/08/44 crashed due to engine failure during flight from Insterburg to Riga, 60% damage.

1211   DT+IK I. Gruppe
15/01/43 shot down by fighters of the 14th F.G. off the coast of Tunisia, 12 killed.

1212   DT+IL II. Gruppe
From 23/09/42 to 28/09/42 conversion aircraft for solo flights by Oblt. Edmund Auer and Oblt. Seidel in Leipheim. 13/04/43 60% damage in failed takeoff at Tunis.

1213   DT+IM I. Gruppe
05/01/43 50% damage in collision with landing Me 323 at Trapani, 1 injured. 01/02/43 damaged in bombing raid on Pomigliano, 08/08/43 65% damage at Pisa, cause not known.

1214   DT+IN I. Gruppe
10/02/43 failed to reach coast for forced landing during flight from Tunis to Naples, 4 killed, 3 injured, aircraft written off.

1215   DT+IO I. Gruppe
16/03/43 mentioned in flight from Tunis to Naples, 05/04/43 45% damage in bombing raid on Tunis.

1216   DT+IP II. Gruppe
30/09/43 shot down by fighter during flight from Tunis to Naples.

1217   DT+IQ

1218   DT+IR I. Gruppe
05/01/43 collision with another Me 323 in Trapani, 45% damage.

1219   DT+IS C8+MB Y1J I. Gruppe

1220   DT+IT II. Gruppe
1942 in Leipheim with name "Himmelslaus", 15/02/43 15% damage in landing at Lvov.

1221   DT+IU II. Gruppe
13/04/43 destroyed in bombing raid on Castelvetrano.

1222   DT+IV C8+BF X1K I. Gruppe
22/03/43 lost engine on takeoff, burned out after crash, 3 killed.

1223   DT+IW II. Gruppe
25/04/43 accident while refueling at Castelvetrano, 2 injured, aircraft written off.

1224   DT+IX C8+EP II. Gruppe
22/04/43 shot down by P-40 Kittyhawks of the SAAF near Cape Bon, 9 killed. A C8+EP is also mentioned in the war diary on 08/03/44: blown up in Uman-Przcekumir "because of nearness of enemy". The aircraft code was apparently reassigned after the loss of the original aircraft.

1225   DT+IY C8+CP II. Gruppe
22/04/43 shot down by P-40 Kittyhawks of the SAAF near Cape Bon, 9 killed. A C8+CP is also mentioned in Lutz's logbook from 28 to 30/09/43 and in the war diary on 27/03/44: crashed while landing at Lvov, 2 killed. Another example of the unit code being reassigned.

1226   DT+IZ C8+DP II. Gruppe
22/04/43 shot down by P-40 Kittyhawks of the SAAF near Cape Bon, 9 killed, 1 injured.

(1227 – 1252: Me 323 D-2 with wooden fixed-pitch Heine two-blade propellers)

1227   SG+RA C8+AG Y1M I. Gruppe
18/06/43 shot down by anti-aircraft fire, 1 wounded (combat report by Oblt. Schalkhauser).

1228   SG+RB C8+AP Y1H II. Gruppe
02/02/43 Obertraubling to Warsaw, 16/07/43 35% in bombing raid on Pomigliano, 28/09/43 forced landing near Mantua due to engine failure and bad weather. Y1H found burnt-out at Pomigliano when Allied forces arrived. Code C8+AP reassigned, aircraft in Goslar on 11/10/43, pilot Uffz. Rößmann.

1229   SG+RC C8+NB Y1B I. Gruppe
16/07/43 35% damage in bombing raid on Pomigliano.

1230   SG+RD

1231   SG+RE I. Gruppe
10/03/43 destroyed in bombing raid on Tunis.

1232   SG+RF II. Gruppe
13/04/43 destroyed in bombing raid on Tunis.

1233   SG+RG C8+AC II. Gruppe
13/04/43 60% damage in bombing raid on Castelvetrano.

1234   **SG+RH I. Gruppe**
20/03/43 shot down by fighters of the 325th F.G. near Villacidro, Sardinia.

1235   **SG+RI C8+GP II. Gruppe**
Me 323 D-2 with two-blade propellers, 13/04/43 40% damage in bombing raid on Castelvetrano. Following repairs the aircraft went to I./TG 5. 22/05/43 40% damage in another bombing raid on Castelvetrano, Allied forces later found aircraft cannibalized.

1236   **SG+RJ**
21/04/43 10% damage in landing at Leipheim (training aircraft with K.Gr.z.b.V. 300 at Schönwalde), later assigned to Ergänzungs-Transport-Geschwader (E.T.G.). 80% damage in takeoff accident on 18/08/43, probably while serving as training aircraft for Me 323 crews.

1237   **SG+RK I. Gruppe**
22/05/43 destroyed in bombing raid on Trapani.

1238   **SG+RL I. Gruppe**
30/05/43 destroyed in bombing raid on Pomigliano.

1239   **SG+RM C8+AC II. Gruppe**
Me 323 D-2 with two-blade propellers. 22/04/43 shot down by P-40 Kittyhawks of the SAAF near Cape Bon, 10 killed. According to the logbook of pilot Obfw. Lutz, beginning on 01/06/44 he flew a Ju 52 with the unit code C8+AC on flights from Tonndorf to Posen.

1240   **SG+RN I. Gruppe**
20/05/43 shot down by fighters of the 325th F.G. near Villacidro, Sardinia, 3 killed, 2 injured.

1241   **SG+RO**

1242   **SG+RP I. Gruppe**
22/04/43 shot down by P-40 Kittyhawks of the SAAF near Cape Bon, 8 killed, 1 wounded.

1243   **SG+RQ**
21/05/43 local flight at Leipheim, Rößmann logbook.

1244   **SG+RR**

1245   **SG+RS C8+DN II. Gruppe**
22/04/43 shot down by P-40 Kittyhawks of the SAAF near Cape Bon, 9 killed.

1246   **SG+RT**
27/03/43 to 29/03/43 familiarization Fl.St.Ing. Walter Baist of E3 by Fl.St.Ing. Bader E2 in Rechlin. 03/04/43 calibration flight, 13/05/43 undercarriage failure.

1247   **SG+RU I. Gruppe**
April 1943, Tunisia, 15% damaged. 10/5/43, Tropani, destroyed in bombing raid.

1248   **SG+RV I. Gruppe**
Me 323 D-2, 22/04/43 shot down by P-40 Kittyhawks of the SAAF near Cape Bon, 8 killed, 1 wounded.

1249   **SG+RW C8+OE X1P I. Gruppe**
18/07/43 60% damage in landing at Pistoia.

1250   **SG+RX**
10/05/43 familiarization Leipheim, Rößmann logbook.

1251   **SG+RY 5. Staffel**
29/03/43 crash-landing at Leipheim, aircraft destroyed in explosion, 2 injured.

1252   **SG+RZ C8+SE X1E I. Gruppe**
07/03/43 flight from Tunis to Naples.

(1253 – 1278: Me 323 E-1 and E-2)

1253   **VM+IA I. Gruppe**
22/04/43 shot down by P-40 Kittyhawks of the SAAF near Cape Bon, 6 killed, 3 injured.

1254   **VM+IB C8+CC II. Gruppe**
22/04/43 shot down by P-40 Kittyhawks of the SAAF near Cape Bon.

1255   **VM+IC C8+LF X1Q I. Gruppe**

1256   **VM+ID C8+CG Y1A I. Gruppe**
17/07/43 destroyed in bombing raid on Pomigliano.

1257   **VM+IE C8+ME X1Y I. Gruppe**

1258   **VM+IF III. Gruppe**
90% damage in landing crash at Obertraubling, 1 killed, 2 injured. Among the injured was Maj. Markus Zeidler. The aircraft was probably being used by the Replacement Training Gruppe of KG.z.b.V. 323 for training.

1259   **VM+IG I. Gruppe**
22/05/43 shot down by Allied fighters over the Mediterranean, 5 killed, 4 injured.

1260   **VM+IH C8+FN II. Gruppe**
07/05/43 blown up by retreating German troops in Tunis, aircraft name "Mücke".

1261 VM+II I. Gruppe
30/05/43 destroyed in bombing raid on Pomigliano.

1262 VM+IJ C8+LB X1L I. Gruppe
05/08/43 45% damage while taxiing on Venofiorita airfield, later found there by Allied forces, partially burnt out.

1263 VM+IK
Visible in photograph: vertical tail without horn balance, probably for flutter tests.

1264 VM+IL C8+QE X1 I. Gruppe
16/07/43 35% damage in bombing raid on Pomigliano.

1265 VM+IM
03/05/43 Regensburg-Göttingen.

1266 VM+IN II. Gruppe
01/08/43 destroyed in bombing raid on Capodichino.

1267 VM+IO C8+DG X1N I. Gruppe
26/07/43 shot down by fighters east of Cape Rera, 3 killed, 6 wounded.

1268 VM+IP C8+TE X1F I. Gruppe
05/09/43 65% damage in bombing raid on Grosseto.

1269 VM+IQ C8+CB X1G I. Gruppe
23/02/44 Me 323 E-2, lost engine, collided with obstacle, 50% damage (Golta).

1270 VM+IR C8+EG X1O I. Gruppe
26/07/43 shot down by fighters near Garibaldi, 5 killed, 4 wounded.

1271 VM+IS C8+AF X1B I. Gruppe
21/07/43 70% damaged in bombing raid on Grosseto.

1272 VM+IT
31/12/43 to 04/03/44 at E-Stelle Tarnewitz. Designated V15, tested as Waffenträger.

1273 VM+IU II. Gruppe
17/07/43 25% damage in bombing raid on Istres.

1274 VM+IV II. Gruppe
30/07/43 80% damage in fighter attack near Barcaggio, Corsica, 4 wounded, pilot Obfw. Walter Honig.

1275 VM+IW II. Gruppe
17/07/43 60% damage in bombing raid on Pomigliano, found there by Allies forces burnt out after end of hostilities.

1276 VM+IX

1277 VM+IY
16/07/43 Me 323 E-1, acceptance flight at Obertraubling by Anton Riediger (his only flight in the Me 323).

1278 VM+IZ II. Gruppe
21/07/43 destroyed in bombing raid on Grosseto.

(1279 – 1299: Me 323 E-2)

1279 SL+HA
Found by Allied forces on Castelvetrano airfield, burnt-out.

1280 SL+HB
29/08/43 Avignon to Pisa, pilot Obfw. Lutz.

1281 SL+HC

1282 SL+HD
09/03/44 Obfw. Friedrich, entry in logbook of Prüfmeister Ebner (Eger) and postcard motif.

1283 SL+HE

1284 SL+HF II. Gruppe
10 to 15/07/43 transport flights Leipheim—Dijon—Istres—Grosseto—Pomigliano—Istres—Grosseto, pilot Fw. Blanke.

1285 SL+HG II. Gruppe
30/09/43 shot down by fighters during flight from Corsica to Elba, 3 killed.

1286 SL+HH II. Gruppe
23/09/43 55% damage in bombing raid on Pisa.

1287 SL+HI II. Gruppe
23/09/43 destroyed in bombing raid on Pisa.

1288 SL+HJ II. Gruppe
23/09/43 damaged in bombing raid on Pisa.

1289 SL+HK

1290 SL+HL

1291 SL+HM
Destroyed at Trapani, found by Allies.

1292 SL+HN
In photo (Dessau)

1293 SL+HO C8+BE I. Gruppe
15/04/44 85% damage in crash at Belgrade.

1294 **SL+HP**

01/10/43 Lvov—Königsberg, air ambulance flight, pilot Obfw. Epke.

1295 **SL+HQ C8+DF X1M I. Gruppe**

28/02/44 forced landing near Kunki, 14 km west of Tomaszow, cannibalized on 31/03/44, probably blown up.

1296 **SL+HR**

1297 **SL+HS**

1298 **SL+HT**

Waffenträger, forward half of code illegible in photo.

130015? **BM+GA**

Recorded in Allied list.

130016 **C8+DS II. Gruppe**

16/04/44 20% splinter damage as a result of bombing raid on Belgrade-Semlin. In the war diary this Werknummer also appears as C8+EG (I. Gruppe), destroyed in the attack on Kecskemét on 16/06/44.

130019? **BM+GE**

Recorded in Allied list.

130023 **C8+EC II. Gruppe**

15/08/44 virtually destroyed (98%) when shot down by Soviet fighters during flight from Riga to Insterburg.

130026 **5./E.T.G.**

Me 323 E-1, pilot Obfw. Fränken, crashed on takeoff at Kecskemét, date and degree of damage not known.

130027 **BM+GM**

V18 25/03/44 to 19/05/44 braking chute tests with 6.5-tonne body at Rechlin and Lärz, pilots Fl.St.Ing. Eisermann and Fl.St.Ing. Hirschberg. 21/05/44 destroyed by enemy action at Lärz.

130028? **BM+GN**

Appears in Allied records.

130030 **C8+HF X1X I. Gruppe**

16/04/44 90% damage in bombing raid on Belgrade-Semlin.

130031 **C8+GP II. Gruppe**

Forced landing 50 km southwest of Uman recorded in war diary on 07/03/44, aircraft blown up on 08/03/44. Aircraft with same unit code destroyed in bombing raid on Wiener Neustadt on 12/04/44.

130033? **BM+GS**

Appears in Allied records.

130036? **BM+GV**

Appears in Allied records.

130037 **C8+CE X1F I. Gruppe**

Me 323 of the corps reserve, 14/06/44 destroyed by American fighters in strafing attack on Kecskemét airfield.

130038 **I. Gruppe**

09/05/44 in Balomir, Romania, 85% damage, reason not known.

130039? **BM+GY**

Appears in Allied records.

130041 **C8+HE X2D I. Gruppe**

14/06/44 destroyed in bombing raid on Kecskemét. Photo exists.

130042 **C8+HP II. Gruppe**

First appears in the war dairy with the unit code C8+ER, on 05/04/44 flight Bacau—Tiraspol—Belgrade. As C8+HP on 16/04/44 40% damage in bombing raid on Belgrade-Semlin.

130043 **C8+CG I. Gruppe**

09/04/44 failed takeoff at Leipzig, Romania, aircraft written off, 1 killed.

130045 **C8+ER II. Gruppe**

16/04/44 75% damage in bombing raid on Belgrade-Semlin.

130053 **C8+AE X1N I. Gruppe**

17/04/44 20% damage in bombing raid on Belgrade-Semlin, on 26/07/43 shot down near Cape Rera. In the Mies logbook there also appears a C8+AE with the tactical code X1D, flight from Warsaw to Uman on 11/01/44, pilots Lt. Balasus, Oblt. Mies.

130055 **C8+DE I. Gruppe**

According to war diary crashed on takeoff at Warsaw on 27/03/44. Subsequent entry, destroyed in air attack on Kecskemét on 14/06/44.

160001 **DU+QZ**

In the book "Safety and Rescue in Aviation" (p. 110-111) this Werknummer and Stammkennzeichen are attributed to the Me 323 V16 (Prototype F1). The aircraft was involved in braking parachute tests for the Do 335 program at the E-Stelle Rechlin. It was destroyed in a crash on its first flight as test-bed on 30/09/44 at Heuberg airfield.

330001 **C8+EE X1J I. Gruppe**

20/03/44 forced landing at Ottynie, Poland, 85% damage, blown up on 31/03/44.

330004 **C8+GC II. Gruppe**
03/08/44 Waffenträger, crashed during transfer flight, 25 killed.

330009 **C8+AP X1H II. Gruppe**
24/03/44 forced landing 5 km southwest Stanislau, blown up on 29/03/44.

330010
Braking parachute test report dated 09/06/44 (assigned to the Do 335 program by XIV. Fliegerkorps).

— **C8+AB I. Gruppe**
Appears in Allied records.

— **C8+AC II. Gruppe**
Ju 52 01/06/44 Tonndorf/Posen, pilot Ofw. Lutz.

— **C8+AN II. Gruppe**
07/04/43 to 11/04/43 flight from Naples to Obertraubling, 15/04/43 Tunis to Naples.

— **C8+AS II. Gruppe**

— **C8+BB I. Gruppe**
13/03/44 blown up at Vinnitsa.

— **C8+BN II. Gruppe**
04/04/43 flight from Tunis to Naples. 22/04/43 aborted takeoff at Pomigliano following loss of engine and blown tire, thus escaped the massacre off Cape Bon on that day, pilot Obfw. Karl Kandzia.

— **C8+BP II. Gruppe**
19/04/43 flight from Tunis to Naples.

— **C8+BR II. Gruppe**
20/03/43 flight from Tunis to Naples.

— **C8+BS II. Gruppe**
17/07/43 flight from Istres to Grosseto, pilot Fw. Karl Blanke. Blanke's last flight end of August 1944 to Skutsch, reassigned after delivery of aircraft.

— **C8+CC II. Gruppe**

— **C8+CF I. Gruppe**
Appears in Allied records.

— **C8+CP II. Gruppe**
01/05/43 to 16/05/43 missions to Naples, Trapani, Villacidro, Venafiorita.

— **C8+CS II. Gruppe**
31/03/44 flight from Biala to Schroda, pilot Fw. Blanke.

— **C8+C? X1R I. Gruppe**
16/03/43 flight from Tunis to Naples, engine transport.

— **C8+DB I. Gruppe**
Ju 52, 14/06/44 destroyed in air attack on Kecskemét.

— **C8+DC II. Gruppe**
07/04/43 flight from Tunis to Naples, engine transport.

— **C8+EF I. Gruppe**

— **C8+EN II. Gruppe**
02/04/43 to 12/05/43 transport flights in the Mediterranean, pilot Walter Honig.

— **C8+ET**
29/08/43 flight from Pisa to Metato, pilot Obfw. Lutz.

— **C8+FC II. Gruppe**
26/09/43 Lagnasco, pilot Obfw. Lutz.

— **C8+FE X1P I. Gruppe**
31/03/44 blown up at Ottynie.

— **C8+FF I. Gruppe**
20/03/43 flight from Tunis to Naples.

— **C8+FG I. Gruppe**
28/11/43 flight from Biala-Podlaska, pilot Obfw. Lutz.

— **C8+FR II. Gruppe**
04/04/43 flight Tunis to Naples.

— **C8+GE X1V I. Gruppe**
17/03/44 crashed at Odessa III with 70 soldiers on board, 63 killed (sabotage).

— **C8+GF I. Gruppe**

— **C8+GN II. Gruppe**
27/03/43 flight from Warsaw to the Mediterranean, pilot Obfw. Lutz.

— **C8+GS II. Gruppe**
08/03/44 blown up at Uman-Przcekumir.

— **C8+IF I. Gruppe**

— **C8+JE I. Gruppe**

— **C8+KB I. Gruppe**

— **C8+LF I. Gruppe**

— **C8+RP II. Gruppe**

— **C8+SE I. Gruppe**

— **C8+TB I. Gruppe**

— **C8+TP II. Gruppe**

Appears in Allied records.

— **X1D I. Gruppe**

19/03/43 flight Tunis to Naples.

— **X1K I. Gruppe**

18/03/43 flight Tunis to Naples.

— **X1T I. Gruppe**

29/03/43 flight Tunis to Naples.

— **X1U I. Gruppe**

13/03/43 and 19/04/43 flights Tunis to Naples, engine transport, crash (date not known).

— **X1Y I. Gruppe**

08/03/43 flight Tunis to Naples.

— **X1Z I. Gruppe**

10/03/43 flight Tunis to Naples.

— **Y1G II. Gruppe**

03/05/43 to 04/04/43 and 15/05 to 17/05/43 Pomigliano, etc., pilot Obfw. Lutz.

— **Y1N II. Gruppe**

??/05/43 attacked by fighter near Sardinia, forced landing.

— **L5+GN 5./E.T.G.**

15/05/44 at Kecskemét, collided with chimney on takeoff, crashed and burned, 6 killed, 3 injured.

— **DU+PD**

— **DU+PK II. Gruppe**

— **DU+PP**

Waffenträger (destroyed, code not confirmed).

— **RD+UE**

09/10/42 test flight Rechlin, pilots Fl.St.Ing. Braun, Dipl.-Ing. Goedicke.

— **RL+UE**

Waffenträger 29/03/44 at Rechlin for tests, pilot Fl.St.Ing. Böttcher, later Warsaw-Okecie.

— **RL+UJ**

Photo

— **??+??**

Waffenträger, parked next to last hangar on south side of Finsterwalde airfield to bolster airfield defenses.

— **SN+HL**

29/03/43 air ambulance flight Nikolayev to Lvov, pilot Fw. Kleinemeyer.

— **G6+FQ IV./TG 4**

Seen in photo, Chrudim 1944.

— **G6+LQ IV./TG 4**

Seen in photo, Skutsch 1945.

— **G6+NQ IV./TG 4**

Seen in photo, tactical code overpainted, Skutsch 1945.

Sources

Documents

Summary of Gnôme-Rhône 14 N variants, Dessau, 05/11/40

Description of the "Bloch" and "LeO" power plants, Me 323 D-1, D-2, D-6 handbooks

Curt Zeiler application to Messerschmitt AG, 28/02/40

Curt Zeiler employment contract with Messerschmitt AG, 05/04/40

Sketch Me 321w, 01/11/40

Sketch Me 323 and Me 321 series vertical tail, 24/03/42

Center of gravity chart for loading the Me 321 dated 24/03/41

Center of gravity check during loading of the Me 321 dated 18/07/41

He 111 Zwilling drawings complete, Heinkel correspondence dated 20/08/41

Report on towing trials with the He 111 H-6, 02/10/41

Flight test with two He 111s, 02/10/41

Instruction on maintaining secrecy "Gigant", 06/10/41

C-Amt Program, delivery plan, 01/12/41

He 111 Z Heinkel conference minutes dated 05/11/41

Me 323 b V1 rough field trials, test report dated 03/12/41

Heinkel works manager, report on He 111 Z prototype, repair of tailwheel, 11/01/42

Heinkel report, He 111 Z performance figures, 18/01/42

Telex He 111 Z production plan, 02/03/42

Telex He 111 Z 2 design team, 13/04/42

Sketch Me 323 horizontal tail with internally-balanced elevator, 25/04/42

Sketch Me 323 horizontal tail with internally-balanced elevator and internally-balanced trim tab, 23/07/42

Sketch Me 321 with Argus pulse-jets, 22/05/42

Trip report by TED Office, Rechlin, He 111 Z V1 dated 29/05/42

Telex Heinkel Berlin Office, deadline for completion of ten He 111 Z contracted for, 23/06/42

Memo Heinkel He 111 Z, conference of 07/07/42

Messerschmitt minutes Me 323 general questions, Augsburg, 11/07/42

Drawing He 111 Z – Me 321 towing harness, 08/10/42

Conference of department heads held 30/10/42 Test Stations Command, Rechlin, 20/11/42

Telex, production delays He 111 Z, 21/11/42

Mission orders DT+IG dated 22/11/42

Sketch Mistel Me 321 – Bf 110, 28/10/42

Program overview Me 321, undated

Program overview Me 323, undated

Messerschmitt letter to GL/C concerning Me 323 delivery program, 05/12/42

Me 323 operational experience report, military post number L 43683, 18/12/42

Messerschmitt AG, departure of secretary Erna Nied, 22/12/42

Me 323 development stages, table, undated

War diary KG.z.b.V. 323

GL/C aircraft program, delivery plan dated 11/01/43

Milch Special Headquarters: status of acquisition of transport aircraft, 13/01/43

Milch Special Headquarters: Aircraft for Airlift to the 6th Army, 13/01/43

Milch Special Headquarters: Overview of the transport gliders and towplanes likely to be available, 16/01/43

GL/C aircraft program, delivery plan dated 28/01/43

Milch Special Headquarters: Delivery Status for Replacement Transports on 31/01/43, dated 18/02/43

Transportfliegergeschwader 5: transport statistics for month of March 1943

Industry delivery plan dated 10/03/43

Messerschmitt AG, Me 323 delivery plan dated 12/04/43

Special Committee F 2: Program Proposal for Continuation of Me 323, 12/03/43

Special Committee F 2: Aircraft Program dated 15/04/43

Milch Special Headquarters: Consideration of One-Time Use of Me 323s, 20/04/43

Order for the reorganization of air transport units, Berlin, 21/04/43

K.Gr.z.b.V. 106 detachment leader, report on daylight mission 22/04/43

Combat report I./KG.z.b.V. 323, command post, 23/04/43

Telex from *Luftwaffe* Operations Staff/Ic/LA dated 23/04/43: Combat Report on Ju and *Gigant* Formation on 22/04/43

K.Gr.z.b.V. "N" *Geschwader* Order No. 20/43, command post 05/05/43

Völkischer Beobachter of 14 May 1943: The Heroic Conclusion of the Courageous Struggle in Tunis

Oberleutnant Peter, Stabsstaffel I./TG 5, combat report dated 20/05/43

Obgefr. Georg Dennerlein, Stabsstaffel I./TG 5, combat report dated 20/05/43

Obgefr. Walter Krüger, Stabsstaffel I./TG 5, combat report dated 20/05/43

Development Me 321/Me 323 Leipheim, 21/05/43 signed Fröhlich

Uffz. Hermann Schladerbusch, qualification certificate as loadmaster for large-capacity aircraft, Munich, 01/06/43

Headquarters Ninth U.S. Air Force A-2 Section: German Me 323 Aircraft, examined at El Aouina, Tunis, June 5, 1943

Special Committee F 2: Aircraft Program dated 15/06/43

Oblt. Schalkhauser, 2./TG 5, report on significant events on 18/06/43

War diary Lg. VII, p. 154 and 165, 21 and 22 June and 9 July 1943.

Messerschmitt aircraft data Me 321, Augsburg, 01/07/43

Messerschmitt aircraft data Me 323 D, Augsburg 01/07/43

Transport Officer Venafiorita: Report on Shooting Down of Me 323s X1O and X1N on 26/07/43

GL/C Aircraft Program dated 15/08/43

E-Stelle Rechlin: monthly report July 1943

He 111 Z DG+DZ flight safety advisory dated 07/08/43

Special Committee F 34: Me 323 Program Change dated 17/08/43

Disbandment of the Lehr- u. Ausb.Kdo. 323, order dated 30/08/43

E-Stelle Rechlin: monthly report September 1943

Luftschiffbau Zeppelin: monthly report August 1943 dated 03/09/43

Special Committee F 34: Me 323 Program Change dated 03/09/43

Special Committee F 34: Jumo 211 power plants for Me 323 F, dated 01/10/43

GL/C Aircraft Program, delivery plan dated 01/10/43

Performance figures Z Me 323 G, LZ, 20/10/43

Special Committee F 34: Modification of Aircraft Delivery Plan 224/1, letter dated 24/11/43

GL/C Aircraft Program, delivery plan dated 01/12/43

Allied Crash Report No. 1354 dated 04/12/43

LZ Flugzeugbau: Weight Distribution Z Me 323 G, 18/12/43

Transportfliegerführer 1, release of *TG 5* from his area of command, H.Q., 11/10/43

German Aviation Research: DFS (Stamer) Towing Method, 20/10/43

Der Adler, 9 November 1943: *"Der Gigant"*, first publication in a German periodical

E-Stelle Rechlin: monthly report November 1943

E-Stelle Rechlin: monthly report December 1943

Flight order Me 323 C8+GR of 01/01/44

Telegram, Order for Reorganization, to TFF 2 / TG 5 Biala-Podlaska, 20/01/44

Telegram to Gen.Kdo. XIV. Fl.Korps, transfer report *Geschwaderstab* Warsaw-Okecie 19/01/44

Telegram from TG 5 to TM 9, disbandment of G.T.F. office in Warsaw-Okecie, 23/01/44

Aircraft Delivery Forecast GL/C-B-2 dated 27/01/44

Aircraft order Me 323 C8+KR dated 31/01/44

Aircraft Delivery Forecast GL/C-B-2 dated 07/02/44

Director Special Committee F 34: Delivery Plan 225/1 concerning Me 323 with Gnôme-Rhône 14 R

Lt. Von Rettberg 2./TG 5, report on forced landing by Me 323 C8+DF on 28/02/44

Program Rationalization through Deletion of Aircraft Types, 10/03/44

Aircraft order Me 323 DU+PK dated 23/03/44

TG 5 operations staff, transport statistics for the month of June 1944

Hptm. Ehrlich 6./TG 5, combat report Me 323 C8+HP, dated 07/04/44

Combat report by Hptm. Ehrlich, Me 323 C8+HP, dated 07/04/44

Lt. Balasus, ATC Semlin, report on transport unit losses in attack on Semlin on 16 and 17/04/44

Special Committee: Aircraft Program GL/C-Pr I dated 15/05/44

TG 5 Operations Staff transfer order dated 19/05/44

Test Report Braking Chute Test for Do 335 with 6.5-tonne Body and Me 323 Test-Bed dated 09/06/44

Special Committee F 34: Aircraft Program Luftschiffbau Zeppelin dated 15/07/44

Telegram to TG 5, transfer of II./TG 5 to Tonndorf, 06/08/44

Gruppenkommandeur I./TG 5, Major Günther Mauß, letter and commemorative print to Prof. Messerschmitt dated 20/06/44

Obfw. Rudolf Pötschke, 5./TG 5, combat report Me 323 C8+EC dated 15/08/44

Mediterranean Allied Photo Reconnaissance Wing: Skutec landing ground, 26/09/44

Luftschiffbau Zeppelin: ZSO 523 large transport, project description dated 30/09/44

War diary KG.z.b.V. "N" (Naples) 13/12/41 to 21/05/43

War diary KG.z.b.V. 323

War diary TG 5 16/10/43 to 10/08/44

Equipment Reports Air Transport Units 31/05/42 to 31/12/44

Uffz. Spitzer: *1. Staffel in Action with the Me 323, Experiences until the Transfer from the Mediterranean Theater to Leipheim* (in poem form), undated

Me 323 as Flying Workshop, general arrangement drawing, undated

Logbooks

Altrogge, Auer, Baist, Beauvais, Blanke, Böttcher, Borsdorff, Braun, Davignon (also diary), Ebner, Eckstein, Eisermann, Endres, Heerling, Hirschberg, Honig, Iser, Lutz, Mies, Reinhardt, Riediger, Rössmann, Storm, Zwick

Literature

Apostolo, Giorgio: *Die grossen Luftschlachten des 20 Jahrhunderts*, Bechtermünz Verlag, Weltbid Verlag, Aubsburg 1997

Ebert, Hans J.; Kaiser, Johannes B.; Peter, Klaus: *Willy Messerschmitt—Pionier der Luftfahrt und des Leichtbaues*, Bernard & Graefe Verlag, Bonn 1992

Frank, Edith and Vilsmeier, Cäcilie: *In Trümmern anfangen aufbauen leben*, Stadt Neutraubling 1996

Green, William: *Warplanes of the Third Reich*, Doubleday, Garden City 1973

Gunston, Bill: *Technik und Einsatz der Kampfflugzeuge*, Buch u. Zeit Verlags-GmbH, Cologne 1977

Haberfellner, Wernfried and Schroeder, Walter: *Wiener Neustädter Flugzeugwerke*, Weishaupt Verlag, Graz 1994

Johnson, Brian: *Streng geheim*, Paul Pietsch Verlag, Stuttgart 1978

Kössler, Karl: *Transporter – wer kennt sie schon!*, Alba Buchverlag, Dusseldorf 1976

Kössler, Karl and Ott, Günter: *Die grossen Dessauer*, Aviatic Verlag, Planegg 1993

Lange, Bruno: *Typenhandbuch der deutschen Luftfahrttechnik*, Bernard & Graefe Verlag, Coblenz 1986

Morzik, Fritz and Hümmelchen, Gerhard: *Die deutschen Transportflieger im Zweiten Weltkrieg*, Bernard & Graefe Verlag, Frankfurt am Main 1966

Munson, Kenneth: *Die Weltkrieg II-Flugzeuge*, Motorbuch Verlag, Stuttgart 1977

Neetzow, Klaus and Schlaug, Georg: *Deutsche Lastensegler 1938 bis 1945*, Grütter, Ronnenberg 1993

Pawlas, Karl R.: *Die Giganten Me 321 – Me 323*, Luftfahrt-Monographie LS 3.

Peter, Ernst: *...schleppte und flog GIGANTEN*, Motorbuch Verlag, Stuttgart, 1976

Ring, Hans and Girbig, Werner: *Jagdgeschwader 27*, Motorbuch Verlag, Stuttgart 1985

Schlaug, Georg: *Geschichte einer Transportflieger-Gruppe im II. Weltkrieg*, Kameradschaft ehem. Transportflieger 1989

Schmidt, Alfred: *Vor 50 Jahren: 2000 Bomben fallen auf Leipheim*, Günzburger Zeitung 23-24/4/1994

Schmoll, Peter: *Luftangriff*, Buchverlag d. Mittelbay. Ztg., Regensburg 1995

Schmoll, Peter: *Die Messerschmitt-Werke im Zweiten Weltkrieg*, Buchverlag d. Mittelbay. Ztg., Regensburg 1998.

Schwabe/Wanka: *Der Flugplatz Mettenheim*, Das Mühlrad Bd. XXX, 1988

Selinger, Peter F.: *Segelflugzeuge*, Motorbuch Verlag, Stuttgart 1981

Shores/Ring/Hess: *TUNISIEN 42/43*, Motorbuch Verlag, Stuttgart 1981

Weick, Jörg: *40 Jahre Flugplatz Leipheim*, Mönch Verlag Coblenz-Bonn 1978

Zentner, Christian: *Lexikon des Zweiten Weltkriegs*, M. Pawlak Verlagsgesellschaft, Herrsching 1977.

Leipheimer Heimatbüchlein 1938, Ulm (Donau) 1938

Photographs

Aders, Air Ministry, Auer, Bernad, Borchers, Bundesarchiv, Charles, Creek, Dabrowski, Daimler-Chrysler Aerospace, Deutsche Aerospace, ECPA, Fricke, Giesecke, Griehl, Haferland, Hellwig, Hoffmann, IWM, Kössler, Koos, Kuettner, Kuntz, Lange, MBB, Myhra, Nowarra, Obermaier, Ostrowski, Ott, Peter, Petrick, Quest, Radinger, Rajlich, Reinhardt, Roba, Rössmann, Roosenboom, Schladerbusch, Schlaug, Schmeelke, Schmoll, Schnittke, F. Selinger, P.F. Selinger, Storm, Stumm, Thiele, U.S. Army, USAF, Vilsmeier, Vogel, Zacher, Zazvonil.

Acknowledgements

The author wishes to thank the following for their assistance with this book.

Auer, Edmund
Bernád, Dénes
Blanke, Karl
Borchers, Wilhelm
Brendes, Dipl.-Ing. Gido
Briegel, Peter
Bukowski, Helmut
Carlsen, Sven
Ebert, Hans Joachim
Edwards, James F.
Fricke, Siegfried
Giesecke, Donald
Griehl, Manfred
Haberfellner, Wernfried
Haferland, Prof. Dr.-Ing. Friedrich
Hellwig, Hans-Werner
Hoffmann, Richard
Honig, Walter
Hood, Erwin
Hörner, Peter G.
Iser, Hellmut
Kandzia, Karl
Koos, Dr. Volker

Kössler, Dipl.-Ing. Karl
Kuettner, Dr. Joachim P.
Lange, Bruno
Leipheim, Stadtverwaltung
Mauß, Günther
Meier, Hans Justus
Molkenthin, Olaf
Mühldorf, Stadtverwaltung
Müller, Franz
Müller, Heinz E.
Müller, Wilhelm
Müller-Romminger, Frederic
Nemecek, Vaclav
Neutraubling, Stadtverwaltung
Niedermaier, Josef
Nowarra, Heinz Joachim
Obertraubling, Stadtverwaltung
Ott, Günther
Peter, Ernst
Petrick, Peter
Rajlich, Jiri
Reden, Horst von
Radinger, Willy
Reinhardt, Dr. Manfred
Riediger, Heinz
Roba, Jean-Louis

Roosenboom, Hellmuth
Rößmann, Egon
Schell, Friedemann M.
Schladerbusch, Werner
Schlaug, Georg
Schliephake, Hanfried
Schmoll, Peter
Schnittke, Kurt
Schwabe, Günther
Selinger, Dipl.-Ing. Peter F.
Selinger, Franz
Sengfelder, Günter
Stangl, Sepp
Stender, Dipl.-Ing. Walter
Storm, Gerhard
Straub, Wendelin
Strzeltz, Siegfried
Thiele, Harold
Truppenübungsplatzkommandantur Heuberg
Uhrig, Emil
Vilsmeier, Cäcilie
Vogel, Erna (geb. Nied)
Wiener-Neustadt, Magistrat